HOW TO RUN A
GREAT
HOTEL

...a Great Hotel is most timely for it addresses the key aspects of management, ...asily implemented responses to assist today's hotelier. With an emphasis on ...tice, Enda Larkin guides the reader through the book by focusing on key ...an uncomplicated and readily absorbed style. Using the themes of professional ...ship, change management and service quality, the author identifies those aspects of ...ole where small changes in management approach can reap disproportionately high rewards. This is vital, for of all the challenges facing the hotel industry, the availability of competent and dedicated people remains by far the greatest.

Philippe Rossiter MBA FIH FTS, Chief Executive, Institute of Hospitality

How to Run A Great Hotel is a must in the hotel industry. Whether you are an experienced manager or just starting a career and focusing on achieving excellence, then this book is your guide to success. I strongly recommend it.

João Eça Pinheiro, Managing Director, Prainhamar Hotel Group, Portugal

How to Run a Great Hotel is the first hotel management book I have read that is actually practical, realistic, informative and cuts through the waffle of 'management mumbo jumbo' which allows you to do exactly what it says on the tin – help you run a great hotel.

Adriaan Bartels, MSc. Hosp. Mgmt, General Manager, Cliff House Hotel, Waterford, Ireland

It is fascinating how Enda Larkin simply breaks down the theoretical background of management theories into practical advice in *How to Run a Great Hotel*. It is not only the easy description of some complicated management theories but also the implementation in clear charts and very useful forms that makes the book into a kind of bible for every hotelier that wants to be successful. It is this easy to understand language and the translation into practical tips that makes the book so useful in daily life, even for the very experienced hotelier.

Beat Wicki, CEO, SSTH Swiss School of Tourism and Hospitality Ltd

How to Run a Great Hotel is a wonderful exploration of strategy, leadership skills, and engaging employees with a strong customer focus to achieve excellence in the hotel industry. Excellence principles tied together by rich personal experiences make it an interesting, powerful and an easy to read format. The publication is practical, with a how-to focus, and includes toolkits which can be used by practitioners and trainers in the field. It is a great text for those interested in achieving excellence in hospitality management and for those who want to experience what leadership and excellence in great hotels is really like.

Kai Partale M.Sc, Partner, Success Consult Germany, experts in tourism and hospitality development and management

In this book Enda Larkin puts people at the centre of success for hotel investors and operators – including leadership development, team coaching and customer relationship management. Industry leaders, hotel developers, hotel general managers, asset managers and brand owners will all benefit by reading the book and pondering its recommendations as relates to their particular area of interest and involvement.

Ian Graham, Principal, The Hotel Solutions Partnership Ltd

This book should be on the desk of every Hotel Manager. Should we search for excellence in the hotel industry? Should we seek to become a leader in the industry? We will feel much more confident making these decisions after reading this book. To help us as we review or develop our hotel business plan, Enda Larkin has included a section with practical steps towards excellence. I feel very fortunate to have learned from his many years of experience and insights.

Khaled Alduais, Dean, National Hotel and Tourism Institute (NAHOTI) Sana'a – Yemen

HOW TO RUN A
GREAT
HOTEL

EVERYTHING YOU NEED TO
ACHIEVE EXCELLENCE
IN THE HOTEL INDUSTRY

ENDA M LARKIN

howtobooks

Published by How To Books Ltd
Spring Hill House, Spring Hill Road,
Begbroke, Oxford, OX5 1RX, United Kingdom
Tel: (01865) 375794. Fax: (01865) 379162
info@howtobooks.co.uk
www.howtobooks.co.uk

How To Books greatly reduce the carbon footprint of their books by sourcing their
typesetting and printing in the UK.

British Library Cataloguing in Publication Data
A catalogue record for this book is available from the British Library

ISBN: 978 1 84528 346 9

Produced for How To Books by Deer Park Productions, Tavistock
Typeset by TW Typesetting, Plymouth, Devon
Printed and bound by Cromwell Press Group, Trowbridge, Wiltshire

NOTE: The material contained in this book is set out in good faith for general guidance
and no liability can be accepted for loss or expense incurred as a result of relying in
particular circumstances on statements made in this book. Laws and regulations may be
complex and liable to change, and readers should check the current position with the
relevant authorities before making personal arrangements.

Contents

Acknowledgements

This book would not have been possible without the contribution of a great many people. Thanks to all the hoteliers who have knowingly and sometimes unwittingly provided inspiration through their dedication and commitment to achieving excellence in hospitality. Thanks to family and friends who supported me as I tried to produce something which would be of value to industry professionals. Particular mention goes to Dr Tony Lenehan for his constant willingness to share his expertise and for all his help and support over the years. Thanks also to Denis Tucker, Tom Conneely and Peter Hutcheson – true believers in excellence – for their guidance. Finally, to Giles Lewis and Nikki Read at *How to Books*, thank you for helping to bring this book to fruition.

Foreword

I am delighted to provide the foreword for *How to Run a Great Hotel* which is a timely publication and essential reading for hoteliers in these challenging days. As the owner and CEO of the Schindlerhof Hotel in Nuremberg, Germany I have always been passionate about excellence. But a business must be profitable too; there can be no pleasure without growth, for growth is the very stuff of life for a company. Our achievements at the hotel show that there is a direct and measurable link between the levels of excellence and profitability.

Since 1984, when I founded the hotel as a 3* property, I have transformed it into a highly profitable 4* hotel which is now the leading Seminar hotel in Germany and one of the best small hotels in Europe. Over that time, we have won many awards, including the EFQM European Quality Award in 1998 and the Best Place to Work Award in 2009, to name just two. Despite what we have achieved, we never stand still and are constantly searching for new mountains to climb.

When people ask why we continually seek these new challenges, I can only give one reason: today we face fierce competition that demands the highest levels of performance. Being as good as your competitors is simply not sufficient. Nor is it enough just to be 2% better. Today we need a real 30% edge on the competition in a number of areas if the public or the spoiled customer is to notice that this guy has really got something. This has been my core philosophy and has guided all our efforts at the hotel, serving as our inspiration to this day.

In his book, Enda Larkin emphasises the importance of striving for excellence as the major driver of business growth and profitability. He helps new and experienced hoteliers to more clearly understand what excellence means in practice, why it is of essential interest today and what practical steps can be taken to bring it alive in your business so that you truly out-perform your competitors. He also describes how learning and innovation can become the life blood of your hotel. All of this is presented in an easy to read format, with lots of helpful tools and resources provided to guide you. The principles he covers are adaptable to suit the needs of any hotel, for there is more than one route to excellence.

Success in business life is never accidental; you create your own destiny. It starts with having a long-term vision for your hotel, supported by clear and measurable goals. Short term planning that is only concerned with next year's cash flow cannot be your starting point. In my experience, you must set your goals so high that the greatest effort is needed to reach them. After all, the greater the goal the less competition you have to fear. Theme 1 of this book will help you to devise appropriate goals for your hotel.

Little can be achieved on the journey to excellence without effective leadership. But leaders alone can't make the result happen; you must set the example and inspire a motivated and thoroughly dedicated team. Then you must give your employees the freedom and desire to act. In doing so, always make sure your people enjoy what they do; have fun at work, because your customers will sense the difference. Themes 2 and 3 in this book are devoted to issues such as leadership and employee engagement and I suggest you take the necessary time to consider your current approach in these areas.

If you want to reach your goals then everyone in your hotel must be committed to what you do; the collective focus must always be on building a great service experience. I cannot emphasise enough the importance of service design, because nothing matters more than satisfied customers. The reward for these efforts is that service quality is nearly impossible for your competitors to copy. You will find some practical guidelines under Theme 4 to help you to create memorable customer experiences.

I firmly believe that the limitations on achievement are not business size, or location but the scale and ambition of your dreams. Today, an increasing number of hoteliers recognise the need for excellence; this is undoubtedly a good development, but at the same time it also serves to constantly raise the bar. As levels of quality increase across the industry, hoteliers which fail to continuously improve their offering will soon be overtaken and eventually left far behind. Only the best hotels will prosper in the future.

I strongly recommend this book as it will undoubtedly be a useful resource as you strive to run a great hotel.

Klaus Kobjoll
CEO and Proprietor
Schindlerhof Hotel
Nuremberg, Germany
April 2009

Klaus Kobjoll is CEO of the Schindlerhof Hotel in Nuremberg, Germany one of the top hotels in Europe. He is a charismatic and motivating speaker and is in constant demand to speak at conferences around the world. His Glow & Tingle seminar business has grown exponentially in recent years to the extent that Klaus currently conducts approximately 180 seminars each year.

Preface

The search for excellence goes on and it continues to be a hot topic across the business world, including in hotels. So too in education, health and science. Even in sport and the arts, it's all the rage. In fact, in every field, it's all about excellence, with models to describe it, magazines to promote it and shiny awards to recognise it. There are even special centres for excellence today.

Yet, for all the hype, excellence remains an elusive concept; hard to explain, even harder to achieve. What does it actually mean in a hotel context? How can it be realised? What is it that makes a great hotel? It is questions such as these which lie at the heart of this book. To begin with, excellence is as much about attitudes as it is about actions. It means having a real desire to not only compete, but to lead.

Most hotel professionals have great hopes for their business and being the best is usually high on their list of desires. But it's easy to lose sight of that goal when faced with the day-to-day challenges of hotel life. In a customer-driven environment, the immediate can overshadow the important; *doing* rather than *thinking* can take precedence. This goes some way to explaining why aspirations and achievements don't always match up when it comes to excellence. Simply wanting it isn't enough.

Becoming a leader in any industry doesn't just magically happen. Nor does it come quickly, or indeed easily. The journey is a long and challenging one, but very rewarding at the same time. The content here will serve to inform that journey, focusing as it does on proven drivers of excellence such as *strategy development, enhancing leadership skills, engaging employees* and *attaining customer focus*. Without clear direction in these critical areas, excellence will only ever be an ideal and never a reality.

The guidance offered throughout this book is the culmination of my 20 years spent managing and consulting in the hotel industry. It is based on first-hand experience, interviews with successful hoteliers and countless observations of best practices seen in great hotels, large and small, around the world.

For all experienced or aspiring hotel professionals this book offers no-nonsense advice, presented in an easy-to-read format, which will make a lasting impact on personal and business performance. It will serve as a welcome companion on the journey to excellence.

Introduction

You don't need anyone to tell you just how competitive the hotel industry is; you are probably all too aware of that fact. Of course, the exact nature of the competition you face depends on factors such as your location and the markets you are in, but for sure, you will be competing with others for your share of the spoils. This is a good thing, even if it doesn't always feel that way, because it forces you to stay on your toes.

The challenges in hotels are compounded by the fact that the industry is particularly susceptible to economic volatility and other shocks which are beyond our control. The current global recession is a good example of that instability. Add to this mix an ever more savvy and demanding customer and it is clear that our industry is as competitive as it gets. In such a dynamic environment, it is not an exaggeration to say that only the very best hotels can prosper over the long term.

It is for this reason that excellence is a paramount concern in our industry. It matters everywhere and to everyone: from the small family-run operation to the large hotel chain, at the budget and luxury ends of the market, in new or well established hotels. Whether you own or manage a hotel, are early in your career or have years of experience behind you, it's an issue for you. Whatever your particular circumstances, excellence matters because customers increasingly demand it and lasting success in our industry stems from an ability to deliver it.

Towards excellence

The path to excellence lies in taking a long-term view of business development and involves constantly questioning what it is you are doing and why you are doing it, with a view to continuously improving every aspect of your operation. Seeking to achieve excellence requires a consistent focus on four central themes which are regularly seen, not only in all great hotels, but in all leading businesses. These themes are shown in the diagram overleaf.

It is these four themes which drive excellence and they will serve as the framework for this book. Although there are many other factors which impact on the operation of a successful hotel, mastering these themes is what helps to turn good into great. Little attention is given here to specific functions such as marketing and finance, not because they aren't important, they are, but without constant attention

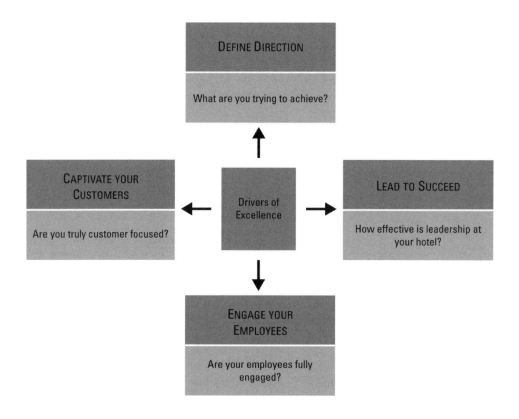

to these four critical areas you can't excel, no matter how well you manage your finances, or market your hotel.

Leading enterprises apply these themes by considering the following points.

❑ *Clear Direction* defining what excellence will mean in the business and converting those broad aspirations into measurable goals, with related strategies and plans designed to make them a reality.

❑ *Effective Leadership* leading the business with passion and energy and harnessing the support of others in realising the defined goals.

❑ *Engaged Employees* genuinely treating employees as stakeholders in the business and recognising that success is ultimately achieved through them.

❑ *Captivated Customers* moving beyond lip service to customers by placing them firmly at the centre of everything you do.

The aim here is to explore these themes in a practical manner so that you can apply them in a meaningful way at your hotel. The intention is not to prescribe what you must do, but rather to give you guidance on what you might do. And that's the key, everything covered in this book can be tailored to meet your specific needs – you will adapt, not adopt based on your own particular circumstances.

Think, Do, Review

Principles and practices of excellence are often made more complicated than they need to be, so we will use a simple conceptual model to guide us as we explore how to bring these themes alive in your hotel. Everything that happens, or should happen within our four themes can be broken down into: *Think, Do, Review.*

In line with this model, the book contains four main sections – one for each theme. Within each section, you will then find three interlinked chapters.

❏ The first chapter in each theme deals with the *think* component of that theme and will provide you with some background information about current thinking in that area.

❏ The second chapter focuses on the *do* part and suggests ways in which you might apply best practice in your operation.

❏ The third chapter helps you to consider how you will *review* progress as you work to continuously improve your business.

A summary and action-planning section is also provided at the end of the book which offers a number of checklists and diagnostics to help you as you move forward. You will also find some useful tools and resources to guide your efforts. Additional online supports are available at www.htc-consult.com.

There are many ways for you to get the most from this book. You might simply treat it as a thought provoker which stimulates you to analyse what you currently do without necessarily applying all the concepts covered. You could also focus on a particular theme that you feel is most relevant to your needs right now. The recommended approach is to use the book in its entirety as a personal and business development resource and, over a period of time, address the range of interlinked issues that it covers.

It is easy to criticise or shout from the sidelines, but you won't find any of that here; those of us who know the industry understand the challenge of hotels. What you will find is practical information targeted at hotel professionals who are as passionate about the quest for excellence as they are about the pursuit of profit. If you want to run a great hotel and are willing to do what it takes to realise that ambition, then you will find a wealth of support as you read ahead.

THEME 1 – DEFINE DIRECTION

Define a clear direction for your hotel

DEFINE DIRECTION

What are you trying to achieve?

> *Efforts and courage are not enough without purpose and direction*
>
> John F. Kennedy

If you were driving somewhere you had never been before, you would probably use a map to guide you. Well, you would if you wanted a hassle-free trip. Without the map, you are more likely to get lost and even if you don't, you are certainly leaving things to chance. The same applies to achieving excellence in your hotel which is also a journey and one with many twists and turns. Having a map to keep you on track is useful. In fact, it's vital, because getting lost in your car is one thing, losing your way in business life is an altogether more serious prospect.

Some hotel owners and managers do lose their way, not because of any lack of ability or effort, but because they don't fully think through what it is they are trying to achieve. They might talk about being the best but they fail to really define what that means in practice, or indeed plan how to get there. Sure, they have a vague idea of where they are going, but this can be as loosely defined as to 'outperform our competitors' or 'maximise profit'.

Such operators lack focus and, as a consequence, end up trying things for a few weeks or months but when they don't see immediate results, they quickly change track. They eventually fall into a damaging cycle of meaningless change driven by an endless search for the next big thing which is going to give them an edge. Next big things are few and far between in the hotel industry today.

Excellence is all about focus and direction. It means knowing the end result you want and planning back from that. In other words, it means having a *strategic map*. A strategic map requires you to direct all your efforts towards first identifying and then realising specific goals that are designed to make you the best. It is an essential component of your journey to excellence because it shifts you away from the short-termism which has inflicted many businesses today; it is well known that goal-orientated individuals tend to achieve more and the same principle applies to enterprises.

As a first step towards excellence you must therefore consider where it is you are going and what you are trying to achieve at the hotel. After all, how can you ever hope to get 'there', if you don't actually know where 'there' is? Even when you do know, you can't make it there overnight, so you must concentrate your energies on specific business areas to see the results you want. This is particularly true in our industry, where much depends on reputation, goodwill and customer loyalty, none of which can be magically built up in the short run. So, now is a good time to consider: *what are you trying to achieve?*

Theme 1 helps you to define what excellence will mean in your business and to devise a strategic map to achieve it. The content in the following three chapters addresses these important questions:

❑ What is a strategic map and how can it help you to achieve excellence?

❑ How can you create a strategic map for your hotel?

❑ How can you measure the impact of your strategic map over time?

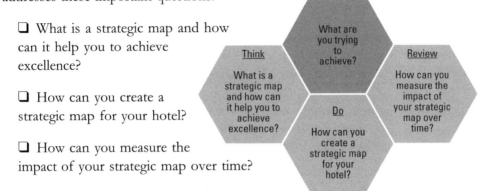

Theme 1 will guide you as you define your journey to excellence, providing down-to-earth advice and practical examples that you can quickly apply to your own circumstances.

1

What is a strategic map and how can it help you to achieve excellence?

Lack of direction in a business significantly increases the risk factor. The owner of a small family hotel recently explained why he had added a spa to his operation, 'My main competitor opened one last year and they seem to be doing very well, so I didn't want to be left behind.' Think about that for a moment: a large chunk of family capital invested with little research on feasibility undertaken to support the move. The danger here should be pretty obvious. What you might not realise is that, although an extreme case, it is far from unusual in hotels both large and small.

When you don't have a framework to guide decision-making, you are essentially making things up as you go along. Worse still, you can be tempted into following your competitors' moves in the hope of getting to a better place – wherever that may be. In the case of this family hotel, it was not a simple change in the offering, or a minor addition to the service mix, but a move posing potential risks for the future survival of a well established business. The owner was a smart guy, yet he made this particular decision on a whim, with no apparent rationale other than to keep up with the Joneses.

Keeping an eye on your competitors is, of course, a must; doing what they do is not, unless it fits with your own goals. If it does, then you should question why you didn't get there first. Do you want to lead, or follow? Operating your hotel solely on the basis of what others are doing, or taking uninformed decisions will get you nowhere in the end because what seems like a smart move today often turns sour tomorrow.

That said, not everything you do in business life can, or indeed should, be planned and analysed to the nth degree. Gut feeling is good and has inspired many great decisions but it shouldn't be the sole driver of the choices you make. Without focused, goal-orientated decision-making, you are essentially drifting; potentially into trouble.

A strategic map will give you the framework you need to excel and achieve lasting business success. With a strategic map you become outcome-driven and, as a result, you reduce the risk of failure because you make informed decisions about the development and growth of your business. Of course, it will always be necessary to respond to changing circumstances; for example you will undoubtedly have to take some difficult decisions to get through the current recession. However, armed with a strategic map in future, any such short-term decisions will no longer be taken in isolation. Your strategic map will create a context for everything you do and will inform every decision you take.

What does having a strategic map actually involve?

Developing a strategic map can at times seem a very convoluted process; google the topic and you will be bamboozled by terms like vision, mission, strategic options, goals, strategy, programmes and plans. Phew, that's enough right there to put you off. But it doesn't need to be so daunting and we will keep it as straightforward as we can.

IT'S ALL IN THE MIND

The ability to create a realistic strategic map for your hotel begins with a particular mindset; everything else stems from that. It's about how you view your business, and as a result, how you operate it. How you think determines how you act, so having a certain mindset supports the creation of your strategic map and indeed the quest for excellence.

Some operators view their business from the wrong perspective, believing that because they have a hotel they have stakeholders, such as customers and employees. Operators who truly believe in excellence take a different approach. They see their stakeholders as being an integral part of their hotel, not external to it, or a result of it. They recognise that without certain stakeholders they do not in fact have a viable business.

YOUR STAKEHOLDERS

Creating your strategic map requires you to become totally *stakeholder focused* and any hotel has a variety of stakeholders.

How you differentiate between primary or secondary stakeholders is in the degree to which they exert *influence* over, or have an *impact* on how you run your hotel. Those who have significant influence and/or impact are seen as primary stakeholders and, as such, require most of your attention. Secondary stakeholders are not unimportant, it is just that they are unlikely to have the same degree of power over the choices you make. However, you do need to consider their needs and address them where appropriate.

For our purposes throughout this book, we will focus on three primary stakeholders as shown. Creating your strategic map involves placing these stakeholders at the forefront of your thinking in terms of the business decisions you make. It also means recognising that the path to excellence lies in satisfying their needs because, in doing so, you are ultimately satisfying your own.

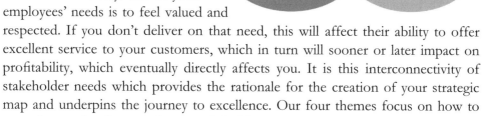

Think of it this way: one of your employees' needs is to feel valued and respected. If you don't deliver on that need, this will affect their ability to offer excellent service to your customers, which in turn will sooner or later impact on profitability, which eventually directly affects you. It is this interconnectivity of stakeholder needs which provides the rationale for the creation of your strategic map and underpins the journey to excellence. Our four themes focus on how to meet the needs of your primary stakeholders to help you run a great hotel.

Elements of a strategic map

Not only can this process of strategic map-making seem confusing at times, but it is also riddled with concepts, models, frameworks and terminology. Worse still, everywhere you look you will find different interpretations of how best to develop your strategic map; it's enough to drive you to distraction and make you want to bang your head against the wall. But when you strip away all the complexity and jargon, you are essentially trying to answer four vital questions in relation your hotel.

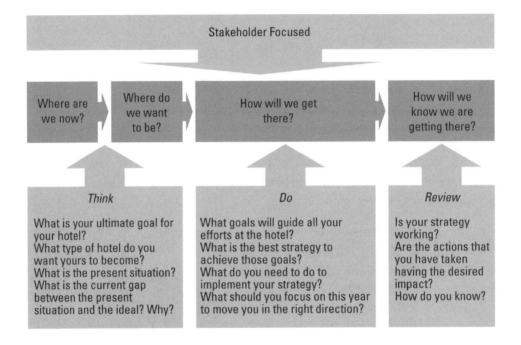

Things start to make a bit more sense when you look at it this way. You know it will be somewhat more challenging in practice, but if you can keep these basic questions in mind, you won't go far wrong. You will notice that building your strategic map fits closely with the *Think, Do, Review* approach which we will follow for all themes covered throughout this book.

❏ You start by *thinking* about the current position of your hotel (*Where are we now?*) and then you describe the big picture (*Where do we want to be?*).

❏ Based on that, you move to the *doing* bit by defining goals and related strategies to achieve them with action taken every year to make it happen (*How do we get there?*).

❑ You will then *review* progress over time to see if you are moving in the right direction (*How will we know we are getting there?*) and the lessons you learn here will be used to adjust elements of strategic focus where necessary.

It is important to re-emphasise at this stage that your strategic map will not be written in stone. Changing economic or competitive dynamics will naturally require you to revisit *where you want to be* or to adjust the *how to get there* part. That is not to say that your strategic map will constantly change from year to year, for that would mean you didn't in fact have a strategic map. Nevertheless, it is a fluid process which you revisit continuously based on internal and external feedback. Even if you are forced to make adjustments, at least you will do so in light of your strategic map which is a far more logical approach than random, impulsive decision-making.

In Chapter 2 we will explore what you need to do to create your strategic map in practice. However, before we move on, many in our industry have misconceptions surrounding the whole area of strategy – let's call them strategic myths – and it is worth tackling some of them now because you may have similar concerns.

Dispelling the strategic myths

NO CONTROL

Some hoteliers, particularly in smaller operations, believe that strategy and related matters are only relevant to very large enterprises which have power in the marketplace. One owner summed this view up well when she said, 'What's the point in having a strategic map when we have no control or influence anyway over what happens in the operating environment? We just need to be good at reacting, and reacting fast.' An understandable concern perhaps, except that having a strategic map does not mean having control. Nobody has control over what happens out there in the general business environment, regardless of size.

However, you *can* have direction and because of that you will be in a stronger position to anticipate, or at least manage change. Having a strategic map is important in a hotel of any size, but if you run a smaller operation, the need for the map is even greater because where larger hotels or chains might survive costly mistakes, you won't. Creating a strategic map for your hotel does not mean trying to be something you're not; it does mean applying proven concepts for success in a manner appropriate to the size and ethos of your business.

THINKING ABOUT THE FUTURE

Another concern frequently raised is that focusing on the future is a luxury that you simply can't afford when you run a hotel. 'That might be great for you consultants, but I live in the real world and have more important things to do than navel gazing', an operator once said to me when discussing the issue. Actually, it is because you live in the real world that you need to think about the future.

KNOWING THE INDUSTRY

The final myth we will touch on is quite prevalent in hotels. A positive feature of our industry is that it offers great scope for ambitious individuals to progress to managing and even owning their own hotel. Maybe you too have taken that route, for many do. The downside of this can be that those who follow this path often believe that it is their experience in the field which will be the major factor in helping them to achieve excellence. So convinced are they by this that they don't bother with all this strategy nonsense. After all, they 'know the industry' so who needs a strategic map?

Unfortunately this sort of thinking often catches up with them in the end. Of course having a hotel background is a big plus, particularly operationally, but without your map, supported by accurate information, then your chances of success are diminished. No amount of industry knowledge or indeed hard work can compensate for lack of direction; effort and excellence are not the same thing.

Considering the realities

Having addressed some of the myths, here are some realities to consider. A strategic map

does not guarantee the achievement of excellence →	it does create a foundation upon which excellence can be built
is not a straightjacket →	it will define what you are hoping to achieve and even if you are forced to change direction in the short term, you have a context to guide those decisions
does not give you control over volatility in the business environment →	it can help you to understand more clearly the forces influencing your business, so that you have a better chance of mastering, or at least managing them
will not in itself resolve the resource issues you face →	it will assist you in channelling limited resources in the right areas for maximum impact
doesn't mean you won't get it wrong from time to time →	it will help you to get it right more frequently. Mistakes are costly, both in financial and reputational terms
doesn't mean you can't change track in future →	it does provide you with a benchmark against which you can measure progress so that you can quickly spot when you do need to change direction

So, if your hotel is in its early stages of development, creating your strategic map should be your number one priority. Even if you are up and running for some time, when did you last sit down and really take stock of where you are now and where you are going? Are you leading, or merely competing? Don't be fooled into thinking that being in a good financial position means that your hotel is heading in the right direction. It is of course a better sign than if you are not, but unless you have mapped out the direction you want to take, you might find that there are shocks hiding behind what currently seems to be a healthy bottom line.

SUMMARY

Understanding what a strategic map is, why it's important and how it can contribute to running a great hotel is a critical first step on your journey to excellence. If the bottom line is your only motive, or if you don't really believe in the benefits of taking a longer-term view to the development of your hotel, then you are likely find the guidelines in the coming chapters more hassle than they are worth. Achieving excellence takes time, effort and, more importantly, direction: Rome wasn't built in a day, as they say.

In the following chapter we will shift our attention to exploring how you can start to create or revise your strategic map. We will, however, end this chapter with a warning. While a strategic map can help a viable hotel to grow and prosper, unfortunately, nothing can turn a frog into a prince. If your operation is based on a bad idea, in the wrong location, at the wrong time then a strategic map will be about as useful as rearranging the deckchairs on the *Titanic*.

2

How can you create a strategic map for your hotel?

DO	**HOW CAN YOU CREATE A STRATEGIC MAP FOR YOUR HOTEL?**

When making any journey, it is only human nature to want to get there as quickly as possible. We all love shortcuts if they save time but still get us to our destination. Whilst there is no harm in looking for the easy route when you are travelling somewhere, it's not such a smart idea when dealing with matters related to the future success of your business.

Unfortunately, many owners and managers do look for the shortcut when dealing with the issue of excellence. There is a natural desire to make things as painless as possible and simple solutions always hold great appeal; something perhaps involving ten steps, or, even better, only five. The bookshelves are full of success formulae but, despite what some authors would have you believe, there are no easy answers to achieving excellence. This can only happen if you remain steadfastly focused on your strategic map.

Creating your strategic map

The first thing to highlight is that your strategic map includes having a strategy, *but is not limited to it*. Strategy tends to get most of the attention, but any strategy is only as good as the information upon which it is based and the resulting measures put in place to realise it. Developing your strategic map is therefore broader in scope than just strategy. It represents a continuous, progressive activity which becomes more specific and detailed as you move through it; an activity which is at all times focused on the needs of your primary stakeholders.

Creating your strategic map does not require you to develop long, written documents. Only realism and accuracy are necessary – in whatever format works best for you. Although from time to time you may need more formal documentation, if you are seeking investment or other forms of support.

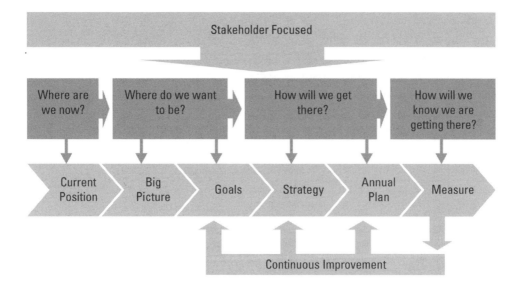

Creating your strategic map requires *reflection, analysis, action* and *evaluation* guided by our four core questions.

An important point to keep in mind as you move forward is that you shouldn't try to create your strategic map alone. You should seek input from your primary stakeholders as you attempt to answer the core questions and involve them as appropriate. It is also useful to get external advice as you tackle this challenge. With the best of intentions, you can't be as objective when judging your own hotel as you need to be, so an outsider can help you to focus on areas that you may overlook. There are generally a range of low-cost mentoring services available from government agencies, industry associations, or indeed your bank, so make use of them.

Where are we now?

As the proverb goes, a jour-ney of a thousand miles begins with a single step. In relation to creating your strategic map this means considering where you are now as a business. Before you go anywhere, you must have a detailed understanding of your current position.

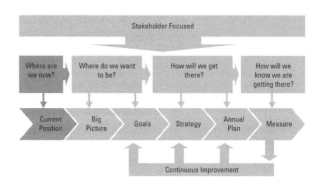

To guide subsequent decisions, you will need accurate and relevant information at hand about your hotel, your market, the industry generally and about any economic and social trends which may impact on the future performance of your hotel. There are many conceptual models and frameworks to support this process, but answering the question *where are we now?* essentially means reflecting upon a series of interrelated sub-questions.

Areas to focus on	Sample questions to consider
Hotel	In essence you are trying to identify the current strengths and weaknesses of your hotel. ❏ How is your hotel performing financially? ❏ How does that compare to other similar hotels? ❏ Who are your customers? Can you divide them into different key segments? ❏ What are your customers' needs? Are you meeting and more importantly exceeding them? What do your customers think about you at present? How do you know? When customers do give you feedback, how often does the word 'excellent' feature? ❏ How does your service offering compare with that of your competitors? Where are the current gaps in what you offer? ❏ Are your employees competent, committed and motivated? Do they play an active or passive role in day-to-day decision-making? ❏ Are you maximising the use of information technology in your hotel? ❏ Is your hotel considered a leader amongst your competitive set?
Market	Here you are trying to get a better feel for the dynamics of the markets you operate (or could operate) in. ❏ Do you have a lot of competitors, or only a few? (Remember, competitors are not just those who are located close by.) ❏ Are you operating in a mass market, or do you offer a specialist or niche experience? ❏ Is overall demand growing, or subsiding in your region? ❏ Is it easy to set up a hotel in your area, or are there barriers to entry such as restrictions on hotel developments? ❏ What drives the market(s) that you are in? Price, quality or both? What trends are you seeing in your markets? Are you increasing market share or losing it in your key markets? ❏ How does the market operate? Do customers buy directly, online or through intermediaries, or all three? Who are these intermediaries and what relationships do you have with them? ❏ How is technology affecting the market dynamics?
Industry	Here you are trying to get a feel for the trends in the industry relevant to your hotel and what supports are available to you. ❏ What are the key trends in the industry? For example, are independent hotels being squeezed out by the major brands? Is there an over/under supply of hotels? ❏ What are the overall projections for the industry in your country/region? ❏ What supports are available for hotels such as yours? Are you maximising your usage of those supports? ❏ Who are the main hotel associations? Do you have a relationship with them?

General	Here you are looking at general economic and social trends which may impact on your hotel, either in the short or long term.
	❏ What is the general economic outlook like where you are for the short and medium term? What is it like in the places where your customers come from?
	❏ How are consumer habits/needs changing? What implications might such changes have for you in the short, medium and longer term?
	❏ Are there any regulations on the horizon which might have implications for the operation of your hotel? What do you need to do to get ready for any such legislation/regulations?
	❏ What are the future technology developments which will impact on hotels generally? How might they impact your hotel?
	❏ What are the environmental issues that you need to respond to?

It looks fairly daunting when you see all these questions and this isn't even an exhaustive list. Let's be honest, research is not everyone's cup of tea but do put in the effort because the effectiveness of any future developmental decisions you take will directly correlate to the accuracy of the answers you find to these questions. In any case, much of this information may already be at hand, or should at least be relatively accessible.

Once you have gathered all the information about your current position, then what? Naturally, to support later decision-making, you must interpret your research to identify the positives and negatives of where your hotel currently lies. A well known tool for facilitating this analysis is the SWOT matrix, which involves summarising the following:

The current internal **s**trengths and **w**eaknesses of your hotel – which in essence helps you to answer the question *where are we now?*

Strengths	Weaknesses
Opportunities	**Threats**

The **o**pportunities and **t**hreats you face in the external business environment which will later influence how you answer the question *where do we want to be?*

SWOT analysis is a widely used, but frequently misused tool. A fairly typical approach to preparing a SWOT in hotels tends to look something like this: a meeting is called where managers sit around the table and everybody chips in what they believe are the strengths, weaknesses, opportunities and threats facing the business. Then, by discussion and agreement the SWOT is finalised. Unfortunately, this is the wrong way to go about it.

Compiling your SWOT analysis based solely on *opinions* is of limited value; you need *facts*. Gather the facts first, and then prepare your SWOT in light of the lessons learned from your research. A fact-based SWOT will give you a clearer and more credible picture of your hotel and the environment within which you operate. More importantly, you will have the right information to help you make smarter choices as you develop your strategic map.

Where do we want to be? Big picture thinking

If a journey starts with a single step, naturally, it should be leading somewhere. In creating your strategic map, you must therefore consider the ideal destination for the development of your hotel. Many operators ignore this phase or only have a vague idea of

where they are headed. But the very purpose of creating your strategic map is to make you more goal-orientated and that can't happen unless you define those outcomes in the first place.

In essence, what you are trying to do here is to visualise what achieving excellence actually means for you and then you work back from that by defining a clear path to get you there. Knowing where it is you want to get to as a business is critical because it creates the framework under which all subsequent decisions are taken.

You explore this big picture component of the strategic map by focusing on the question *where do we want to be?* In answering this, you are trying to put into words what you ultimately want to achieve for your hotel and what type of hotel you want to operate; you will often see this big picture thinking described as your *vision* and *mission* statements.

A lot of hoteliers tend to run a mile from these concepts because they can initially seem a bit corny, or worse still, they sound like MBA speak. One manager attending a workshop on this topic asked me when the 'group hug' was coming – a clear indication of what his views were about these statements. And he is far from alone in thinking that way.

There is plenty of cynicism surrounding the notion of developing vision and mission statements. They get a lot of bad press, much of which is deserved because they are widely abused in how they are applied in enterprises. But don't dismiss the idea just yet. When used properly, and properly is the key word here, vision and mission can serve as a powerful driving force for your hotel and can both define and guide the journey to excellence. Let's explore how you might get the most from them.

GETTING THE MOST FROM YOUR VISION AND MISSION STATEMENTS

A good place to start is to clear up the widespread confusion surrounding vision and mission. The two terms are often used interchangeably and wherever you look for advice on this, you tend to get varied explanations on what the statements are intended to do. But as with everything else we do, we will keep it simple. For our purposes, we will describe them as the following:

Vision is what you ultimately want to achieve in your hotel. It is your snap-shot of what 'excellence' will look like.

Mission describes what type of hotel you will operate as you work towards that vision.

In other words, vision broadly refers to the destination, whereas mission relates more to the journey and describes the type of hotel you want to operate as you move towards your vision, with reference to your primary stakeholders.

One of the main causes of the scepticism surrounding vision and mission statements is that although many enterprises do prepare them today, they often do little else with them. Frequently they end up as extravagant but empty statements pinned to a wall somewhere, slowly discolouring and curling up at the edges; a monument to lost opportunity. When this happens, it is a sure sign that the people involved have missed the point. Unfortunately, missing the point in relation to vision and mission is a frequent occurrence.

Here is an example of how one group of hotel managers wasted their time and effort.

Recently the management team at a hotel, established for many years, were seeking to refocus their efforts by creating a strategic map. Working closely with an external advisor they decided that as part of their map they would develop a vision and mission for the business and agreed to complete the task over a number of weeks.

During a later meeting with their advisor, they presented their statements, which at the time seemed very familiar to the advisor. Further exploration revealed that the managers in question had simply downloaded the statements verbatim from the website of an international hotel company they admired and just changed the appropriate words . . .

Now, it should be pretty clear what's wrong here, but you would be amazed how often this kind of thing occurs. It happens because people are simply going through the motions and ticking things off the strategy 'to do' list. They make the mistake in believing that it is the statements themselves which are of paramount value, which is not the case at all.

The written statements are useful as a communication tool, but the real benefits of having a vision and mission for your  business come from first *developing* them and then more importantly *living* them every day. So, we need to look at both these dimensions.

DEVELOPING YOUR VISION AND MISSION

It is in the process of developing your vision and mission where the initial benefits will arise for you. Defining what you want to achieve, in consultation with your primary stakeholders, is valuable because it forces you to stand back from day-to-day operations and think about, in broad terms, what your ultimate goal is. Do you want to grow your hotel to the fullest extent, or have you other priorities? Are you really serious about excellence and, if so, what does excellence actually mean for you? What are you trying to deliver for your customers? What matters to you about your employees?

It is this process of *reflection* which adds value, not necessarily what ends up in your statements. The more people in your hotel that you include in the development of vision and mission the better. Allowing key employees to be involved as appropriate in the process is a good way of building team spirit and generating commitment to what you are trying to achieve.

Clarifying your vision

As you are the most important stakeholder in your hotel, it is logical to first define your vision in conjunction with any owners/investors/partners you might have in the business. You should begin by thinking about what you want your hotel to achieve:

Try to describe what your vision for the hotel is. Put into words what is probably already in your head!

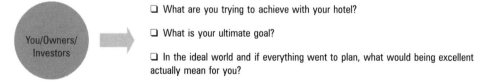

❏ What are you trying to achieve with your hotel?

❏ What is your ultimate goal?

❏ In the ideal world and if everything went to plan, what would being excellent actually mean for you?

Something is driving you, what is it? Does it matter to you whether you are the best or the worst? Of course it does and that is what you are trying to express; it's your dream translated into words.

To give you an idea of what a vision statement might look like, let's use a fictitious example of a medium sized, independent four-star hotel situated in London. We shall define the vision for this hotel as being the following.

> ### Vision
> To become the leading independent four-star hotel in London providing excellent products and services at reasonable prices to every customer, every time.

You can see how the vision for this hotel defines their overall aim for the business. We won't debate the merits of this statement, but it will give you a sense of what is required. Your vision should signpost the future and represent a real challenge for the hotel; not something that is easy to achieve or that you are doing already. Being the best hotel in a ten-mile radius isn't much of a stretch, but to be the best in your city, country or even continent would be! But it also has to be realistic and describe what you actually want to achieve.

Vision concisely outlines what your general aspirations for your hotel are in terms of excellence and should serve as the overall guiding force for everything you do in future. All subsequent decisions and actions should be geared towards moving you closer to that vision; you may never get there, but you are always striving to.

Defining your mission

Having considered your vision, you will then need to prepare the mission for your hotel. The mission refers to your primary stakeholders and is where you start translating your *stakeholder focus* into words by outlining, again in broad terms, what you are trying to deliver for them.

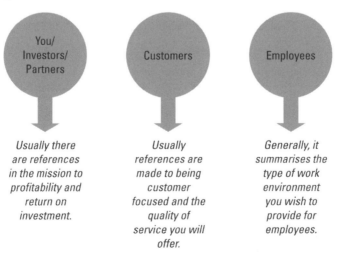

You/ Investors/ Partners — Usually there are references in the mission to profitability and return on investment.

Customers — Usually references are made to being customer focused and the quality of service you will offer.

Employees — Generally, it summarises the type of work environment you wish to provide for employees.

Mission describes what excellence will look like in relation to your ongoing dealings with your primary stakeholders. For our fictitious hotel in London, the mission might read something like this.

Mission

Our customers are our priority and we will provide them with a quality experience which is second to none. We recognise the importance of our employees in achieving this and we will create a positive working environment which encourages their loyalty, commitment and hard work. We strive to be excellent leaders and will undertake all our business activities in an honest and ethical manner to provide a fair return on our investment.

You can see that the mission describes how the hotel will operate, making reference to the primary stakeholders: *owners, customers and employees.*

Your mission does not have to be a long, wordy statement but should simply summarise in a couple of sentences what really matters to you with regard to your primary stakeholders. It should also provide a window into the culture of your business and use words which give a flavour of what is unique about your values. Some organisations also develop a separate *values statement.* You can do so if you wish, but by choosing the right words, you can incorporate your values into your mission.

TIP

The content covered under 'Culture' in Theme 3 will also be helpful as a thought provoker when you come to develop your vision and mission.

In preparing the vision and mission statements for your hotel, you must naturally keep in mind what you have already learned about your current position when you answered the question *where are we now?* These statements should challenge you, but at the same time, they need to be founded in reality too. Creating unrealistic or unattainable vision and mission statements just means that you enter into the realm of fantasy and as such they cannot be used in any practical way to guide the development of your hotel.

So, it's about getting the balance right; define where you want to be in challenging terms but at the same time consider what is possible, based on a realistic assessment of where you are now. When you do develop or revise the vision and mission statements for your hotel, keep the following in mind.

❑ **Don't be constrained in how you go about it.** Be creative and do whatever works best for you, but do involve all the relevant stakeholders in some way during the process.

❑ **If you don't want statements** then just use memorable phrases which have real meaning for you.

❑ **If you don't want two statements** just have one, once it incorporates the principles of vision and mission.

❑ **If you don't like the terms vision and mission** then call them something else – just make sure you end up with your 'meaningful sound bite(s)'.

❑ **Embrace a challenge, but be realistic too.** Reach for the stars as they say but at least stay in our solar system.

Whatever you actually come up with in terms of the content of the written statements is fine, once they are based on the principles outlined here, accurately reflect what you want to achieve for your hotel, describe what excellence means to you and give a flavour of the type of business you want to become. In the end, it's what you do with them that matters, so let's move on to exploring how you can live these statements once you develop them.

Living your vision and mission

Once developed, you should then consider how your vision and mission statements can actually add value to your hotel in the long term. After all, if you go to the trouble of preparing them, you want to ensure that you see some results for your efforts. You certainly do not

want to end up like many businesses where they are forgotten about after a couple of weeks.

The lasting benefits of these statements will *only* be seen if you truly live them every day. That is what excellent hotels do at any level. Vision and mission (or whatever you decide to call them) are tangible, living commitments which really mean something to those working in the business. They are the written down blueprints which guide the journey to excellence. But how can you really live these statements in practice?

FROM VISION AND MISSION TO GOALS

An easy first step in this is to make sure that your primary stakeholders actually know about them by communicating your vision and mission widely and frequently. This can be done, for example, by incorporating them into all your promotional tools, through staff training or on signage and notice boards. By informing your stakeholders, you are effectively making public commitments to them and this puts pressure on you to deliver, which is a good thing. So communication plays an important role with regard to increasing awareness about your vision and mission.

However, in order for these statements to actually become the true driving force in your hotel, you must translate the broad aspirations outlined within them into concrete goals; then you must plan how to realise those goals. *In this context, we are using the term goals to mean measurable targets.*

Goals are important in any walk of life. Think of an athlete seeking to break a world record or to win an Olympic gold medal. Very few do, but the serious ones not only have talent, they always have goals even if it is just to beat their personal best. In fact, for successful athletes you might say they are goal obsessed – their whole training system, diet and the events they select to compete in are based on what they want to achieve. When they do achieve their goals, they don't just stop there, instead, they raise the bar even further by setting new and more challenging targets.

It is this focus and determination which sets the great apart and achieving excellence in the hotel industry is no different. As an aside, it is worth mentioning that athletes who attempt to take shortcuts to achieve their goals, such as through doping, usually suffer in the end. There are no shortcuts to excellence.

The goals you develop will relate directly to what you described in your vision and mission and should be SMART: **s**pecific, **m**easurable, **a**chievable, **r**ealistic and **t**ime bound. Your strategic goals will serve a number of important functions and they will:

❑ define in more concrete terms what excellence will look like

❑ guide you in preparing strategies and plans

❑ allow you to measure progress at a later stage as to whether you are living your mission and ultimately whether you are getting closer to your vision.

To help us demonstrate how your vision and mission statements can be translated into more specific goals and related strategies, let's return to the examples from our hotel in London.

Vision

To become the leading independent four-star hotel in London providing excellent products and services at reasonable prices to every customer, every time.

Mission

Our customers are our priority and we will provide them with a quality experience which is second to none. We recognise the importance of our employees in achieving this and we will create a positive working environment which encourages their loyalty, commitment and hard work. We strive to be excellent leaders and will undertake all our business activities in an honest and ethical manner to provide a fair return on our investment.

Reading these statements gives a strong sense that this management team want their hotel to be a step above the norm; they want to excel. If what is stated in their vision and mission was lived up to in reality, this would truly be a great hotel. But they are only words and for these statements to be of any real benefit, the management team would need to break these broad aspirations down into more tangible goals to guide their efforts in future. Sample goals for this hotel derived from their vision and mission could be:

Converting Vision and Mission into Goals

Vision		Sample Goals
'To become the leading independent four-star hotel in London providing excellent products and services at reasonable prices to every customer, every time' ➜	What does 'leading' entail? How can this be achieved in practice? Perhaps the goal could be to win industry recognition, or an award of excellence within a certain timeframe ➜	❑ To win the *Customers' Choice Award* in the coming year ❑ To achieve the Hotel Association's *Best Hotels Award* within two years

To translate the mission into goals, let's break it down into its constituent parts. The mission related to three different primary stakeholders:

1. Our customers are our priority and we will provide them with a quality experience which is second to none (*Customers*)
2. We recognise the importance of our employees in achieving this and we will create a positive working environment which encourages their loyalty, commitment and hard work (*Employees*)
3. We strive to be excellent leaders and will undertake all our business activities in an honest and ethical manner to provide a fair return on our investment (*Owners/Managers*)

Mission		Sample Goals
'Our customers are our priority and we will provide them with a quality experience which is second to none.'	How can this be translated into more concrete terms? What does 'quality experience' mean? Goals would be required in areas such as: overall number of customers, % of repeat customers, customer satisfaction levels, quality audits scores etc.	❏ To increase the number of repeat customers to 40% within three years. ❏ To increase customer satisfaction levels to 90% within two years. ❏ To continuously increase our scores on internal and external quality audits.

Mission		Sample Goals
'We recognise the importance of our employees in achieving this and we will create a positive working environment which encourages their loyalty, commitment and hard work.'	What does this specifically mean? How will they know they are achieving this? Goals would be required here in areas such as employee turnover and employee engagement to guide their efforts.	❏ To reduce employee turn-over to 20% within three years. ❏ To achieve an average rating of 75% from employee engagement surveys. ❏ To introduce a bonus scheme for all employees within three years.

Mission		Sample Goals
'We strive to be excellent leaders and will undertake all our business activities in an honest and ethical manner to provide a fair return on our investment.'	What does 'excellent leaders' actually mean? What exactly does 'fair return' mean? What returns are acceptable, or indeed necessary? Defined financial targets would have to be developed, such as *revenue*, *cost* and *profitability* targets.	❏ To improve leadership effectiveness annually based on our leadership competence model. ❏ To increase net profit to 15% of sales within two years. ❏ To increase RevPar by 5% annually. ❏ To increase restaurant throughput to 1,500 covers per week within two years. ❏ To reduce food cost to the industry average of 35% in the coming year without reducing quality. ❏ To reduce labour costs to 40% within two years.

It is important to point out that these sample goals are only for demonstration purposes – we can't set real goals, as we don't know where this hotel is starting from. But we will assume that they are challenging, but achievable based on the hotel's current position. You should also recognise that it is these goals which must be achieved if this hotel is to live its vision and mission and achieve excellence. Having goals is a far cry from just hoping 'to be the best' as they define what that means in real terms.

The key message you should take from this example is how vision and mission are brought to life in a business through goals. Your goals will, of course, relate to your own vision and mission and you can have as many as you like or indeed need.

How will we get there?

Having vision, mission and goals for your business – no matter how realistic and well thought out – will be meaningless unless you actually do something about making them a reality. With that in mind, once you identify your goals, based on your own vision and mission, you

must then decide what you intend to do in order to realise them. This is where strategy comes in.

For some reason, a lot of people are daunted by the term strategy. But don't be. Your strategy simply describes the general route you will take towards achieving your goals. In reality, you are likely to have a number of integrated strategies to achieve each set of the stakeholder-focused goals you have defined. In identifying their strategies, the management team at our fictitious hotel would need to ask themselves certain questions based on their defined goals.

Linking Goals to Strategy

Vision	Goals	Strategy
'To become the leading independent four-star hotel in London providing excellent products and services at reasonable prices to every customer, every time.'	❏ To win the *Customers' Choice Award* in the coming year. ❏ To achieve the Hotel Association's *Best Hotels Award* within two years.	The management team at this hotel must decide what is needed to make this happen.

Mission	Goals	Strategy
'Our customers are our priority and we will provide them with a quality experience which is second to none.'	❏ To increase the number of repeat customers to 40% within three years. ❏ To increase customer satisfaction levels to 90% within two years. ❏ To continuously increase our scores on internal and external quality audits.	The management team at this hotel must decide what needs to be done to achieve this. How will they define their customers' expectations? How will they improve the quality of service they offer? How will they measure customer satisfaction in future?

Mission	Goals	Strategy
'We recognise the importance of our employees in achieving this and we will create a positive working environment which encourages their loyalty, commitment and hard work.'	❏ To reduce employee turnover to 20% within three years. ❏ To achieve an average rating of 75% from employee engagement surveys. ❏ To introduce a bonus scheme for all employees within three years.	The management team at this hotel must determine what has to happen to achieve these goals. What will their *Human Resource* strategy be? How will they define their employees' expectations? How will they create a better working environment? How will they measure employee engagement in future?

Mission	Goals	Strategy
'We strive to be excellent leaders and will undertake all our business activities in an honest and ethical manner to provide a fair return on our investment.'	❏ To improve leadership effectiveness annually based on our leadership competence model. ❏ To increase net profit to 15% of sales within two years. ❏ To increase RevPar by 5% annually. ❏ To increase restaurant throughput to 1,500 covers per week within two years. ❏ To reduce food cost to the industry average of 35% in the coming year, without reducing quality. ❏ To reduce labour costs to 40% within two years.	The management team at this hotel must define what their expectations of leaders are and how this can be achieved. They also need to develop both *financial* and *marketing* strategies to achieve the specific performance goals. Will they increase sales with their existing products or will they develop new ones? Will they try to increase market share in existing markets or develop new ones? Will they go for a lower cost strategy or seek to become a premium, quality operation? How will they reduce food and labour costs, without impacting on quality?

By answering these questions, the managers at the hotel would arrive at general strategies for achieving the goals they set. Of course, the strategies you identify will depend upon your own vision, mission and goals.

Strategies are essentially choices you make, or options you take by answering similar questions to the samples provided above. They are designed to help move you from your current position (*where are we now?*) towards the goals you want to achieve (*where do we want to be?*). Strategies should also help you to play to your strengths, address your weaknesses, capitalise on opportunities and prepare for threats.

You should by now recognise that as you move through the process of creating your strategic map, you are simply getting more specific as you go. It is a very logical and coherent process because:

❏ each new phase builds on the previous one, so there is at all times strong linkages from broad aspirations to concrete actions

❏ you remain stakeholder focused throughout, so you ensure that your strategies and actions are geared towards meeting their needs

❏ you define a specific path to guide your journey to excellence.

From strategies to annual plans

Whatever goals and related strategies you come up with, it is clear that it will take more than one year to realise them, so you need to ensure that you take the necessary steps each year to implement your strategy. For this you will need an annual business plan. Un-

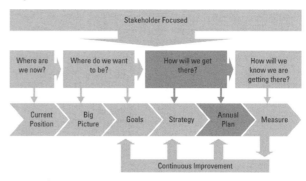

doubtedly, you already plan things in your hotel. You couldn't run a business of any kind without some degree of forward thinking. However, you might need to review the nature and effectiveness of that planning as you create your strategic map.

Most of what is termed planning in our industry tends to have a short-term focus, day to day, week to week and is designed to facilitate the ongoing operational demands of hotel life. This type of *operational planning* is of course critical and you must continue to do it. But, having a structured *annual business plan* is essential too because it is only through planning, not hoping, that you will actually move closer to your goals and become the best.

An important distinction to make here is that your financial budget is not an annual plan, although it will naturally be part of one. Budgets only focus on outcomes, so they do not provide you with the necessary guidance on how to get there. In any case, if your goals are genuinely stakeholder focused, as per our example hotel, many of them will be non-financial, so you need more than a budget to guide you.

One manager recently explained his approach to annual planning: 'At the beginning of the year I do have in mind what I hope to achieve and stick to it as best as I can. But every day is so different in this industry that sometimes I don't always get around to doing the things I hoped to do. But we have a budget and things aren't going too badly, so I must be doing something right.'

This approach to planning is reminiscent of a desperation tactic used in American football called the 'hail Mary' pass. It's deployed when a team is losing with only seconds remaining and the quarterback lobs the ball into the end-zone and prays that somebody catches it: essentially the hit-and-hope approach. Unfortunately, many hotel owners and managers adopt this mentality to annual planning – they hope for the best without consistently doing enough to influence the result.

Planning of all kinds is essentially about discipline and our industry does present unique challenges in this regard. In a customer-facing environment, it is harder to structure each day and as a result it's not that surprising that planning might not always be as effective as it could be. Some operators make the mistake of believing that because things are going reasonably well, then lack of planning is not a problem for them.

You need to be careful with this kind of thinking. It takes time to see the benefits of effective planning, just as it does to see the damage that arises from not planning. Just because things look good today, it doesn't mean that there aren't seeds growing which will produce problems later.

Whereas operational planning is concerned with *doing things right* so that the hotel runs smoothly, annual planning is focused on *doing the right things* so that you are actually implementing your strategies, progressing towards your goals, living your vision and mission and, as a result, heading for excellence. If you are really serious about achieving the goals you have set, then you will need to attach high priority to developing an annual business plan.

Your annual plan should address the range of finance, marketing, human resources and operational actions necessary to implement your strategies in any given year. The approach you take to developing this plan is of course a matter for you to decide but whatever process you adopt, it should be structured, organised and occur within a defined timeframe usually aligned to your financial year.

A five-step procedure for preparing and implementing your annual plan is suggested in the diagram on page 30, based on a calendar financial year.

Your annual plan doesn't have to be a detailed document but simply well thought out with actions defined, implementation schedules and responsibilities agreed.

Sample activities in the annual plan for our example hotel related to implementing their strategies and achieving their goals are shown on pages 31–2.

You can see from the example on the following pages how the planned actions for the coming year relate directly back to their goals. There are undoubtedly many other activities which need to happen in this hotel during the year, but it is these

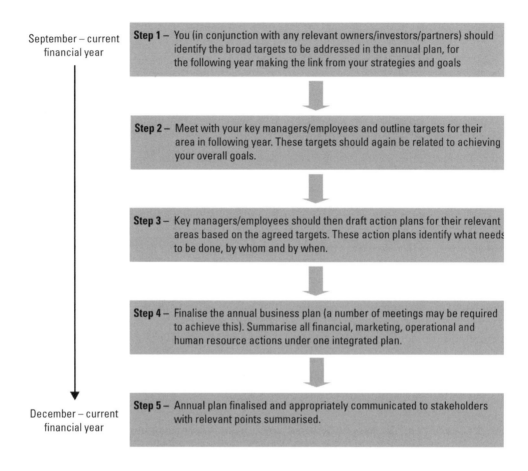

September – current
financial year

Step 1 – You (in conjunction with any relevant owners/investors/partners) should identify the broad targets to be addressed in the annual plan, for the following year making the link from your strategies and goals

Step 2 – Meet with your key managers/employees and outline targets for their area in following year. These targets should again be related to achieving your overall goals.

Step 3 – Key managers/employees should then draft action plans for their relevant areas based on the agreed targets. These action plans identify what needs to be done, by whom and by when.

Step 4 – Finalise the annual business plan (a number of meetings may be required to achieve this). Summarise all financial, marketing, operational and human resource actions under one integrated plan.

December – current
financial year

Step 5 – Annual plan finalised and appropriately communicated to stakeholders with relevant points summarised.

sample actions which are required to implement their strategy; as such they are critical and must be planned in advance annually.

Your annual plan will define the actions necessary in any given year for you to progressively implement your strategies. Obviously, when you prepare your plan, you need to be more specific in terms of allocating responsibilities for each action point and in defining the deadlines for completion, but you have hopefully got the feel for what is required from this example.

From Strategy to the Annual Plan

Vision

'To become the leading independent four-star hotel in London providing excellent products and services at reasonable prices to every customer, every time.'

→

Goals

- To win the *Customers' Choice Award* in the coming year.
- To achieve the Hotel Association's *Best Hotels Award* within two years.

→

Strategy

The management team at this hotel must decide what is needed to make this happen.

→

Current Year Actions

- Conduct self-assessment for *Customers' Choice Award* – by end of January.
- Prepare action plan based on findings of self-assessment – by the end of February.
- Complete all outstanding improvements – by the end of May.
- Apply for the Award – by the end of June
- Award assessment to take place – by the end of July
- Meet with hotel association to define requirements *Best Hotels Award* – by the end of August

---

Mission

'Our customers are our priority and we will provide them with a quality experience which is second to none.'

→

Goals

- To increase the number of repeat customers to 40% within three years.
- To increase customer satisfaction levels to 90% within two years.
- To continuously increase our scores on internal and external quality audits.

→

Strategy

The management team at this hotel must decide what needs to be done to achieve this. How will they define their customers' expectations? How will they improve the quality of service they offer? How will they measure customer satisfaction in future?

→

Current Year Actions

- Hold focus group meetings with regular customers to identify areas where service improvements need to be made – by the end of January.
- Review current system for gathering customer feedback – by the end of February.
- Prepare a plan for improving service quality at the hotel – by the end of March.
- Provide customer care training for all full and part-time employees – by the end of April.
- Review internal and external approaches to quality auditing – by the end of May.
- Identify options for upgrading hotel interior – by the end of June.
- Prepare plan and budget for upgrading hotel to begin next year – by the end of September.

Mission	Goals	Strategy	Current Year Actions
'We recognise the importance of our employees in achieving this and we will create a positive working environment which encourages their loyalty, commitment and hard work.'	❑ To reduce employee turnover to 20% within three years. ❑ To achieve an average rating of 75% from employee engagement surveys. ❑ To introduce a bonus scheme for all employees within three years.	The management team at this hotel must determine what has to happen to achieve these goals. What will their *Human Resource* strategy be? How will they define their employees' expectations? How will they create a better working environment? How will they measure employee engagement in future?	❑ Introduce staff forum to meet monthly to discuss work related issues – by the end of January. ❑ Review current approach to recruitment and selection and propose improvements – by the end of February. ❑ Develop a more structured approach to training and development. Agree and implement – by the end of March. ❑ Design and implement annual employee engagement survey and conduct in April and October annually – by the end of March. ❑ Explore initial option for application of bonus scheme – by the end of August.

Mission	Goals	Strategy	Current Year Actions
'We strive to be excellent leaders and will undertake all our business activities in an honest and ethical manner to provide a fair return on our investment.'	❑ To improve leadership effectiveness annually based on our leadership competence model. ❑ To increase net profit to 15% of sales within two years. ❑ To increase RevPar by 5% annually. ❑ To increase restaurant throughput to 1,500 covers per week within two years. ❑ To reduce food cost to the industry average of 35% in the coming year without reducing quality. ❑ To reduce labour costs to 40% within two years.	The management team at this hotel must define what their expectations of leaders are and how this can be achieved. They also need to develop both *financial and marketing* strategies to achieve the specific performance goals. Will they increase sales with their existing products or will they develop new ones? Will they try to increase market share in existing markets or develop new ones? Will they go for a lower cost strategy or seek to become a premium, quality operation? How will they reduce food and labour costs, without impacting on quality?	❑ Review current rostering system to evaluate effectiveness – by the end of January. ❑ Review current marketing approach and define potential opportunities – by the end of January. ❑ Provide cost management training for all kitchen staff – by the end of February. ❑ Formulate new marketing strategy – by the end of March. ❑ Develop a leadership competence model and provide leadership training to all managers at the hotel – by the end of March. ❑ Develop and launch new website for the hotel – by the end of May.

SUMMARY

The approach to creating or revising your strategic map outlined so far will take time to implement, but it offers an easy-to-understand framework which you can adapt to fit the specific needs of your hotel. The larger your hotel, the more structured the process is likely to be and the more input you will need from other managers and stakeholders. But the steps involved in creating your strategic map are basically the same, regardless of the specific nature of your operation.

Following these guidelines will help you to define what achieving excellence actually means for your hotel and to translate that into goals, strategies and an annual plan to make it happen. By adopting this approach you become results-driven and as those outcomes are based on your stakeholder needs, you plant the seeds for running a great hotel.

The final phase in creating your strategic map is to consider how you will measure progress and this will be our focus in the following chapter.

3
How can you measure the impact of your strategic map over time?

As we turn our attention to measuring the impact of your strategic map, it is helpful to think again about the athlete example we used earlier. Not only do great athletes set goals, but they also constantly monitor whether they are progressing towards those goals.

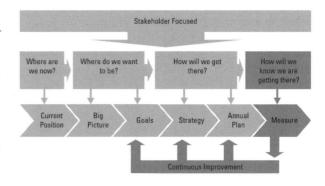

Each race is in fact a measure for them, but so too is every training session and even a timed lap helps them to gauge how well they are doing.

If results indicate that they are not moving in the right direction then they re-examine every aspect of what they are doing and make adjustments where necessary. They might even find that their goals were unrealistic in the first place, given their capabilities.

You too can learn lessons from athletes in terms of how the best are constantly striving to be better, which you can apply to your hotel. The previous chapter helped you to answer questions such as *where are we now?*, *where do we want to be?* and *how will we get there?* in relation to achieving excellence. The final part of developing your strategic map requires you to consider, *how will we know we are getting there?*

How will we know we are getting there?

The answer to this question can only come from measuring progress, analysing the implications of the results you get and taking action to continuously improve. Continuous improvement is a feature of all excellent companies and is only possible within a culture where there is genuine concern, dedication and a willingness amongst managers and employees to constantly get better at what they do. Hence, everyone in your hotel will have a role to play in the process, but you must naturally take the lead here.

A basic framework for managing continuous improvement, which we will use throughout this book, can be described as:

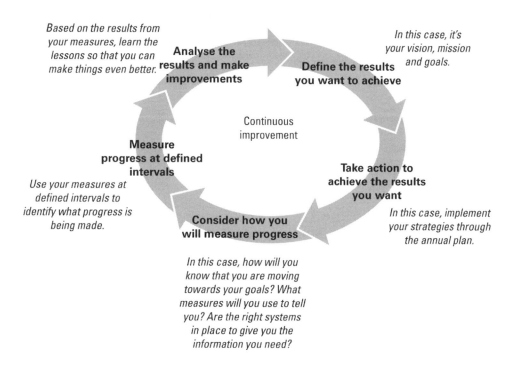

Focusing on continuous improvement with regard to your strategic map requires you to consider the issues in the following sections.

Define the results you want to achieve

You will already know what you want to achieve here. It's your goals, which define excellence in concrete terms and have been developed based on your vision and mission. As we work through our continuous improvement framework, we will continue to use our fictitious hotel example to help make sense of the process. As a reminder, here are the goals which they were seeking to achieve:

Sample Goals

Vision	Goals
'To become the leading independent four-star hotel in London providing excellent products and services at reasonable prices to every customer, every time.' →	❑ To win the *Customers' Choice Award* in the coming year. ❑ To achieve the Hotel Association's *Best Hotels Award* within two years.

Mission	Goals
'Our customers are our priority and we will provide them with a quality experience which is second to none.' →	❑ To increase the number of repeat customers to 40% within three years. ❑ To increase customer satisfaction levels to 90% within two years. ❑ To continuously increase our scores on internal and external quality audits.

Mission	Goals
'We recognise the importance of our employees in achieving this and we will create a positive working environment which encourages their loyalty, commitment and hard work.' →	❑ To reduce employee turnover to 20% within three years. ❑ To achieve an average rating of 75% from employee engagement surveys. ❑ To introduce a bonus scheme for all employees within three years.

Mission	Goals
'We strive to be excellent leaders and will undertake all our business activities in an honest and ethical manner to provide a fair return on our investment.' →	❑ To improve leadership effectiveness annually based on our leadership competence model. ❑ To increase net profit to 15% of sales within two years. ❑ To increase RevPar by 5% annually. ❑ To increase restaurant throughput to 1,500 covers per week within two years. ❑ To reduce food cost to the industry average of 35% in the coming year without reducing quality. ❑ To reduce labour costs to 40% within two years.

The management team at this hotel know precisely what it is that they are aiming for. You of course will have different goals, but the principles remain the same; you will simply want to know whether your goals are becoming a reality. Otherwise, they are just pipe dreams.

Take action to achieve the results you want

Once you are clear on what results you want, you must then take action to make them happen. In relation to your strategic map, this means implementing your strategies through your annual plan as described. After all, if you don't actually do the work in the first place then measuring impact is pointless, so make sure that the defined actions are addressed within the agreed timeframes.

Consider how you will measure progress

Measuring progress in relation to your strategic map has two dimensions: *implementation* and *impact*. Measuring implementation is relatively straightforward and essentially means that you ensure that the actions agreed in your annual plan are actually carried out within the agreed timeframe through regular review during the year. In other words, did you actually take the action necessary to achieve the results you want?

Measuring impact is somewhat more complicated but more valuable in terms of what it can tell you about your progress towards excellence. It is a critical area to consider and will require you to think about how you will actually measure progress towards your goals in the months and years ahead. This will not only involve defining potential measures, but may also necessitate putting systems in place to gather the relevant data. It is such an important area that you should give it a lot of thought early on in the process, so that you will have the information you need, when you need it later.

You will probably have already heard of terms such as key performance indicators/measures and even scorecards but, as with everything else, we will streamline the jargon here too.

No doubt you already measure impact in certain areas and you certainly evaluate financial performance. However, when we talk about identifying progress toward your goals, there may be measurement gaps to be bridged because clearly not all the goals in your strategic map will be financial in nature. So, what measures will you actually need?

Naturally, this will depend upon the goals you set and the key point here is not to overload yourself with measures; you only need those that are of value for you. Taking our hotel example, this might involve the following sample measures.

Sample Measures

Goals		Sample Measures
❏ To win the *Customers' Choice Award* in the coming year.	➡	❏ Achievement of the *Customers' Choice Award*
❏ To achieve the Hotel Association's *Best Hotels Award* within two years.	➡	❏ Achievement of Hotel Association's *Best Hotels Award*.

Goals		Sample Measures
❏ To increase the number of repeat customers to 40% within three years.	➡	❏ Repeat customers %
❏ To increase customer satisfaction levels to 90% within two years.	➡	❏ Overall customer satisfaction %
❏ To continuously increase our scores on internal and external quality audits.	➡	❏ Quality audit scores.

Goals		Sample Measures
❏ To reduce employee turnover to 20% within three years.	➡	❏ Employee turnover %
❏ To achieve an average rating of 75% from employee engagement surveys.	➡	❏ Employee engagement %
❏ To introduce a bonus scheme for all employees within three years.	➡	❏ Actual implementation of bonus scheme.

Goals		Sample Measures
❏ To improve leadership effectiveness annually based on our leadership competence model.	➡	❏ Results from leader performance appraisals ❏ Employee satisfaction with leadership
❏ To increase net profit to 15% of sales within two years.	➡	❏ Net profit %
❏ To increase RevPar by 5% annually.	➡	❏ RevPar
❏ To increase restaurant throughput to 1,500 covers per week within two years.	➡	❏ Number of covers
❏ To reduce food cost to the industry average of 35% in the coming year without reducing quality.	➡	❏ Food cost %
❏ To reduce labour costs to 40% within two years.	➡	❏ Labour cost %

Without the sample measures identified above, the management team in our example hotel couldn't determine whether or not they were on the right track. You will also notice that their mix of measures gives them feedback relating to each of their primary stakeholders, *owners*, *customers* and *employees*, so they will have a very holistic feel for how the hotel is performing.

DO YOU HAVE THE NECESSARY SYSTEMS IN PLACE?

Having identified the measures you will use, you must then consider whether you have the systems in place to give you the data you need at the times you need it. To be in a position to measure anything, information systems are required and whilst these do not have to be complicated, they must provide you with the feedback on actual progress against projected in the relevant areas.

In a larger operation you probably already have the required systems in place but in a smaller hotel you may not. Every business regardless of size needs regular information to support ongoing decision making. Of course this might present resource challenges for you, but if you are serious about excellence, you must find ways to address the issue. Without the right data, you cannot measure impact, make informed decisions, take corrective action or indeed continuously improve. In short, you cannot excel. In any case, think of any costs incurred here as an investment, the return on which will be improved decision making and ultimately a better hotel.

Based on the goals and measures for our example hotel, the management team would need to consider the following information requirements.

Having the systems to give you the information you need, when you need it

Measures		
Measures ❏ Achievement of the *Customers' Choice Award*. ❏ Achievement of Hotel Association's *Best Hotels Award*.	➡	❏ These particular measures are easily evaluated. It will be a yes/no answer; they either get the awards or they don't.
Measures ❏ Repeat customers %. ❏ Overall customer satisfaction %. ❏ Quality audit scores.	➡	❏ The management team would need to consider what customer-related measures they currently have in place. Do current systems enable them to track repeat customers for example? ❏ Can they compile an overall customer satisfaction percentage from the feedback mechanisms they already use? ❏ Do they have a system for auditing quality and does it provide them with overall scores that they can track?
Measures ❏ Employee turnover %. ❏ Employee engagement %. ❏ Actual implementation of bonus scheme.	➡	❏ In this case, the management team would need to ask themselves whether or not they currently measure employee turnover and engagement. If not, they would need to decide how they can do this. ❏ Do they have the systems in place which would allow them to devise and implement a bonus scheme?
Measures ❏ Results from leader performance appraisals. ❏ Employee satisfaction with leadership. ❏ Net profit % ❏ RevPar ❏ Number of covers ❏ Food cost % ❏ Labour cost %	➡	❏ The management team would need to consider whether their existing systems enable them to appraise the effectiveness of leaders at the hotel. Can they track employee satisfaction with leadership? If not, they would need to decide how this information could be generated. They would also need to ensure that performance appraisals were effective and that employee feedback on leadership effectiveness was actually sought. ❏ In addition, the management team would need to consider whether or not their financial systems could produce the various measures they require.

As part of creating your own strategic map, you should therefore think about what your information needs will be in future, what you currently have available and put the appropriate systems in place to bridge any gaps.

TIP

In later chapters, you will find guidance on implementing structured feedback mechanisms with customers and employees which will help you in devising appropriate information systems for your business.

Measure progress at defined intervals

At defined intervals in the future, you will obviously need to produce the measures you have identified so that you can track progress. For some measures, such as financial data, you will produce them frequently. For others, such as an employee engagement percentage, it takes more time to see results. Such measurements might be taken quarterly, bi-annually or annually depending upon the scale of your operation.

Analyse the results and make improvements

The final stage of the continuous improvement cycle is the most important component and is really the cornerstone of your journey to excellence. Depending on actual results achieved against those expected you will be faced with some decisions. If progress is not matching expectations, you must identify what's causing the shortfall and take corrective action. Even when the result is positive, you still need to learn the lessons, so that you can make it even better in future.

This analysis phase will require you to investigate root causes and might involve, depending upon the specific measure, a range of actions such as:

❑ If customer satisfaction is below par, you will need to communicate directly with your customers to determine why.

❑ If employee engagement levels do not meet expectations, this again will require you to communicate with them to find out why.

❑ If financial targets are not met, you will naturally explore in detail where things went wrong.

Based on what you learn from this analysis, you then plan for the next period to make improvements so that you actually do get better. You might even be forced to re-examine your strategies or maybe even to conclude that the goals you set were simply over ambitious in the first place. Also as part of this analysis and improvement phase, you will be able to identify trends in your key measures over time and this will help you to determine whether you are consistently improving.

Benchmarking your results

To strengthen your understanding of how your hotel is performing against the defined goals, you should also explore ways in which you can *benchmark* your results against industry norms. These benchmarking relationships can be informal in nature, agreed with what you consider to be comparable hotels, or they can be more structured systems. For example, many hotel associations or government agencies now produce sector-wide performance data and you can use this to determine how well your business is performing against your peers. After all, you might show improvement in key areas within your hotel year on year, but if similar hotels are generating even greater results, then you are still under-performing.

This concept of constantly striving to be better based on accurate feedback is the essence of continuous improvement; it is also the frame of mind which underpins excellence. Being the best means never standing still, always pushing up the bar and having the right data to guide improvement decisions. You should always aim to be better in all your key activities a year from now than you are today, for to stand still is in reality to go backwards in a competitive industry like ours.

Managing continuous improvement does not have to be a complex undertaking but it does need structure and is dependent upon having the right information to guide you, if you want to see positive results.

SUMMARY

The ability to know what information you need, generate it and then act on what the results tell you will support you as you raise the performance of your hotel. In this chapter, we have explored the concept of continuous improvement in relation to your strategic map, but we will return to this model as part of the 'review' section under each of our themes.

There is no magic pill for achieving excellence but the principles we have covered in these first three chapters will set you on a course where becoming the best is a more realistic aspiration. All great hotels, whether they are large or small, independent or part of a chain, succeed in large part because they know what they want to achieve, implement a range of integrated actions to make that happen, track their progress and continuously improve based on the results they get. You now have the tools to help you apply those principles to your hotel.

Finally, take a key message with you from Theme 1: hard work and effort without clear direction to guide it is essentially self-defeating and will hurt your hotel in the end. Excellence is not achieved by chance.

THEME 2 – LEAD TO SUCCEED

Strengthen leadership effectiveness at your hotel

LEAD TO SUCCEED

How effective is leadership at your hotel?

> *In the past a leader was a boss. Today's leaders must be partners with their people, they no longer can lead solely based on positional power.*
>
> Ken Blanchard

Theme 1 focused on defining the overall direction for your hotel and provided guidance on how to convert your broad aims into concrete goals and related actions. Continuing with our stakeholder focus, the remaining three themes will concentrate on *you*, your *employees* and your *customers*. Leadership effectiveness, employee engagement and captivating your customers will be important issues in helping you to realise whatever goals you define for your hotel as part of your journey to excellence.

We begin with *you* because it is the quality of your leadership, and that of other leaders in your hotel, which will be the key driver of improved performance. You might have noticed that few subjects in the world of business are as hyped as leadership; the soundbite culture thrives, gurus flourish, and there are literally thousands of leadership development programmes out there to choose from. Yet, for all the attention it gets, feedback from employees across industry lines consistently shows high levels of dissatisfaction with the quality of leadership at work.

In hotels we depend heavily on our employees, more so than in many other fields, because it is they who ultimately make or break the customer experience. Given the financial constraints associated with running any type of hotel, there is rarely any 'fat in the system', so you need every employee to work to their full potential if your hotel is to thrive.

We will explore later in the book what can be done to more fully engage your employees in your business but getting the best from them begins with you and your management team; the collective quality of your leadership impacts heavily on employee productivity and directly influences their willingness to work to a high standard. As you continue on your journey to excellence now is the time to ask yourself: *how effective is leadership at your hotel?*

It should come as no surprise to you that employees perform better in an environment where leadership is strong than when it's not. You may not be so clear about what leading people means in practice.

Theme 2 helps you to enhance leadership effectiveness at the hotel through exploring important questions such as:

❑ What does leading people actually involve?

❑ How can you improve leadership effectiveness at your hotel?

❑ How can you measure leadership effectiveness over time?

How
effective is
leadership
at your
hotel?

Think

*What does
leading
people
actually
involve?*

Do

Review

*How can you
measure
leadership
effectiveness
over time?*

*How can you
improve
leadership
effectiveness
at your hotel?*

In the following three chapters you will see that being an effective leader is as much about who you are and how you think as it is about what you do. Understanding the mindset, qualities and skills which facilitate strong leadership will provide you with a solid foundation as you seek to improve your talents in this area.

As you progress through the content in Theme 2, you should initially reflect on your own leadership capabilities because you are the primary source of inspiration in your hotel. You should then think about the potential of the other leaders you employ and how their capabilities might be enhanced. After all, there is no point in you seeking to develop your leadership skills, if they don't.

4

What does leading people actually involve?

THINK	**WHAT DOES LEADING PEOPLE ACTUALLY INVOLVE?**

A few months ago, I was consulting with a hotel group which had a number of properties in different city-centre locations. These hotels had fairly similar offerings, mainly directed at the corporate market and operated under comparable economic and competitive conditions. In general, the performance of all the hotels was living up to expectations, except for one.

Having spent time in this underperforming hotel, it quickly became clear that things weren't right; the atmosphere within that property was very different to that of the others. Morale was low, employee turnover was higher than the norm and customer feedback was not at the level normally seen across the group.

In working with the general manager to identify ways to improve things at the hotel, the issue of employee motivation naturally arose. During our discussions, he made a comment which was pretty blunt, but very telling: 'Look, these people are paid to do a job and I expect them to do what they are paid to do. If they don't like it, then they know where the door is.' The reference to 'these people' says it all really. This comment offered but a glimpse into his overall approach and no prizes for guessing that the problems at this hotel were not resource, marketing or product related; they were a direct result of poor leadership.

Now there is no suggestion, I repeat no suggestion, that this sort of attitude is reflective of hoteliers generally, but many do struggle with the notion that there is a need to lead and not only manage people today. You should recognise that just because you own, or manage the hotel, this doesn't guarantee that your employees see you as a leader. Equally, others in the hotel who act in leadership roles must understand that whilst they might have the name badge, there is no automatic entitlement for employees to look up to them.

Gaining the respect and support of employees doesn't come from the position you hold and thinking solely in terms of managing people is not enough; people need to be led today. Unless you fully appreciate why this is so, then you are unlikely to strive continuously to enhance leadership effectiveness, so we will first explore this need to lead.

Balancing the human equation

Employees are the key to success in the hotel industry and you ignore the people component at your peril. The reason for this becomes clearer when you analyse what actually happens in your hotel every day, based on three simple dimensions of work: the *what*, the *how* and the *who*.

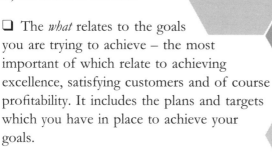

❑ The *what* relates to the goals you are trying to achieve – the most important of which relate to achieving excellence, satisfying customers and of course profitability. It includes the plans and targets which you have in place to achieve your goals.

❑ The *how* refers to the manner in which the work is done and includes issues such as productivity, efficiency and quality.

❑ The *who* is concerned with the people you employ to do the work and includes issues such as their commitment, competence and motivation.

We can depict these three considerations as a basic equation:

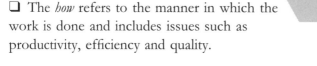

The Who		The How		The What
Commitment competence and motivation	leads to	Productivity, efficiency and quality	contributes to	Achieving excellence, satisfied customers and profitability
Employees		Processes		Results

You don't have to be Einstein to figure out that, in our industry, the *what* and the *how* are ultimately dependent on the *who*. It is through the commitment, competence and motivation of your employees that you achieve greater productivity, efficiency and quality – all of which contribute to achieving excellence, customer satisfaction and in turn to the overall profitability of your hotel. You cannot succeed without your employees and that applies whether you have ten or a hundred. This fundamental principle provides the rationale for the need to lead.

What's the difference between leading and managing?

If you aren't too sure how to differentiate leadership from management then rest assured, you are not alone. The distinctions are not so easy to explain and although we won't get too hung up on the theory of it all, they are not the same thing, so you do need to give it some thought. Don't make the mistake that 'leadership' is just some fancy term to make management sound more interesting. It isn't.

Although the differences between the two are often subtle, they have a major impact in terms of employee engagement and hence business performance. These differences initially lie in the approach taken to getting the results you want; leading and managing are in essence two very different mindsets. In fact, they are in many ways like chalk and cheese. A leader thinks and therefore acts differently from a manager, although they carry out the same functions and want the same results.

Perhaps one of the most common misconceptions about leadership is that leaders are in some way less concerned with results than are managers. This is simply not the case and leadership is as keenly focused on excellence and profitability as management. However, the approach taken to achieving those desired results can differ greatly. But how is it different?

Leaders recognise that if you concentrate too much on the *what* and *how* elements of our equation, then this will cause problems. Of course they are important, but as we have said they are achieved through employees, so you need to focus on the *who*. Whereas management, particularly old style approaches, seeks to 'push' employees towards goals, leadership is about trying to 'attract' them there by first attracting them to you by the way you think, act and behave as a leader. Those who only see their role as being to manage tend to rely on their title or position as their main source of power. Those who lead use their personality and related behaviours to achieve their aims and have highly developed people skills.

Leadership has assumed greater importance in recent decades because of changing attitudes to work. Once upon a time, you didn't really have to be concerned about employees, it sufficed to simply tell them what to do and they just did it. If you told them to jump, they asked how high. Clearly those days are now long gone and your employees will not respond well to being told what to do all the time.

Adopting such a limited approach today at best creates robots – people who just do what they are told to do – at worst, it is likely to lead to resistance, disgruntlement, conflict and eventually, disengaged employees.

It is only through effective leadership that you can get the best from your employees and comfortably deal with the range of people and problems that you encounter every day. It can be argued that in a hotel setting, the need to lead is even greater, because you interact so closely with your employees on a daily basis. Some employees are easy to motivate but, sadly, they are often in the minority. The majority require a bit more effort. There are also those special ones who seem to drift through life at work, so much so, that the only way to tell they are actually breathing is to place a mirror under their nose!

Without strong leadership, you cannot master the challenges that people at work present and the real test of effective leadership is not what happens when the leader is present but what goes on when they are not around. When you really think about it, it's not so hard to figure out. Everyone wants to work for someone who values and respects them and if they get that, most people will respond in a positive way.

Leadership seeks to create a working environment where people want to work to the best of their ability, not because they have to, but because they feel part of something they value. There is no pretence that this is easy to achieve, but you will find that the results are worth the effort.

THAT'S ALL FINE IN THEORY, BUT . . .

A significant concern often raised about leadership is that because it focuses on the employee side of the equation as a means to getting results, becoming an effective leader is just too time consuming and unrealistic when faced with the constant pressures of hotel life. One operator described these concerns nicely when she said 'you would end up trying to create a happiness camp at work. When would the actual work get done?' This and other concerns crop up time and time again in relation to leadership and you may feel this way too. For this reason, it is worth exploring further what leadership is and is not concerned with.

Leadership means genuinely seeing your employees as stakeholders in your hotel and acting in a way that reflects that belief. If you don't truly see your employees as an integral part of your business, then leadership isn't going to work for you. At the same time, it is always a two-way street and you expect them to deliver the goods for you in return for your approach.

Leadership:

is about focusing on your employees	→	but not at the expense of quality performance and results.
does mean involving your employees in the running of your hotel	→	but does not mean allowing the 'tail to wag the dog'.
is about working consistently to engage your employees	→	but not without seeing a return in terms of improved performance.
does mean allowing employees freedom and autonomy when appropriate	→	but does not mean that you allow them to do whatever they want.
does not take more time	→	but does require more thought.

There are of course those who refuse to accept this need to lead and they cling to their 'my way or the highway' approach. Can they succeed? Well, that depends on how you quantify success. *Getting the job done* and *getting the job done to a high standard* are not the same thing. When people work in an environment where leadership is lacking, a number of things usually happen. Over time the good employees generally leave, which causes problems with continuity and quality in the business. Those who don't have the same options might well stay, but they do the job because they have to, which does not mean they give their all.

Real leadership is required if you want great employees and ultimately a great hotel. It is not a cliché to say that you cannot manage people towards excellence; you can only ever hope to lead them there.

Leaders are different, but still human

Many people shy away from the term *leader* because they believe that only the select few can become one; you need to be born at some magic time when the planets are in alignment if you want to lead. This is inaccurate. Of course, there have been great leaders throughout history whom you can say were born or destined to lead, but leadership in a work context is different.

Everyone can develop their ability to lead at work, if the desire is there to do so. Naturally some people will be more gifted at it, but that's the same in every walk of life; we can all learn to swim, but that doesn't mean we will all be competing in the 100 metres breaststroke at the Olympics. Being a leader is not only for the chosen few, nor is it something to be feared.

The core to becoming an effective leader is having a real desire to lead and being prepared to translate that commitment into action all day, every day. You have to want to do it and be ready to work hard at improving your abilities. The best leaders do possess certain qualities and skills, which we will explore in the next chapter but as a minimum they are always passionate about what they do and are continuously striving to be better. They are in tune with human nature and accept that no two people will think and act the same, nor should they be expected to. Leaders see this, not as a problem, but as a challenge and recognise that they will get better results if their attitude and approach to their employees is right.

Probably the greatest difference between a leader and a manager is that managers often view leadership as being one of the many functions they must perform as part of their management role. Leaders see things in a different light. They perceive leadership not as a duty, but as something which defines them. Leaders are different because they:

Think Differently		Act Differently
recognise that attitudes to work today are radically different and the concept of 'managing people' is becoming less and less relevant.	→	apply innovative leadership approaches in order to bring the best out of people.
understand that just telling employees what to do might seem be easier but it doesn't get the best results over the long term.	→	involve employees in decision making, when appropriate, and regularly utilise two-way communication channels.
realise that it is the people who ultimately achieve business outcomes.	→	strive to engage their employees, not just occasionally but all the time.
accept that people are all different and as such will not all act in the same way or respond to the same approach.	→	develop their people skills to a high level and have flexibility in their approach.
acknowledge that the past cannot be changed, only learned from and continuously look to the future.	→	have a clear view of where they are going, which they continuously communicate to their employees.
understand that the days of 'do as I say, not as I do' are long gone.	→	are role models for those around them – not perfect or infallible by any means, but continuously striving to be better.

SUMMARY

Effective leadership means focusing on people in order to increase their commitment, competence and motivation so that they improve their productivity, efficiency and the quality of their work. This in turn helps to achieve excellence , increase customer satisfaction and leads to greater profitability . Seeking to improve the quality of leadership in your hotel is impossible unless you, and all those in leadership roles buy into the general principles described here.

It is therefore worth taking time out to talk with your managers and supervisors to determine what their current attitudes are in relation to leadership. You will likely find that many do not see their role as being to lead, but they can never improve their potential as leaders, unless they first accept the idea that leadership is essential today. In the following chapter, we will explore how you can enhance leadership effectiveness in practice.

5

How can you improve leadership effectiveness at your hotel?

DO	**HOW CAN YOU IMPROVE LEADERSHIP EFFECTIVENESS AT YOUR HOTEL?**

When did you last sit down and really think about how you can improve overall leadership effectiveness at your hotel? If you are like most owners and managers, you probably feel that there are far more practical matters to worry about. Indeed, there are many pressing issues which require your attention every day, but there are none more critical than leadership. Don't underestimate the strength of the correlation between strong leadership and excellence.

When you did devote time to thinking about leadership in the past, it was perhaps in the context of organising some form of training, either for yourself or for the other leaders you have at the hotel. Whilst training is of course an important consideration, leadership effectiveness is not delivered through training alone, so we need to reflect more deeply on the subject.

Here's what not to do . . .

As you begin to consider how to improve leadership effectiveness, here is an example of what not to accept at your hotel. Remember our underperforming manager from the previous chapter? His problem was that he was a very belligerent character and his leadership style was the equivalent of a blunt instrument; the big stick and in his case with nails in it too! Essentially, he had a fairly explosive temper and regularly blew a fuse because he lacked self-control. It is the daily consequences of that approach which are of interest, as we consider how to enhance the quality of leadership.

Some of his employees described their reactions to his outbursts as 'riding out the storm' and they readily admitted that when he lost it with them, they just stood there and waited for him to calm down. One or two of his more senior staff, the stronger characters, described it differently: they called it 'kangaroo boxing' (don't ask me why, but the fact that this manager was Australian might have had something to do with it). What they meant by this was that they gave as good as they got and heated arguments and battles regularly ensued.

In both instances, the employees didn't take on board what were often valid concerns of their manager because you could say that his style overshadowed his substance. Whatever you think of this manager's approach, you certainly couldn't call it leadership and the damage he caused should be pretty clear. In fact, it's more a case of self-harm, because he suffered most in the long run and he was rightly blamed for the hotel's poor performance.

Of course, we all get it wrong from time to time – we're not machines – but his was a repetitive pattern of aggression, which is different. He was not a bad chap, but he did have a spectacular talent for shooting himself in the foot. In short, he was not a leader. Whatever approach you take to enhancing leadership effectiveness, one thing you should never accept at the hotel is aggression; it only serves to damage performance, not improve it.

This chapter provides you with an opportunity to undertake a root and branch review of leadership throughout your business. In doing so, you should consider it from three perspectives.

1. Before you can enhance the quality of leadership at the hotel, you need to create an overall context for it.

2. You should also give some thought as to what leadership effectiveness will actually mean, in measurable terms, in your business.

3. Based on this definition of effectiveness, you should then consider how you and all the leaders at the hotel can, individually and collectively, improve.

These three aspects of leadership will be our main concern in this chapter and we will first turn our attention to how you might create an overall context for leadership.

Creating a context for leadership at the hotel

As it is with all our themes, it is important to initially define the general parameters in relation to leadership at the hotel. Creating an overall context for leadership will help you to identify specific goals to guide all future improvement activities in this area. You create this context when you prepare your mission statement, for it is here that you broadly outline what you are trying to achieve as leaders.

As a guide, let's look again at how the management team at our example hotel from Theme 1 described their overall aspirations with regard to leadership.

> ## Mission
> Our customers are our priority and we will provide them with a quality experience which is second to none. We recognise the importance of our employees in achieving this and we will create a positive working environment which encourages their loyalty, commitment and hard work. **We strive to be excellent leaders and will undertake all our business activities in an honest and ethical manner to provide a fair return on our investment.**

Clearly these are nice sentiments, but they didn't stop there. Instead they defined some tangible goals regarding leadership, which were the following.

Mission		Goals
'We strive to be excellent leaders and will undertake all our business activities in an honest and ethical manner to provide a fair return on our investment.'	➔	❑ To improve leadership effectiveness annually based on our leadership competence model. ❑ To increase net profit to 15% of sales within two years. ❑ To increase RevPar by 5% annually. ❑ To increase restaurant throughput to 1,500 covers per week within two years. ❑ To reduce food cost to the industry average of 35% in the coming year without reducing quality. ❑ To reduce labour costs to 40% within two years.

The mission and related goals created the context for leadership at this hotel. But what would be required to achieve those goals? As part of their overall strategy, the management team would have to devise a competence model, which specified what leadership effectiveness meant in practice. From that, it would be necessary over time to develop the capabilities of all leaders at the hotel to deliver on those competences.

You too will be faced with the same challenge. First, you must think about the big picture and incorporate your general intentions regarding leadership into your mission for the hotel. From that, you should develop specific goals and an overall strategy for enhancing leadership effectiveness. As part of that strategy, you must devise a leadership competence model, if you don't already have one, to guide all your efforts at developing individual and collective leadership capabilities.

Defining a leadership competence model

Leadership effectiveness is a fuzzy term at the best of times; it can mean different things to different people. You can't really use such a vague concept to drive improvement efforts and you certainly couldn't measure progress in future against something so intangible. This is why you need a competence model.

There are many possible approaches to developing a leadership competence model which vary in complexity, but we will keep it fairly straightforward here and consider one in line with our three dimensions of work; the *what*, the *how*, the *who*. Based on these components, you could develop specific criteria to describe leadership effectiveness which might include some or all of the following points (see opposite page).

These are just sample criteria for you to consider, but you get the idea; you are translating leadership effectiveness into something more concrete. You might use these criteria as they stand, or you can develop others to reflect your own requirements. In doing so, you will generate a user-friendly definition of what you expect from the leaders at the hotel.

Think of it this way: if any given leader in your hotel was meeting all of these sample criteria, they would be very effective and adding a lot of value to your business. The competence model you develop will also be useful in other areas such as recruitment, training and performance management, so it is certainly a task worth undertaking.

Improving individual and collective leadership performance

With leadership goals and a competence model in place, you can then turn your attention to building your own capabilities and those of other leaders at the hotel to deliver on those competences. This will involve a range of measures including training, coaching and indeed mentoring around leadership.

To support you in this, the remainder of the chapter will focus on the personal qualities which underpin effective leadership and some core competences which would be an integral part of any model you might develop. Your competence model will naturally contain a broad range of skills but it is not the intention to address all of them here. Instead, the emphasis will be on two critical competences which are fundamental to success in any leadership role. As you read ahead, consider the content in relation to yourself first and then think about what you need to do to build those capabilities in others.

		Sample criteria to define leadership effectiveness
The What →	Define leadership criteria which are related to meeting specific performance targets. →	Specific measures and targets could be defined for leaders which might include an ability to: ❏ meet revenue targets ❏ achieve cost percentages ❏ increase customer satisfaction ratings for their area ❏ lower employee turnover in their area ❏ reduce the number of accidents in their area ❏ meet the requirements for training hours provided to staff
The How →	Develop leadership criteria which are related to a leader's ability to get the work done to a high standard. →	❏ demonstrate *commitment* to the hotel's vision and mission ❏ understand their *roles* and *responsibilities* and demonstrate high levels of competence ❏ continuously *develop* their own skills and knowledge ❏ effectively *plan* and *organise* the workload in their department ❏ *manage resources* to achieve the objectives agreed for their area ❏ provide clear *direction* and *guidance* to their employees ❏ ensure that work in their area is consistently carried out to the *standard* required ❏ constantly strive to improve overall *quality* and promote continuous improvement in their area ❏ address *underperformance* in a proactive and constructive manner ❏ adopt a structured approach to *training*, *coaching* and *developing* their team ❏ provide regular constructive *feedback* to employees ❏ *solve problems* and show initiative in finding creative solutions to work-related problems
The Who →	Develop leadership criteria which are related to their ability to lead others. →	❏ be *self-motivated* and set a positive example for employees by their attitude and performance ❏ demonstrate high levels of *energy*, *enthusiasm* and *professionalism* ❏ show *concern* for their team members and interact with them in a positive manner ❏ treat all team members *equally* and *fairly* ❏ apply flexible *leadership styles* and regularly demonstrate an ability to adjust their approach to deal with different people and situations ❏ communicate in a structured and effective manner with their team ❏ build and sustain effective *relationships* with employees and customers ❏ *motivate* others to improved performance.

What makes a great leader?

What is it then that makes a great leader? Naturally, leaders require certain skills and you have already seen some of them in the sample competence model. However, there is often too much emphasis placed on the skills of leadership; develop specific competences, it is proposed, and you will become a better leader. Unfortunately, this is a bit misleading. Let's be clear, the skills of leadership are critical, but they are somewhat secondary.

Success as a leader stems from how you think and who you are, and not solely from what you do. There are certain personal attributes which facilitate effective leadership, so you should consider them first. With these qualities in place, you are in a better position to apply the skills of leadership; without them you will struggle.

Here is a simple example: our Australian manager was told by his boss that unless he adjusted his management style, he wouldn't have much of a future with the company. To their credit, his superiors gave him lots of support and signed him up for a prestigious leadership course where he covered skills such as communication and leadership styles. But he found little value from this programme back at work. Why? Because he never managed to control his temper, so he wasn't able to apply the skills he learned in any meaningful way. He did try to become a better communicator, but every time he found himself under pressure or stressed, he lost it and all the learning went out of the window.

An important message to take from this should be that successful leaders need certain characteristics to succeed; these qualities help the skills and competences to 'stick'. Therefore the first practical step you can take in seeking to improve your ability to lead is to increase your *self-awareness* and explore what strengths and areas for improvement you currently have in relation to the leadership profile. You then need to act on what you learn about yourself, of course.

So, what is this leadership profile? Obviously, there isn't a perfect model, as all leaders are different, so one size does not fit all but there are common attributes which are proven to support effective leadership. We can define them by again referring to our three dimensions of work: the *what*, the *how* and the *who*.

DRIVING QUALITIES – HELPING YOU TO GET RESULTS

Leaders need certain attributes which help them to achieve the *what*. We'll call them *driving qualities* in the sense that they support you in driving results in your hotel.

❑ A key quality here, which we have already discussed, is to be *goal-orientated*: having a clear view of what your hotel is trying to achieve, which you constantly 'sell' to others. The best leaders get buy-in from their employees for business goals, so much so, that they feel they are their own.

❑ Being *committed* is also critical, because how can you ever expect others in your business to show commitment, if you don't? Obviously, you are likely to be committed, but are the other leaders in your hotel as committed to what you are trying to achieve?

❑ Being *self-motivated* is vital, and successful leaders in any field are driven by the quest for excellence. As you well know, running a hotel is not a bed of roses and there are plenty of days when you feel like being somewhere else. But real leaders can raise their game, even when they don't feel like it.

❑ Finally in this area, you need to have *energy* and *enthusiasm*. Being positive and passionate about what you do is infectious and will spread to others; as will negativity. The best leaders have high energy levels which makes people feel good about being around them. They are never the dark cloud on the horizon.

DIRECTING QUALITIES – HELPING YOU TO GET THE WORK DONE
This set of qualities relates to your ability to deal with the *how* component of work. We'll call them *directing qualities* because they support you as you direct how the work is carried out.

❑ At the heart of this is being *competent* at what you do and it goes without saying that you need to know the tasks you expect others to undertake. This is particularly true in a hotel context where you often have to jump in and support your employees when they are under pressure; there is nothing worse than a boss who causes chaos when they try to help out!

❑ Allied to being competent is the need to be *knowledgeable* about aspects of the work your employees do. Providing insightful advice and guidance is not only essential to overall performance, but also helps you to build your credibility and levels of respect.

❑ One point that is often overlooked by leaders is the need to be *innovative*. Finding creative solutions to problems which arise at the hotel is clearly not solely your responsibility. However, an ability to find better ways of doing things will not only lead to improved performance but will also raise your profile in the eyes of your employees.

❑ Lastly in this area you need to be *consistent* both in your own behaviour and in the direction you offer your employees. Nothing winds people up more than a moody boss who, for no apparent reason, changes the way things are done or who gives conflicting direction from one day to the next. Change is of course critical when it leads to improvement, but we are not talking about that here. Inconsistency has nothing to do with change and only leads to frustration and disillusionment.

DRAWING QUALITIES – HELPING YOU TO ATTRACT OTHERS

Leaders also need to have certain attributes which help them to deal with the *who* dimension of work. We'll call them *drawing qualities* in the sense that they help draw others towards you.

❑ To start with, you need to have *concern for others* if you want to be an effective leader. This doesn't mean that you will like all of your individual employees to the same degree, but as a unit you must care about their levels of motivation and satisfaction with their work environment. If you can see that everyone around you has their head down and this doesn't bother you, then you can't be an effective leader. It is only by showing concern for your employees that you can develop trust, appear approachable and build relationships.

❑ Another important quality in terms of building relationships with your employees is the ability to be *open and honest* with them. If you truly view your people as stakeholders, then you should recognise that they need to know what's happening at the hotel. Even when you can't give them the information they want, at least be honest with them as to why; they may not like the answer, but they will respect your honesty.

For as much of the time as you can though, try to avoid running your hotel like the CIA – keep everyone informed as to what is going on and if it concerns sensitive information such as financial data, talk to them in percentages if you don't want to give precise details. The more you provide feedback and supply information, the more your employees feel part of your business.

❑ *Empathy* is a key drawing quality and the ability to understand where someone is coming from is essential in a leadership role. Take the example of the negative employees that you encounter from time to time. Your initial reaction is likely to be that you want to get rid of them as quickly as possible. You may end up having to do that, but behind their negative exterior often lie intelligent, strong-willed characters who have the potential to deliver a lot for a business, if handled correctly.

Human beings are not mass-produced goods, they are individuals and as such have different approaches to life; at times they need support and you need to identify these situations and respond accordingly. You also need to know when people are trying to pull the wool over your eyes, of course.

This leads us to the final quality in this area, *self-control* which we have already referred to in relation to our Australian friend. If you do not have self-control, then in reality it is other people and situations which are controlling the way you behave. Particularly if you are constantly aggressive, you become like a walking time-bomb, creating an atmosphere of fear and anxiety, which has obvious repercussions. But being too passive with your employees will also damage your ability to lead. The goal here is to be assertive or 'in-control' of how you behave.

When we combine these three sets of qualities, we end up with a honeycomb matrix which describes an ideal leadership profile. It is these qualities which are more commonly seen in good leadership.

There are others to consider, such as that elusive quality called charisma; great if you have it, but don't confuse it with arrogance if you do. Now, unless you are superhuman, it is unlikely that you will shine in all these areas but you should at least have strengths across a range of them. Without that, your ability to lead is diminished. Whilst you can learn skills and techniques, it is these qualities which actually enable you to apply them effectively.

You should also recognise that developing your personal qualities is no easy task and it takes time and effort. Maybe that's why they are so often overlooked – they don't fit conveniently with the quick-fix approach often promoted in relation to leadership. You did not become the person you are overnight, so changing your personal qualities and related behaviours won't happen in a flash. Indeed, you can only ever hope to improve, if you show a real desire and commitment to change.

At this point it is probably useful for you to think about your current strengths and areas for improvement against this leadership profile. Consider the following questions to help you:

❏ Do you genuinely believe that your employees are stakeholders in the hotel? How do you currently demonstrate this in practice?

❏ Do you have a clear vision and goals for how you want the hotel to develop? Have you communicated them to your employees?

❏ Are you strongly committed to the hotel and to your employees? How do you show this commitment in practical ways?

❏ Are you highly self-motivated and can you raise your performance, even when you don't necessarily feel like doing so?

❏ Are you passionate about running a great hotel? Does your energy and enthusiasm reflect that every day?

❏ Are you genuinely concerned about the welfare of your employees? What proactive measures do you take to create a positive working environment for them?

❏ Do you make a conscious effort to be open and honest with your employees? When was the last time you sat down and updated them on the hotel's performance?

❏ Do you work hard at seeing things from other peoples' perspectives and do you try to be objective when dealing with your employees?

❏ Do you have excellent levels of self-control and can you prevent individuals, or situations from making you act in a way that you later regret?

❏ Are you competent at what you do and do you have you a strong understanding of the hotel industry in general and hotel operations in particular?

❏ Are you good at analysing problems and finding creative ways of improving how you do things at the hotel?

❏ Are you consistent in your behaviour and approach or do you change what you think, or want from one day to the next?

❏ Do you make yourself available to meet with your employees, individually and collectively, at regular intervals? Do they feel comfortable in coming to speak to you?

❏ Do you let things at work get you down or do you always try to see the bright side?

❏ Can you build trust between yourself and other people?

Self-assessment is of limited value but if you are honest with yourself, it can at least serve as an indicator as to the areas you might need to focus on. Even better, you could ask others whom you know and trust in a work context for their opinion about you. Whatever you decide to do to increase your self-awareness, don't underestimate the importance of the personal qualities needed to succeed as a leader.

To further motivate you in addressing your areas for improvement in this regard, consider the leaders you have worked for over your career. Try to think of one whom you really enjoyed working with and one you didn't. When you compare the two, it is likely you will find that the difference between them was that the good leader had more of these personal attributes than the bad one. Leadership can be a complicated subject, but in some ways, it's pretty easy to figure out.

Core leadership competences

Having considered where you currently fit in relation to the leadership profile and identified what you need to work on, you can now begin to look at two core skills which underpin effective leadership. Leading in practice every day is essentially about managing relationships and certain competences are critical in this regard.

It is these core competences which are fundamental to your ability to lead. In particular, how effectively you communicate impacts on everything you do, so we will deal with this first.

Mastering the art of communication

At the heart of any positive relationship lies effective communication; it is the life blood of human interactions. Great leaders are great communicators, it's as simple as that. Without an ability to 'reach others', you can never hope to lead them in the direction you want them to go.

There is sometimes a misconception that communication in hotels is easier because it's a people business and we interact closely with one another all the time; we are not hidden behind partitions all day. This isn't necessarily accurate. Yes, the nature of communication in hotels may be more personal and at times more informal, but that too can create problems. It is not an exaggeration to say that the majority of people problems you see at work can be traced back to some form of communication breakdown. Hotels are no different.

At one level, communication should be a fairly easy process to master because we have all done it, in some shape or form, since the day we were born, so you would think we would have mastered it by now. You might ask: what's all the fuss about anyway? After all, it simply involves sending messages back and forth between two or more parties. But, as we all know to our cost, something which sounds so straightforward is in fact one of the most regular problems we face, not only in business life, but in our private lives too.

There are an infinite number of reasons why communication breaks down: poor skills of the sender, bad timing and misperceptions – intentional or otherwise – on the part of the receiver to name but a few. In fact, the list goes on and on, so it's understandably frustrating to know where to start and what to do in seeking to become a better communicator.

The best way to deal with the issue is to break it down into manageable bites. To begin with, improving your ability to communicate requires you to act on the areas for improvement that you identified regarding the leadership profile, as many of those personal qualities also directly impact on how you communicate.

Building from there, you need to consider two distinct aspects of communication, *personal* and *structural*. Personal relates to your own capabilities as a communicator in face-to-face situations and this area will be our immediate focus. Structural means the channels and mechanisms that you use to communicate with your employees. We will only touch on that aspect here, but will return to it again in later chapters.

BALANCING CONTENT AND CONTEXT

From the personal perspective, when you communicate directly with others, the message you try to get across has two further components to consider – let's call them *content* and *context*. Content relates to the words you choose whereas context is about how you transmit those words and includes tone and body language. Don't get hung up about the relative importance of words, tone and body language, instead, you should recognise that communication fails when content and context don't match and support each other.

Becoming a better communicator therefore requires you to work on both the content and context of your messages. Obviously they go hand in hand, but as getting the content right is somewhat more straightforward, we will start with that.

What did you say?

The goal of any communication is to develop a common understanding between the parties involved and without that result, the process has failed. Every face-to-face communication situation has a sender and receiver, whether that is one, or many; the receivers are your audience and the content of your message must be constructed to resonate with them. So preparation is the key and you must choose your words for best effect.

Naturally, if you were making a presentation or holding a meeting, the need to prepare is obvious, but even for everyday conversations you must think about what you say. How many times have you opened your mouth and afterwards realised that you should have thought things through more clearly before you spoke? Here are some simple tips for getting the content right.

❑ It goes without saying that you always need to know what you are talking about. Make sure you fully understand the subject under discussion – this in itself helps your confidence as a communicator.

❑ Speak in everyday terms. Don't be metaphor man or woman and avoid being that person who fills their messages with phrases like 'going forward' or 'thinking outside the box'. Recently, whilst sitting in on a management meeting at a hotel, the general manager used the following terms in the space of thirty minutes: 'as you know we are facing into a mega week with the conference coming up, so it's all hands on deck for the next few days . . . I want to make sure we are all singing from the same hymn sheet on this one . . . we need to get the team on board ... at the moment there's a bit of cat herding going on ... making a mess of this conference isn't going to happen on my watch'. People only laugh at you if you overuse silly metaphors.

❑ You should also avoid using too much hotel jargon if your audience might be unfamiliar with those terms.

❑ When transmitting the content of your message, speak clearly and concisely; people don't like wafflers, so get to the point, without being blunt.

There is no step-by-step solution to getting the content right, it's largely common sense. Ask yourself: what do the receivers need to know, what do they already know and how can I put it into words that will grab their attention and resonate with them? Then follow the golden rule by thinking first, then speaking.

It's not what you say; it's the way that you say it

Whilst it is fairly easy to understand what you can do to get the content of your messages right, addressing the context part is far more challenging. The starting point here is to recognise that all your face-to-face communications are emotional to some degree. When angry, your tone and body language changes, as it does when you are insecure, confident, happy, sad and so on. It is this emotional element which is transmitted through the context of your messages – your tone and body language – and this is why context so often overshadows content, disrupting the process of understanding.

To become a better communicator you have to manage the emotional element of communication; you are *not* trying to remove emotion from your communications, for to do so would turn you into an automaton. What you are trying to do is minimise the impact of uncontrolled, negative emotions and maximise the controlled, positive ones.

When uncontrolled emotions increase, something else goes in the opposite direction – your ability to be rational. This is where most of us struggle because our emotions can take over, often without us even realising it. These emotions are individual and situation-dependent and can be anything from anger to shyness and everything inbetween. But, they all have one thing in common – they come out through our tone and body language.

Improving the context of your messages is difficult because first of all, you need to understand what it is you do well and what you don't and then you might have to change the habits of a lifetime. This is made even more challenging by the fact that rarely do our perceptions of what we do match reality. But unless you have an out-of-body experience, how can you actually see what it is you do? It is for this reason that we all need feedback from others we respect; it helps us to see what we can't see ourselves.

There are so many emotional components to consider that in offering guidance on how to improve the context of your messages, it is only possible to focus on extremes and to show symptoms but not causes. The table below demonstrates what happens when you are too aggressive on the one hand or too passive on the other, with the ideal, assertive approach inbetween.

	Passive	Assertive	Aggressive
Tone of Voice	❏ Too softly spoken ❏ Sounding nervous ❏ Overly apologetic ❏ Mumbling	❏ Firm ❏ Calm ❏ Clear ❏ Concise ❏ Enthusiastic	❏ Loud ❏ Raised ❏ Shouting ❏ Sarcastic
Eyes	❏ Uncomfortable making eye contact ❏ Looking down or away a lot	❏ Maintaining good eye contact ❏ Not seeking to intimidate	❏ Staring down ❏ Eyes bulging ❏ Trying to intimidate
Hand Gestures	❏ Nervous gestures ❏ Fidgeting ❏ Hand wringing	❏ Open hand gestures	❏ Lots of pointing ❏ Clenched hands ❏ Thumping table
Body Language	❏ Inward posture ❏ Obviously uncomfortable ❏ Hunched, self protecting	❏ Upright posture ❏ Head up ❏ Using active listening	❏ Forward posture ❏ In your face ❏ Leaning ❏ Threatening

These are just samples of what can happen and your emotions can also influence the words you choose, which is why aggressive people use foul language a lot or people who are very passive say sorry all the time.

Seeking to get the context right means using your tone and body language to support what you are saying and not to detract from it. When you are transmitting a positive message, your tone and body language should reflect that. However, even when you are annoyed and angry with someone you need to control the urge to scream and shout by remaining calm but firm and using assertive not aggressive gestures. None of this is easy of course because we are 'conditioned' to behave in certain ways, so we all get it wrong occasionally.

Where you need to be concerned is if your predominant style of communicating is overly aggressive or indeed overly passive. If you suffer from either, that is a problem which not only affects your ability to communicate but, as we shall see, will also influence your capacity to apply different leadership styles. Only you can take action to find out what your areas for improvement are and only you can do something about it.

SILENCE MAKES A POWERFUL NOISE

As well as thinking about how you send messages, in trying to become a better communicator, you should also think about how you receive them. You must be a good listener too and it is important to view listening as being both a frame of mind and a skill in its own right.

Effective leadership means that you should always be prepared to listen to your employees, individually and collectively. There should be structured communication channels in place, which provide opportunities to sit down and listen to their concerns. In addition, on a day-to-day basis you will need to make time to listen to the people around you, in an appropriate way and at an appropriate time. We will return to this structural aspect of communication later.

You must also view listening as a skill to be developed, designed to encourage your employees to open up and to prevent you from doing all the talking in any given situation. Becoming a better listener means using simple active listening techniques such as:

❏ **Maintaining eye contact** Obviously, this not only shows you are actually willing to listen, but it also helps you to read body language, which can often tell you that something that the other person is saying doesn't add up.

❏ **Nodding** This again is an obvious sign that you are attentive and it encourages the speaker to keep going.

❏ **Encouraging** Simply interjecting on occasion with 'Yes, go on' gets the speaker to continue to open up. This has less impact if you are not making eye contact at the same time. Saying it whilst shuffling through your papers doesn't work!

❏ **Allowing short silences** Most of us hate silences and often try to quickly fill the gap. Don't be afraid to let short silences occur, as it lets the other person know that you are not automatically going to jump in. Often this will encourage them to continue.

❏ **Paraphrasing** This means showing the person that you have got the gist of what they have said by saying things such as: 'So what you are saying is . . .'

❑ **Summarising**   This means confirming in precise detail what they have said to show that you have understood.

Active listening is about concentration. Some people help us to do this because they are good communicators and make us want to listen, whilst others can drone on and drive us to distraction. In a leadership role, you must be a good listener regardless of the context that the other person uses for their delivery.

Developing your ability to communicate is such an important area in business, and in life generally, that not improving isn't an option. You certainly cannot excel as a leader without mastering the art of communication. To help you to reflect on the points raised here, consider the following questions.

❑ Are you open minded when you communicate with people and are you prepared to change your opinion based on the valid opinion of others?

❑ Do you prepare for all communications and think things through before you speak, even for everyday conversations?

❑ Do you tailor your messages to suit the needs of the listener(s)?

❑ Are you a good listener and do you find it easy to let others speak without interruption?

❑ Do you consciously use positive body language signals to improve how you communicate?

❑ Are you good at making eye contact with others when speaking with them?

❑ Are you strong in reading the body language signals of others?

❑ Are you a confident speaker and do you speak in a clear and calm voice even when stressed?

❑ Are you good at getting to the point without being blunt, or do you have a tendency to waffle a lot?

❑ When other people are shy and quiet, are you good at encouraging them to open up?

❏ Are you comfortable in dealing with difficult individuals and can you do so in a controlled manner without losing your cool?

❏ Do you regularly use a range of communication channels to interact with your team?

❏ Are you confident at managing effective meetings? Do your meetings lead to a common understanding of what was discussed and agreed?

❏ Do you over-rely on written forms of communication?

❏ Are you comfortable in dealing with criticism from others?

Without strong communication skills, discussing what leadership styles you can use is difficult because applying any leadership style is simply a form of interaction. Leadership and communication are soulmates. So, devote the necessary time to identify what you need to do to improve how you communicate.

Leading with style

A second core skill likely to be found within any leadership competence model is the ability to apply different styles of leadership in practice. You are faced with many challenging people-related situations every day in your hotel and it is clear that you need to adjust your approach accordingly; the key word when talking about leadership styles is therefore *flexibility*. The best leaders can change their style, depending on the individual or the situation they are faced with, but can do so in a way that is subtle.

This is all marvellous in theory but not so easy to do in reality. Being flexible requires you to adopt different styles of leadership depending on certain factors and this is a skill which takes time (and lots of patience) to develop.

There are numerous theories which describe different leadership styles that you might use and whilst they are helpful at a conceptual level, they are not all that useful in describing how to lead on an every day basis. We will try to be a bit more practical here and will again look at this area with the help of our three components of work: the *what*, the *how* and the *who*. Your daily life at work is essentially about getting the right balance between these three components.

The focus from a leadership perspective should be on your employees (the *who*), as a means of ensuring the work is done to a high standard (the *how*), in order to get the results you want (the *what*). In seeking to balance this equation on a daily basis, you need to consider questions such as:

The What and How	How much *direction* will you give your team and how much *control* will you exercise over their actions?
The Who	How much will you *involve* your team in the decision-making process and how much *autonomy* will you give them in the completion of their duties?

You should quickly see that the more *direction* and *control* you exercise, the less *involvement* and *autonomy* your employees will have. So, in effect they are polar opposites and if you are high on one, you will naturally be low on the other.

The different styles of leadership which can be applied in practice are therefore defined by where you place your emphasis; this can be influenced by the levels of mutual trust and respect between you and your team. The higher that is, the more likely you are to involve your team in decision making or to allow them greater autonomy. Based on these factors, we can define some general styles as follows:

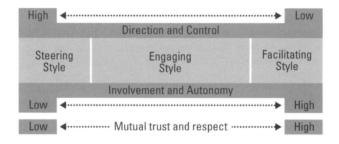

You can see from our simple model that there are essentially three styles of leadership which can be applied, depending on certain factors. Don't view these three styles as boxes that you jump in and out of, but rather as a sliding scale that you subtly move back and forth upon, depending upon what you are faced with. How will you know which one to use? Naturally experience helps, but a number of issues will influence the style you choose.

❑ **Employee engagement**   The level of engagement of your employees will influence the style of leadership you adopt.

❑ **Individual performance**   The ability and willingness of an individual to work to the standard that you want determines the style you adopt with them.

❑ **Different situations**   Different situations will always require the application of different styles.

USING THE STEERING STYLE

The *steering style* is one where you exercise high direction and control over the actions of your employees, which naturally means they have low involvement and autonomy. Steering simply means that you are guiding them as a unit, or individually, in the direction you want them to go. It is an essential style, for example, when confronted with individual or collective underperformance, or when you are faced with a situation where quick action is required, such as when a function is booked at short notice. You might also use it with a new employee, or when an employee is not acting or behaving in an acceptable manner. In fact, you use it at any time where you feel things are not happening as they should be, or when you need to implement decisions where they are not open to debate.

It is important to stress here that *steering* does not mean aggressive; aggression, as we have said, is not part of any leadership approach. When using the steering style you may well be firm at times, or even direct, but the behaviours and communication style you adopt are non-aggressive and you are always in control of your emotions. This is an example of the clear linkages between the way you lead, the way you communicate and the leadership qualities you possess; it's about what you think, who you are and what you do. All three have to be 'in sync' for you to lead effectively.

USING THE ENGAGING STYLE

The *engaging style* is one which involves reducing direction and control and increasing the involvement and/or autonomy of your team. This can be achieved for example by including your employees in decision making, or allowing them to propose solutions to given problems. It might entail different levels of engagement; on some occasions you might simply explain decisions you have taken, on others you might actually involve employees in the decision making process itself. Certain situations, such as when seeking to implement change, can be ideal for the engaging style.

The engaging style shows that you value input and involvement. Employees generally respond well to it and ideally you should be using this approach most of the time. Being prepared to engage your employees does take courage, but it is the most logical approach if you genuinely believe they are stakeholders in your hotel.

USING THE FACILITATING STYLE

The *facilitating style* is one which involves allowing your employees, individually or collectively, high levels of involvement and autonomy in how they do their work;

you would most likely use this approach with truly engaged employees. In some ways, when using this style, you are a passenger in the sense that your employees are almost self-managing. Naturally, you can only use this approach where relationships are strong and levels of mutual trust and respect would have to be very high here.

In particular, you should adopt this approach with your more engaged employees by increasing their levels of autonomy and involving them heavily in the running of the business. Not only does this recognise their abilities and commitment, but it also encourages them to stay with you where otherwise they might go elsewhere to broaden their experience. However, you should remember that the facilitating style means low, but not no, direction and control.

These three styles are not so hard to understand and in fact, you most likely use them every day to some extent without even thinking about it. If you don't, then ask yourself what is your predominant approach at present and is it working as effectively as possible? Consider the following questions to help you reflect on your current leadership style.

❑ Do you believe that your real authority as a leader comes not from your title or position, but from how you behave and interact with your team?

❑ Do you regularly think about how you lead others and are you constantly trying to improve your performance?

❑ Do you lead by example? How?

❑ Do you treat all your employees equally and fairly?

❑ Are you aggressive in your leadership style? Would your employees consider you to be a bully?

❑ Do you have the ability to be flexible in how you apply your leadership style in practice?

❑ Can you actively apply different styles to match the requirements of each given situation? Think of examples where you have done this.

❑ When an individual is not performing to standard, can you deal with them in an effective manner or do you lose your temper easily?

❑ Have you consistently shown an ability to bring people back on track when they underperform?

❑ Do you encourage your employees to be more involved in decision making? Think of examples where you have done this.

❑ Do you allow your employees a degree of autonomy when appropriate?

❑ Do you regularly acknowledge the efforts of your employees and do you give them praise when it is justified?

❑ Do you ensure that high performing employees have the ability to develop their skills even further?

❑ Do you delegate to these high performing employees?

❑ Do you believe that you are a positive role model for your employees?

SUMMARY

Leadership effectiveness is such an important area that you should devote a lot of attention to it. Your first priority should be to create the overall context for leadership at the hotel and in particular to develop the related competence model to guide your efforts.

As well as enhancing your own talents as a leader you must also consider the other leaders at the hotel. Ask yourself:

❑ Do they have the right personal qualities to succeed?

❑ Do they have the competences you expect based on the model you come up with?

❑ Are they effective communicators?

❑ What leadership styles do they currently adopt and do they match what you expect from them?

If they don't stack up against these questions, then you have to do something about it.

Improving leadership effectiveness at the hotel means ensuring that all those in leadership roles are proactively applying the principles covered here all day, every day. In the next chapter we will explore ways in which you can measure whether the quality of leadership in your hotel is improving over time.

6

How can you measure leadership effectiveness over time?

REVIEW	HOW CAN YOU MEASURE LEADERSHIP EFFECTIVENESS OVER TIME?

The idea of measuring leadership effectiveness in a formal way might seem like an unnecessary activity, great if you had little else to do but somewhat of a luxury for a busy hotelier. One general manager reflected this view well when he said: 'If people aren't happy with leadership at this hotel, they will just leave won't they, so why do I need to measure it?' That's a fair point, in one sense. After all, if people do stay with you then you can reasonably assume that they are happy with the way you are leading them. Unfortunately, there are a couple of flaws associated with that viewpoint.

First, striving for excellence does not sit well with the notion of simply accepting things as they are. It means constantly aiming to make everything better in the spirit of continuous improvement; that includes leadership. Unless you have some concrete measure of how effective it is, or isn't as the case may be, how can you ever hope to improve it? Second, just because employees stay with you does not necessarily mean that they aren't unhappy, or that there aren't at least certain aspects of leadership at the hotel with which they have issues. If there are problems, isn't it better to know about them? To do that you need to measure leadership effectiveness in a structured way.

This chapter will explore some general principles as to how leadership effectiveness can be measured which you can apply in a manner appropriate to your own situation.

Continually improving leadership effectiveness

In essence, what you are trying to do here is to generate feedback regarding the quality of leadership at the hotel, so that you can learn the lessons and make things better over time. Our framework for managing continuous improvement can be a useful guide again here in terms of how you might do this:

To be in a position to measure leadership effectiveness you will therefore have to address the following challenges.

Define the results you want to achieve

You will already know what results you want in this area. You are seeking increased leadership effectiveness, as represented by the criteria in the competence model that you agree. Clearly, you couldn't actually measure 'leadership effectiveness' – it's too general – but you will be able to measure each leader's performance against the specific competences that you have agreed. The sample competences defined earlier are shown again in the table opposite.

As well as measuring individual leader performance, you will also want to know whether the collective quality of leadership at the hotel is having a positive impact on those most impacted by it, i.e. your employees. So, you also need to consider how you can get their feedback on this aspect of work life.

Take action to achieve the results you want

If you want to see improvements in leadership effectiveness at the hotel, you actually have to do something to make that happen. This means taking on board the messages from the previous chapter and ensuring that the competence model

		Sample criteria to measure leadership effectiveness
The What	→	❏ Meets revenue targets ❏ Achieves cost percentages ❏ Increases customer satisfaction ratings for their area ❏ Lowers employee turnover in their area ❏ Reduces number of accidents ❏ Meets the requirements for training hours provided to staff.
The How	→	❏ Demonstrates *commitment* to the hotel's vision and mission ❏ Understands their *roles* and *responsibilities* and demonstrates high levels of competence ❏ Continuously *develops* their own skills and knowledge ❏ Effectively *plans* and *organises* the workload in their department ❏ *Manages resources* to achieve the objectives agreed for their area ❏ Provides clear *direction* and *guidance* to their employees ❏ Ensures that work in their area is consistently carried out to the *standard* required ❏ Constantly strives to improve overall *quality* and promotes continuous improvement in their area ❏ Addresses *underperformance* in a proactive and constructive manner ❏ Adopts a structured approach to *training*, *coaching* and *developing* their team ❏ Provides regular constructive *feedback* to employees ❏ *Solves problems* and shows initiative in finding creative solutions to work-related problems.
The Who	→	❏ *Self-motivated* and sets a positive example for employees by their attitude and performance ❏ Demonstrates high levels of *energy, enthusiasm* and *professionalism* ❏ Shows *concern* for their team members and interacts with them in a positive manner ❏ Treats all team members *equally* and *fairly* ❏ Applies flexible *leadership styles* and regularly shows an ability to adjust their approach to deal with different people and situations ❏ *Communicates* in a structured and effective manner with their team ❏ Builds and sustains effective *relationships* with employees and customers ❏ *Motivates* others to improved performance.

is agreed and adhered to, both by you and all other leaders. This will also involve addressing issues such as training, coaching and mentoring to help your leaders to individually raise their game.

In addition, it will require you to rethink how you recruit and select leaders to ensure that you are appointing the right people into leadership roles; right meaning that they can deliver on the criteria you defined for leadership effectiveness. You may even find over time that some of your existing leaders cannot meet expectations, regardless of how much you try to develop them. This may require tough decisions to be made in future.

If you don't take proactive steps to improve the quality of leadership then seeking to measure its effectiveness is a waste of time and effort because you won't actually see any improvements, and even if you did you wouldn't know what caused the better result.

Consider how you will measure progress

An important consideration here will be to decide how you will actually measure leadership performance at the hotel. There are many ways to do this, none of which need to be overly elaborate, and some suggested approaches are outlined here for you to consider.

ADOPT A SELF-ASSESSMENT APPROACH

The most basic option is to use some self-assessment tools to judge your own leadership effectiveness and to get other leaders in the hotel to do the same. Obviously, the downside of self-assessment is that it is very hard for any of us to be truly objective about our own performance, but it is at least a starting point. Deep down, all of us intuitively know where many of our strengths and areas for improvement lie, but whether we are always prepared to admit the latter is another point. However, in an environment of openness and trust self-assessment has some merit.

The criteria in the competence model, or the general questions around the leadership profile, communication and leadership styles which you considered in the previous chapter could be easily converted into simple self-assessment tools. These can then be completed annually and areas for improvement defined as part of mentoring your leaders to better performance. Samples of self assessment tools which you might use are included in the Tools and Resources section at the end of this book.

HARNESS THE POWER OF APPRAISALS

A more credible approach to evaluating the quality of leadership is to use structured performance appraisals. Appraising the performance of your leaders will help you to determine how well they are individually living up to expectations based on the competence model. Using the sample competences, a leadership appraisal form along the lines of the template shown opposite could be developed.

Appraising your leaders using this template will allow you to track their personal effectiveness and identify areas where they need support. Appraisals are an extremely important tool, and everyone at the hotel should have an annual appraisal, not just leaders. However, they can lead to problems if not delivered effectively and we will return to the issue of performance management and appraisals in greater detail under Theme 3.

ANALYSE EMPLOYEE PERCEPTIONS OF LEADERSHIP

The only true measure of leadership effectiveness can come from those who are impacted by it, so your employees must be involved in the measurement process.

Leadership Appraisal

Name:						Date:	

Area	1	2	3	4	5	Comments	Totals
The What							
Meets expected revenue targets							
Achieves required cost percentages							
Increases customer satisfaction ratings for their area to required levels							
Lowers employee turnover rate in their area							
Reduces number of accidents							
Meets the requirements for number of training hours provided to staff							
The How							
Demonstrates *commitment* to the hotel's vision and mission							
Understands their *roles* and *responsibilities* and demonstrates high levels of competence							
Continuously *develops* their own skills and knowledge							
Effectively *plans* and *organises* the workload in their department							
Manages resources to achieve the objectives agreed for their area							
Provides clear *direction* and *guidance* to their employees							
Ensures that work in their area is consistently carried out to the *standard* required							
Constantly strives to improve overall *quality* and promotes continuous improvement in their area							
Addresses *underperformance* in a proactive and constructive manner							
Adopts a structured approach to *training, coaching* and *developing* their team							
Provides regular constructive *feedback* to employees							
Solves problems and shows initiative in finding creative solutions to work related problems							

Poor — Average — Excellent

The Who							
Self-motivated and sets a positive example for employees by their attitude and performance							
Demonstrates high levels of *energy, enthusiasm* and *professionalism*							
Shows *concern* for their team members and interacts with them in a positive manner							
Treats all team members *equally* and *fairly*							
Applies flexible *leadership styles* and regularly shows an ability to adjust their approach to deal with different people and situations							
Communicates in a structured and effective manner with their team							
Builds and sustains effective *relationships* with employees and customers							
Motivates others to improved performance							

Summarise strengths and areas for improvement

Personal development plan

Performance targets for next period

Sales targets		Employee turnover in their area	
Cost percentages		Number of accidents targets	
Customer satisfaction ratings for their area		Training hours provided to staff	

After all, it is they who are most closely affected by what you do, or do not do as leaders, so their feedback is vital.

You can generate employee feedback about their perceptions of leadership at the hotel informally though direct contact with them and more formally from an employee engagement survey. We will examine how to develop and implement such surveys to include feedback on leadership effectiveness in Theme 3.

USE HARD MEASURES

As well as the financial measures related to leadership effectiveness such as meeting sales or cost targets, you can also use your *employee turnover percentage* as a general indicator as to whether or not leadership is effective at the hotel. When you break down this figure by department, you can also identify where there might be specific problems with the performance of a particular leader.

However, on its own, the employee turnover percentage is not ideal as a measure of leadership effectiveness because the result you get, whether good or bad, may or may not be solely as a result of leadership. Clearly there are many other issues which could influence employee turnover. But it is an indicator and when coupled with the qualitative feedback arising from the employee engagement survey, you will have a stronger indication as to whether the quality of leadership is getting better over time.

DO YOU HAVE THE NECESSARY SYSTEMS IN PLACE?

When you have decided upon which methods to use to measure leadership effectiveness, you then need to consider whether you have the right systems in place to give you the information you need. This might involve answering questions such as:

❏ Do you currently have a performance appraisal system in place?

❏ Do you currently use an employee engagement survey?

❏ Do you have the capabilities to measure costs and revenue targets relevant to individual leaders?

❏ Do you currently measure employee turnover, globally and by department?

Depending upon your answers to the above, it will be necessary to introduce or adjust systems and procedures so that you can generate the data you will need.

Measure progress at defined intervals

As with all measurements, the results should be produced at defined intervals so that you can determine whether leadership is actually improving. The financial and other hard data related to leadership effectiveness will generally be produced regularly at the hotel, so tracking individual leadership performance in one area at least should be relatively straightforward.

Leadership appraisals must happen at least once a year, but as a medium-term goal, you should seek to run them every six months to give a more rounded and up-to-date view; the same principle applies to the employee engagement survey.

Analyse the results and make improvements

Based on the results you get from your various measures of leadership effectiveness you will know whether things are getting better or not, and you obviously need to act accordingly. If you are finding from your appraisals that individual leaders are not matching your expectations in terms of effectiveness, you need to be clear as to why and then take steps to address the problem.

Your employee engagement survey will provide you with overall perceptions of leadership and the results you get here will also have to be followed up. This might involve further consultations with employees to determine what lies behind the results, whether that is good or bad, with action taken to counteract shortcomings or build on the positives. In particular, over time you should see an upward trend in employee perceptions of leadership. If not then your efforts are not having the desired impact and you would need to determine why.

You might also consider how you can benchmark your leadership effectiveness against other comparable hotels but to do so would require that they measured 'effectiveness' in a similar manner to you.

SUMMARY

Measuring leadership effectiveness does not have to be a complex process but it must provide you with accurate and reliable feedback which you can act upon to make things better. Effective leadership is such a fundamental component in achieving excellence that it warrants devoting significant time and resources to it. By tackling the leadership issues described in these three chapters, excellence will become a more likely possibility, so it is worth any and all the effort you put into this area.

Finally, take a key message with you from Theme 2: excellent businesses come in all shapes and sizes and span industry fields but a common thread binds them together; strong leaders driving improved performance.

THEME 3 – ENGAGE YOUR EMPLOYEES

Bring the best out of your employees

ENGAGE YOUR
EMPLOYEES

Are your employees fully
engaged?

Loyal employees in a company create loyal customers, who in turn create happy shareholders. The process sounds easy but it's not, and it has defeated some of the bigger organisations of the twentieth century.

Sir Richard Branson

Recently a hotel manager made an amusing comment to me. When asked how many people worked at her hotel, she replied: 'depends on what mood they are in'. We had a good laugh at this but quickly realised the challenge she was referring to: how can you get your employees to consistently work to their best? Employees naturally have their good and bad days, but it is their overall pattern of performance which is of concern because you cannot achieve excellence without satisfied employees. Actually, you want them to not only be satisfied but also to fully engage with your business which, as we will see, is not necessarily the same thing.

Increasing employee engagement means creating an overall environment within your hotel which fosters commitment and encourages your employees to go above and beyond the call of duty for you on a regular basis. Is this easy to achieve? Of course not, but it is a worthwhile goal; studies consistently show that engaged employees deliver higher productivity, focus more on your customers and stay with you longer, so the effort required to engage them pays off.

As you begin to focus on this important area, now is the time to ask yourself, *are your employees fully engaged?*

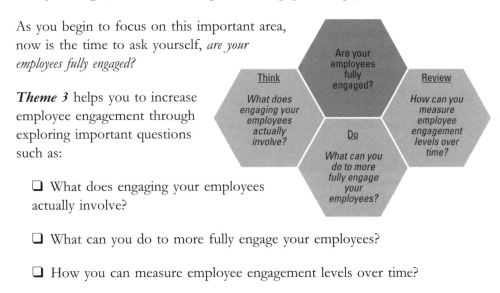

Theme 3 helps you to increase employee engagement through exploring important questions such as:

❑ What does engaging your employees actually involve?

❑ What can you do to more fully engage your employees?

❑ How you can measure employee engagement levels over time?

You won't be shocked to learn that there are no simple answers to the challenge of employee engagement. It is fraught with difficulties and there isn't one thing on its own that will achieve it. Instead, you must address a number of factors in unison if you want to make it happen. And you must address them consistently if positive results are to be seen. The good news is that you are probably doing many of them already to some extent.

In the following three chapters you will find useful advice to help you to apply the principles and practices of employee engagement for the benefit of your hotel.

7
What does engaging your employees actually involve?

THINK	**WHAT DOES ENGAGING YOUR EMPLOYEES ACTUALLY INVOLVE?**

An interesting incident occurred during a workshop which I recently delivered for employees working in a busy hotel. During an ideas session on how to improve business performance, one talented, but extremely demotivated employee, surprisingly suggested several positive things which would make a difference. When later asked why he had not previously told his manager about these ideas, his response was fairly revealing: 'I don't get paid from the neck up'.

Here was a guy who was so disengaged that he saw his role as being to do, but not to think. You might wonder why he stayed, or even why he was allowed to stay, but the fact was that he was there and was not contributing as much as he could to the business. Although an extreme case, he is far from alone; respected national and international research commonly shows that as few as 30 per cent of employees are actively engaged in the companies they work for.

Think about that for a moment: in practical terms this could mean that for every ten employees you have, as few as three of them are likely to be fully engaged – believing strongly in what you do and giving their all. Five will be only somewhat engaged and there will be one or two who are completely disengaged. It's a disturbing thought and not something you can easily ignore.

Lack of employee engagement is a hidden cost and you can never hope to achieve your goals or deliver excellence unless your employees roll in behind that ambition. But what exactly does engaging your employees involve?

The twelve factors of employee engagement

Employee engagement has emerged as an important issue in recent years and whilst it might be a current 'in' term, it's not necessarily a totally original concept. Issues like teambuilding, motivation, satisfaction and empowerment have always been important and engagement is essentially an umbrella concept which pulls all these strands together.

An engaged employee is not only happy in their job but also translates that satisfaction into higher productivity. They believe in what you are trying to achieve, are eager to help you realise your goals and play an active role in making your hotel a success. Their job has meaning for them and they see a real purpose in what they do. As such, employee engagement involves addressing any issue which impacts on an individual's ability or willingness to give their all and concerns a range of factors such as individual motivation and commitment, team effectiveness, overall employee satisfaction and productivity.

Employee engagement is primarily concerned with raising the performance of your employees to maximise the *contribution* that they, individually and collectively, make to the business.

As you well know, engaged employees do not magically appear on your doorstep. Some individuals are of course more naturally inclined to give their best, but unless the conditions are right even they can drop their performance, or more likely move somewhere else in search of an environment where they can grow and develop in return for their efforts. In seeking to identify how you can engage your employees more fully, there's a long list of things for you to consider. The following framework is helpful in highlighting the key factors which can directly or indirectly impact on employee engagement.

It's a bit daunting when you look at it first and this isn't even the full list, but these twelve factors are the priority. OK, don't throw the book away just yet. You are likely to be addressing many of these issues already for you couldn't run any type of hotel without tackling them to some degree. But even if you are, there is always scope for improving the levels of employee engagement.

It is these twelve factors which combine to create a working environment where the potential for engagement is higher. It is important not to see these factors as being independent of one another, for they are not; instead, they are interlinked and what you do within one will often have a spin-off effect on another. In the remainder of this chapter, we will explore why these factors are important and in the next chapter we look at how to address them in practice, with clear guidelines and suggestions offered as to what you might do in your hotel.

Leadership, leadership, leadership

At the risk of sounding like a broken record, effective leadership will be at the centre of your efforts to engage your employees. You can have all the employee engagement measures you like, but if you don't lead effectively, you will not see the results you want.

People may be employed by organisations, but they work for and with other people every day. Leaders have the ability to directly influence, in a positive or negative way, how employees feel about where they work. Strong leaders bring the best out in people and it is for this reason that we have placed so much emphasis on the quality of your leadership and that of others at your hotel. Unless leadership is strong, engagement will be weak.

The link between culture and engagement

Culture is a difficult concept to describe but you can sense it, even if you can't easily explain it in words. Think of the various places you have worked in your career, they all likely had a distinctive 'feel' about them. In certain jobs you probably felt very comfortable working there, in others you might have wanted to jump ship quickly. This feel or climate which you find in different workplaces is linked to culture, and is often a reflection of the owner, or senior leaders. Of course there are short-term occurrences which can influence the general atmosphere, but it is culture which determines the overall feel in the business over the long term.

Forgetting about the theory of it all, at its simplest, the culture in your hotel is made up of the things you believe in, what is acceptable to you in how you operate the business, what your beliefs and values are and what has become the 'norm' over the years. Culture often has a hidden impact on the daily working environment but it does influence how your employees think and behave; everything you do and how you do it is in some way touched by the culture in your business.

Let's look at a simple example of culture in action. A number of years ago whilst consulting for a hotel, which was part of a state-owned group, the effects of culture became very evident. In this hotel, the majority of employees were long serving and a very negative culture had built up over the years; this resulted in a 'them and us' mentality between managers and employees. Jobs were very strictly defined and there were so many rules, regulations and accepted practices governing how things could be done that it was a wonder how anything actually did get done.

In this environment, employees had become completely inflexible. For example, the hall porters would only vacuum the lobby area to a certain line in the carpet, when it then became the responsibility of the banqueting porters. They wouldn't even pick up a piece of litter if it was over that line, but would instead return to the concierge desk and telephone the banqueting porters to tell them to do it. I kid you not!

Change was impossible within this culture as employees were very entrenched and they certainly were not engaged. When local competition increased, the hotel ran into trouble because the prevailing culture didn't permit it to quickly respond to the new competitive dynamics.

This is just one example of how culture can impact everyday work life. Although it is very intangible, culture is a powerful energy force in any business and certain cultures, like the one described above, destroy employee engagement, whilst others encourage it. You need to be concerned about culture because you cannot achieve excellence unless you create an environment which facilitates employee engagement.

The impact of team composition

The composition of any team determines the likelihood of its success and influences whether the individuals within it will fully engage. You want employees who are team players and have the right mindset to 'fit' with the culture of your hotel. Despite the importance of getting this balance right, some owners and managers still don't pay enough attention to their recruitment process. When talking about how he hires his team members, one owner said to me, only half-jokingly: 'the first thing I look for is whether they have two arms and two legs, the next is whether they can speak, anything after that is a bonus.'

In fairness, he wasn't that bad in reality, but he didn't give much thought as to who he brought into his team. What attention he did give it tended to focus on what someone could do, rather than who they were: both are important. Skills are of course vital, but so too is attitude. Unfortunately, even today, recruitment processes often concentrate too much on the skills part. There is little point in recruiting someone with the wrong mindset, no matter how skilled they are, as engaging them fully will be an uphill battle. In short, you want people who not only can do the job, but who have a 'can do' attitude as well.

Clarity facilitates engagement

If someone asked your employees what it is you are trying to achieve at your hotel, would they know? Do they get the big picture? Do they individually know what their duties are and what your expectations are of them? Clarity in these areas is important and you should define both *aspirations* and *expectations*.

Your employees do need to know what's out there on the horizon and how they can help get you there, because it makes them feel part of something. If, as a first step, they don't understand what you are trying to achieve at the hotel, don't expect them to be able to help you realise your goals. Unsurprisingly, when you treat an employee like a stakeholder, they are more likely to start acting like one.

At the same time, employees must also be very clear as to what you want from them in terms of their performance. If they don't know what you expect from them at work, don't expect them to deliver what you want.

Lack of clarity on these issues will affect an employee's willingness and ability to engage. Defining your aspirations for the hotel and your expectations of them will not on its own increase employee engagement, but it will provide a foundation upon which that engagement can be built.

Competence supports engagement

It is an obvious requirement that all your employees must be able to do the work they are employed to do, so competence is an important issue in its own right. However, it is of specific concern from an engagement perspective for two reasons.

First, if certain employees are not fully competent at their jobs, others in the team have to compensate for those weaknesses by picking up the slack. This creates disharmony which over time will affect engagement, as who wants to continuously do the work that someone else is paid to do?

Second, on a broader scale, most employees want to learn and grow in their jobs, so helping them to build their competence and capabilities also increases their willingness to engage. Some hoteliers can be a bit short-sighted in this regard and one manager reflected a not uncommon concern when she said: 'Why would I spend time and money training people when all they'll do is soak up the learning and go on to a better job?' It's hard to argue with this in some ways. Well it is, if you only view training in cost terms, when in reality it is an investment.

Employees move on, that's life, but they are more likely to engage whilst they are with you, or at least to perform to a higher standard, when they are competent than if they are not. In any case, when employees feel that they are developing in a job this can actually influence their decision to stay longer with you, as they see it is in their self-interest to do so. Making the effort to increase the competence of your employees pays off in a number of ways and is therefore worth doing.

Engagement and cooperation are interdependent

The levels of cooperation in your hotel are both a driver of employee engagement and a reflection of it. The more that your employees cooperate with one another the stronger the team spirit that develops amongst them. Feeling part of a successful team is a proven driver of engagement. Conversely, when employees are engaged, you will also find that cooperation between them is naturally higher, because when they see themselves as a team, the desire to support each other is greater. So, the more you can do to get your employees working and interacting with each other the better, because building team spirit and cooperation across your hotel will increase engagement.

One problem which sometimes arises in our industry is that although employees can work well within their own area, different departments can actually work against each other, intentionally or otherwise. The classic example of this problem is the kitchen versus restaurant syndrome. There is often too strong a focus on 'my department' in hotels and you should break down these barriers at every opportunity. There should be only one team at your business.

Control and engagement are not enemies

Control and engagement may not seem like obvious bedfellows but there is an important relationship between them. To see how they are linked we need to explore the issue from two perspectives.

ADDRESSING UNDERPERFORMANCE

Amidst all this talk of employee engagement, there's still a need for the work to be done to a high standard if you want to run a great hotel. Therefore supervision and control are not the enemies of employee engagement and remain at the core of what you do. Monitoring performance and maintaining discipline are vital concerns, using effective leadership approaches of course. When individuals who consistently underperform (be that in relation to the quality of their work or their behaviour) are allowed to do so without correction, this reduces the potential for engagement of others around them who are making the effort.

Here is an example of the damage that ignoring underperformance can do. In one hotel, there was a long-serving member of the team, we'll call him Johnny, and he was, to put it mildly, a complete pain. He did his work, although not to any great standard but he never did anything bad enough to warrant his dismissal; he could at times be charming to customers, which is probably what saved him. However, he spent most of his working day moaning about one thing or another and everything was a problem in his eyes.

The harm that this guy caused to the hotel was immeasurable and apart from his own average performance, anyone who was positive and engaged was quickly worn down by exposure to the 'moan fest' that was Johnny. Many good employees left the hotel because they couldn't cope with the negativity.

Yet, for all of this, he was never dealt with properly by the management team. His performance was simply put down to 'ah sure, that's Johnny for you' and he was tolerated as if he was some sort of loveable eccentric.

Allowing people to continuously get away with underperformance in one form or another makes engaged employees question why they should bother. So, when you tackle employees who are not delivering for you, you send out a message to engaged employees that their effort is worthwhile. It also lets any other slackers around the place know that they won't be tolerated either.

EMPOWERING YOUR EMPLOYEES

The second aspect of control to consider here is the degree to which your employees are *empowered* at the hotel. People need to feel that they have meaningful input into decisions which affect them and that they have a degree of autonomy to act on their own initiative. This doesn't mean you let them run the show, but everyone needs to feel that they have some control over their lives at work. Engagement is always higher in an environment where empowerment is strong.

Effective communication builds engagement

The association between engagement and communication is very strong and where there is open, two-way and effective communication the levels of employee engagement will always be higher. We talked earlier about the *personal* aspects of communication and improving your own abilities as a communicator will contribute to engaging your employees.

However, from an engagement point of view, the *structural* components of communication are critical. One of the most frequently heard complaints from employees is that they get fed up with not knowing what's going on, which is often reflected in the simple phrase 'nobody tells me anything around here'. Employees often jokingly call it mushroom management – being kept in the dark and fed . . . well, you know the phrase. It can impact heavily on engagement levels when you don't communicate with your people in an effective way.

There should be a range of formal channels in place which allow you to interact with employees on a daily, weekly, monthly and yearly basis. In addition, you should ensure that there are regular social or teambuilding events which are great for stimulating informal communication and lifting morale, which in turn contributes to increasing the levels of engagement.

More challenged means more engaged

An important factor in determining levels of engagement is how challenging employees believe their work is; most people eventually get bored doing the same thing day in day out. Luckily in our industry there is plenty of variety but even so, it can still become a bit mundane over time, especially for experienced employees. Once an employee has mastered the needs and demands of their own particular job, the sense of learning and stimulation can quickly dissipate which reduces their potential for engagement.

To counteract this, you should explore ways in which you can increase the sense of challenge associated with their work; that concept of challenge will naturally have a different meaning from one person to the next. Some individuals might simply be happy to come in, do their job and go home and if they are productive and work to a high standard, then you can ask no more. But others will have higher expectations and ambitions and it is these individuals for whom addressing the challenge issue is particularly important.

Conflict and engagement are linked

It might initially seem somewhat unusual to associate conflict with employee engagement but there is actually quite a direct link. Conflict is a feature of all organisations and is normal and indeed sometimes necessary. What is abnormal about conflict is not that it happens but often how it is dealt with. When conflict at work is poorly managed, it can have a detrimental impact on employee engagement.

Constructive conflict can be positive when it focuses on issues not personalities. Such conflict is healthy because it leads us to challenge each other and as a result we often find better ways of doing things. It can also enhance employee engagement, because employees feel that they can question, in an acceptable fashion of course, the decisions which affect them.

Constructive conflict should not be stifled, for to do so is to potentially stifle not only creativity but engagement too. However, you do have to ensure that individual behaviours or approaches do not shift away from the issue to the personality; it simply needs to be managed.

Destructive conflict where it is personality driven, not leading to any benefits, accompanied by damaging behaviours or creating a negative atmosphere should be dealt with firmly and proactively. This form of conflict is also a feature of every business; sometimes it can be low level and other times more serious; both are problematic. Although those who are directly involved in the conflict can often be quite comfortable with it, indeed some even thrive on it, others who are not involved suffer the consequences.

Sometimes the 'bystanders' feel pressurised to take sides and at the very least the conflict can poison the atmosphere they have to work in every day. Who wants to have to put up with that? Allowing destructive conflict to continue, or fester will impact on employee engagement so you do need to respond to it, even though it is not always nice to have to do so.

Compensation influences engagement

In this case, we will explore compensation in the broadest sense, not just restricted to pay, although that is naturally important. On the pay side, the question is often asked, if you pay people more, will they be more engaged? The emphatic answer is no, not unless the other factors which impact on engagement are addressed too. Clearly, pay has a role to play – people need to feel valued for their work – but if engagement was only dependent upon pay then your hands would be tied, as there is always a limit to what you can pay and people always want more.

Taking a more holistic view, it is essential for your employees to feel 'compensated' or valued for their efforts and pay is a factor in that, but far from the only one. Compensation in the broader sense relates to other issues such as how your employees are rewarded for performance beyond the norm, beginning with a simple thank you right up to structured recognition mechanisms and performance-related pay.

You should maximise the use of informal and formal structures which allow you to acknowledge and, where appropriate reward, good performance; feeling undervalued will serve as a negative force on employee engagement.

Change is a factor in engagement

Continuity and a degree of certainty are important in any business because too much change can be frustrating for many people, particularly if it isn't leading to improvements. You often hear employees sneering about the 'flavour of the month' referring to new initiatives which they know will eventually disappear if they keep their heads down. Constant meaningless change erodes the potential for employees to engage because they simply get fed up of the lack of direction.

However, continuing to do things a certain way just because 'we have always done it this way' is equally as damaging to engagement, as there is no sense of challenge or desire to raise the bar. Change and innovation processes can contribute to improved engagement but only when they are well managed, inclusive, based on solid rationale and lead to improved working practices or results. The manner in which you manage change at your hotel will therefore have a strong role to play in engagement levels.

SUMMARY

How well you master these twelve factors will determine the overall levels of engagement you will see in your hotel. You are never likely to get every employee to generate the same level of engagement but by consistently paying attention to these issues you can, over time, encourage all employees to contribute more to your business. Before we move on, you should give some thought now as to how well you currently address these factors in your hotel.

In the following chapter, we will look at practical things you can do within each of these twelve areas to make a real impact on the levels of engagement seen in your employees and as a result the performance of your hotel. But don't expect overnight results, it takes time and consistent focus.

8
What can you do to more fully engage your employees?

DO	**WHAT CAN YOU DO TO MORE FULLY ENGAGE YOUR EMPLOYEES?**

Engaging your employees will be a significant challenge; hopefully you recognise that the rewards make that effort worthwhile. Here is an example of how one engaged employee made a real difference to the customer experience: having travelled for almost twelve hours, suffering the usual chaos that is air travel today, I arrived at my destination in less than good humour. Whilst checking in, I was informed that the kitchen had just closed, so there was no hot food available but sandwiches were on offer and could be ordered from the room.

Shortly after I arrived in the room, the phone rang. It was the head chef. She informed me that although she was just about to go home, she had heard that I could do with a hot meal and proceeded to offer me some available alternatives. An excellent meal duly arrived shortly thereafter.

Now this is a minor incident, but massive in what it tells us about the value of employee engagement and certainly memorable from a customer's point of view. Wouldn't it be great if all employees would engage to that extent? That's probably an unattainable goal, but the majority are prepared to give more when the environment at work is conducive. So what concrete steps can you take to more fully engage your employees at your hotel?

We saw in the last chapter the twelve factors which can help achieve this, and our focus here will be on how to practically apply those factors. However, before you do anything in this area, you should stand back a little and really think about how you view your employees and what they actually mean to you. This goes back to what we said earlier about the stakeholder mindset and if you don't truly see your employees as being an integral part of your business, then engaging them is unlikely to hold high priority for you.

Seeking to engage your employees actually begins when you develop your mission statement for your hotel, where you give an overall flavour of what type of work environment you intend to create. Looking back to our hotel example from Theme 1, their mission included the following reference to their employees.

Mission

Our customers are our priority and we will provide them with a quality experience which is second to none. *We recognise the importance of our employees in achieving this and we will create a positive working environment which encourages their loyalty, commitment and hard work.* We strive to be excellent leaders and will undertake all our business activities in an honest and ethical manner to provide a fair return on our investment.

You get a real sense from reading this sentence that the management team do see their employees as stakeholders. Again, they are only words. What set this hotel apart is how these general intentions were translated into concrete goals to guide all their employee engagement efforts. Their goals were:

Mission		Goals
'We recognise the importance of our employees in achieving this and we will create a positive working environment which encourages their loyalty, commitment and hard work'	➜	❑ To reduce employee turnover to 20% within three years. ❑ To achieve an average rating of 75% from employee engagement surveys. ❑ To introduce a bonus scheme for all employees within three years.

In particular the goals relating to *reducing employee turnover* and *increasing engagement levels* set some pretty challenging targets for that hotel. How would they deliver on these goals? The only way to make them a reality is through developing and implementing a strategy to more fully engage their employees based on the twelve factors.

Your first priority therefore should be to incorporate your aspirations about employees into your mission. Naturally, you will end up with different employee-related goals from those above, but whatever they end up being, you will still need a strategy to realise them and that strategy will have to focus on some or all of our twelve factors. The advice offered in this chapter will give you some practical suggestions as to what you might do as part of that strategy, or how you might further build on what you are doing already.

How does effective leadership help?

Hopefully you get the point about leadership by now. Unless you apply the principles and practices we covered earlier, you can never hope to engage your employees to the level of our kindly chef.

As we define practical things you can do to strengthen engagement, it is worth highlighting the relationship between levels of engagement and leadership styles. We can do this by referring back to our leadership styles model (see p. 71).

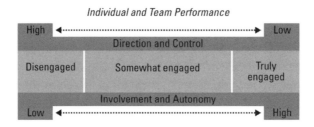

You will quickly notice that individuals and indeed teams can shift between different levels of engagement in terms of their level of contribution to your business: *disengaged, somewhat engaged and truly engaged*. Occasional fluctuations will always occur, but you want as many of your team to be truly engaged for as much of the time as possible. There is somewhat of a chicken and egg dilemma here; there is a direct linkage between the quality of leadership and the levels of engagement of your employees, but in turn, their levels of engagement can determine the style of leadership needed.

Where an individual, or employees as a unit, are *disengaged* the steering style is needed because you have to drive performance. When people are *truly engaged*, the facilitating style works best because you know that they will do the work to a high standard. Your goal should be to use the engaging style for as much time as possible because, by its very nature, it encourages employees to engage more.

It is critical to match leadership style to the state of engagement because overuse of the steering style with someone who is truly engaged will actually reduce it. Equally, trying to use the facilitating style with an unengaged employee is ineffective because they are simply not ready for it.

How can you impact the culture in your hotel?

We have placed a strong emphasis on having clear direction for your business to guide your journey to excellence. But all the strategising or planning in the world is of limited value unless you have a supportive culture at the hotel which engages your employees to the extent that they actively support you in the achievement of your goals. Strategy and culture must therefore always be in alignment.

Nobody can determine what culture is best in your hotel; that decision rests with you and in any case there is no 'right' culture which fits every business as it is unique to each enterprise. However, it should be clear that there are obvious pitfalls to avoid, such as creating a 'top-down' culture or one where employees feel undervalued. In addressing the cultural component of your business, you simply want to ensure that the overall environment within your hotel is one which brings the best out of people.

An obvious starting point here is to think about the current culture at your hotel, to determine whether it facilitates employee engagement or not. You can consider this issue by reflecting on the following questions which are once again based on our three dimensions of work: the *what*, the *how* and the *who*. You will already have touched upon some of these questions in previous reflection exercises.

THE WHAT

❑ What are you trying to achieve at the hotel?

❑ What values are important to you in the way you run the hotel?

❑ What five words could summarise those values?

❑ What is the one thing you would like to change about the culture at the hotel?

❑ What attracts people to come and work in your hotel?

❑ What makes people leave?

❑ What would your customers say about you if you went out of business tomorrow? Why would they miss you?

❑ What happens when you're not at the hotel? Does the work get done to the same high standard as when you are there?

THE HOW

❑ How would you describe the leadership styles at the hotel?

❑ How would you describe the nature and style of communication at the hotel, top-down or inclusive?

❑ How are decisions made and problems solved at the hotel? Do you involve employees in the process?

❑ How are failures dealt with? Are they seen as opportunities for punishment or learning?

❑ How do you recognise and reward individual and collective successes?

❑ How is quality achieved at the hotel? Is there a sense of ownership amongst employees or do you have to drive everything?

THE WHO

❑ Who works for you? What type of people are they? Do you have a stable team at the hotel or is it constantly changing? Why?

❑ Do your employees really believe in what you are doing? Are they proud to work at the hotel?

❑ How do your employees interact together? Are they committed to, and supportive of, each other?

❑ How diverse is your team? Do they respect each other?

❑ Do your employees individually and collectively make a contribution that meets your expectations?

❑ What is the most common feedback you receive from customers about your staff?

These questions are designed to get you thinking in practical terms about the culture within your hotel. You should also talk to your employees to get a sense of what their views are about it. Obviously, there is no point in asking them directly about culture as you are likely to be met with blank stares, but simplify it into questions relating to what they like/dislike about working at the hotel, how valued they feel, what's important to them about their work and so on. It will be interesting to see if their views match your own.

You might also communicate with your regular customers who know the hotel well to get their viewpoints. It is only through this holistic examination that you can build up an accurate picture about the culture at the hotel.

The results from these reflections will lead to one of two conclusions; either you will find that there is a positive culture which supports employee engagement and is helping you move towards your goals, or you may realise that it isn't as you would like.

If it does match your expectations, give yourself a pat on the back and spend time thinking about how that was achieved. Did it just happen, or did you do certain things to get it right? Can you do even more to make it stronger?

If your culture isn't as you would wish, then you need to be clear about where the gaps lie and why they are there. If you own the hotel, then you may have to hold your hand up and accept responsibility. If you manage it, what might you be doing that is contributing to the cultural problems, or have you inherited difficulties created by others who may have gone before you?

Whatever the reasons, if you want to really to engage your employees you cannot sidestep the culture issue. You should also recognise that cultural change in any business of any size is far from easy and will not be achieved in the short term.

PRACTICAL STEPS TOWARDS CHANGING THE CULTURE OF YOUR HOTEL

Some practical steps which you could take to either begin the process of changing the culture, or to build on the positive one you already have are the following.

❑ If you haven't developed your vision and mission, then that's the first thing you should do, based on the lessons learned earlier. As part of that, incorporate words which reflect the values which are important to you. In our example hotel, they used phrases in their mission like: *quality experience, positive working environment, excellent leaders* and *honest and ethical manner*. These were not random words, chosen because they sound nice, instead they broadly described the values which mattered to them.

❑ If you already have your vision and mission, do they accurately describe the culture and values you want? Are they reflective of where you want the business to go in light of the content we have covered? If not, redefine them to match the new reality.

❑ No matter where you are with regard to your vision and mission, always involve your employees in the design/redefinition process; consult with them, get their ideas and opinions.

❏ Launch or re-launch your vision and mission to your primary stakeholders.

❏ Always be a role model for the culture you are trying to create in the hotel and, in particular, apply the leadership principles we have identified. Do not allow other leaders, or indeed any employees, to act or behave in a way that does not mirror your preferred culture.

❏ Review all training programmes which you may have at the hotel – make sure that behaviours and attitudes reflective of your preferred culture are promoted during these sessions.

These initial steps won't change the culture at the hotel, but they will get the ball rolling. If you take action on the remaining factors outlined in this chapter and indeed on the key messages throughout this book, this in itself will drive cultural change over a period of time.

How can you manage the composition of your team?

One of the most important areas where you can influence employee engagement is when you recruit new team members. You need to, as far as is possible, employ individuals who match the culture of your hotel and have the greatest potential to engage. As you consider this area, make sure that whatever approach you adopt to recruitment places a strong emphasis on not only finding out what a person can do, but also who they are.

It is one thing to say that you need to recruit the right type of people, but what practical steps can you take in this area? You should begin by reviewing your existing approach to recruitment and selection. Ask yourself the following questions.

❏ Do you have a structured approach to recruitment and selection?

❏ Are there defined roles and responsibilities to underpin the process, with appropriate support tools in place?

❏ Are those who are involved in recruiting employees competent at it?

❏ Is your current approach to recruitment and selection generating the right type of employees for you, or are you having problems finding people who match your needs?

❏ Do you find that a significant number of the people you employ don't live up to your expectations?

❏ How many employees start working for you and then leave after a short period of time?

❏ When you look at the employees you have, do they make you proud or drive you to despair?

❏ Is diversity embraced and managed at the hotel?

If you find you have problems in these areas, then you probably need to look again at how recruitment and selection is conducted at your hotel. Even if you feel it is quite strong, you will still find some useful tips as you read ahead to make it even stronger.

It is not intended here to examine the recruitment and selection process in full, but rather to point out some of the common pitfalls which lead to poor candidate selection. We will do this by focusing on three important questions, the answers to which will help you to improve the quality of people you recruit.

WHAT DO YOU WANT EMPLOYEES TO DO?

Knowing what it is you want your employees to do is a fairly basic requirement and most hotels now have defined *job descriptions* in place for every position in the hotel. If you don't have them, you should address this weakness immediately. Don't assume that your employees are on the same wavelength as you when it comes to what their job involves and what results are expected. If you already have them, make sure they remain current and reflective of what is required and adjust them where necessary.

When using job descriptions as part of recruitment, the earlier that you give them to potential candidates during the process the better, because before you interview them, you want to at least be sure that they know what the job will entail and are comfortable with that. Apart from their use in recruitment, job descriptions also play an important role in managing performance because how can you ever measure an employee's contribution, if you haven't clearly outlined to them what they are supposed to do? They can also be used in training and development to help identify individual training needs, so they are vital tools.

One of the benefits of preparing or reviewing your job descriptions is that it makes you think about how the work is structured and organised at the hotel and as part of that you can often identify better ways of doing things in terms of job design.

However, job descriptions only describe what you want a person to do; as part of recruitment, you also need to know what type of person you want for any given job.

WHAT TYPE OF EMPLOYEES ARE YOU SEEKING?

You can generally find out what a candidate can do by analysing their CV or by looking at the past jobs they have held. When you compare that to the job description you can get a fair idea as to whether they are right, in a competence sense, for a particular job. But when you seek to fill a vacant position at the hotel, do you also have a defined picture in mind of what type of person you want, or is it a bit vague?

Unfortunately for a lot of hoteliers, it's the latter and they only have a general idea of what they are looking for. Consequently, their approach to interviewing goes somewhat like this: the first person who comes for interview on the day sets the benchmark. The second is either better or worse than the first and so on down the line. The problem with this approach is that each candidate is compared against the previous one, so you can be easily swayed by those who put on a good show at interview.

You avoid this trap by devising a profile of the 'ideal candidate' which serves as the basis for how you select from the pool of interviewees available. You may not find the ideal but you measure all candidates against that profile and select the individual who most closely matches it. An employee profile essentially identifies the characteristics of the person you want to fill a particular position. You do not need a different profile for every position as you do with job descriptions, but you can have one for a reception position, one for restaurant/bar, housekeeping and so on. So it's not a major task.

Although it depends on the job you are recruiting for, in developing a profile of the ideal candidate, our three dimensions of work can again be a useful way of highlighting what a profile consists of.

THE WHAT

❑ What *education* or *training qualifications* do you expect the ideal candidate to have to be able to do the job?

❑ What level of *work experience* are you looking for?

THE HOW

❑ What specific *skills and knowledge* must they already have to do the job to the standard you require?

❑ What *communication skills* do they require?

THE WHO

❑ What overall *personality/disposition* are you looking for in the person?

❑ What *personal attributes* must they have? *Define them very clearly.*

It is only through answering these questions and then clearly mapping out what you are looking for that you will enhance your prospects of recruiting someone who is more likely to engage with your business. After all, an interview is supposed to help you determine if a candidate is the 'right' person for the job, but you can never do so unless you clarify what 'right' actually means.

In particular, you need to be very clear about the *who* part of the profile and clearly define the attributes you are ideally seeking. Skills and knowledge can be developed, but moulding an individual into your way of thinking is much harder, if not impossible, so finding people with the right attributes is crucial. You should also note that there shouldn't be anything discriminatory in your profiles.

By having employee profiles, you can then devise a series of questions to draw out whether the candidate matches the profile and use these as part of your interview plan. As an example, let's say you were looking for someone who was a team player. Of course you wouldn't devise a question such as, are you a team player? That's not going to tell you anything. Instead you might devise questions along the lines of:

❑ Give me some examples of where you felt you made a positive contribution to your team in the past?

❑ What do you think your previous team mates would say about working with you?

❑ What can you bring to our team that would set you apart from other candidates?

Developing and using well structured questions, based on the employee profile, will help you to get behind the mask that most people wear at interviews so that you get a better insight into a candidate's true personality.

HOW DO YOU SELECT THEM?

The third question in relation to getting team composition right relates to how you select people as part of the recruitment process; this will likely depend on the size of your operation and the support structures you have in place.

Predominantly, interviews remain the main selection tool used in hotels, but there are a range of options available such as psychometric tests and assessment centres which can be used in conjunction with the interview to really test suitability against the employee profile. If you have access to such tools then use them widely, particularly for recruiting leaders, as they improve the effectiveness of the selection process. We will, however, focus solely on how to make your interviews more effective.

Clearly, interviews are by no means a perfect way of truly learning about a candidate. They are even less effective when you don't have an ideal profile in mind. Think of an interview as being somewhat similar to a fishing net, whereby badly run interviews leave major gaps which unsuitable candidates can get through. But even well run interviews, held by experienced interviewers, only serve to make the holes in the net smaller; you will still get caught out occasionally, but less frequently.

The golden rules of interviewing

Consider the following golden rules to make your interview process more rigid.

❑ *Nobody should interview candidates for jobs at your hotel, without first having had training in that area.* Experience helps of course, but only if it is based on doing the right things. A lot of people believe that holding interviews is easy; it isn't and doing it well requires specific training and then practice gained through experience.

❑ *Use your job descriptions and employee profiles to screen CVs and only call the most suitable candidates for interview.* As a rule, interview fewer candidates for longer, so you have a better chance of really getting to know them. A 15-minute interview tells you nothing about a person – you should be thinking in terms of at least half an hour per candidate and significantly more with applicants for leadership roles.

❑ *Ensure that you prepare for interviews in advance.* Read the application/CV before the interview, not during it. It's amazing how many times you see interviewers reading through a CV or application when a candidate is talking. Apart from being bad manners, by not making eye contact with the candidate, it is off-putting for them and you miss out on all that can be learned through watching their body language.

❑ *Don't interview in public areas.* This is disrupting both for you and the candidate. Again you commonly see potential employees being interviewed in the bar or lobby area. Find a private setting, not too formal, where you and the candidate can both concentrate.

❑ *Interviews should* always *follow a plan.* Incorporate the structured questions based on the relevant employee profile and issues which you have identified from their CV or application into your interview plan. A suggested format for an interview plan is provided in the Tools and Resources section at the end of the book.

❑ *Don't make your judgement too early.* Very often, the interviewer makes up their mind in the first few minutes. This is totally subjective and causes you to subconsciously alter how you interview the candidate, which does not allow them a fair chance.

❑ *Use effective question techniques*, avoiding closed questions which enable candidates to give yes/no answers.

❑ *Ensure that you follow the same question plan for all candidates.* It is only through having common questions which you ask all candidates that you can compare like with like and increase your chances of finding the candidate who most closely matches the ideal profile.

❑ *The majority of your questions should seek to draw out, or to probe who the candidate is, not only what they can do.* The concept of probing at interviews does not

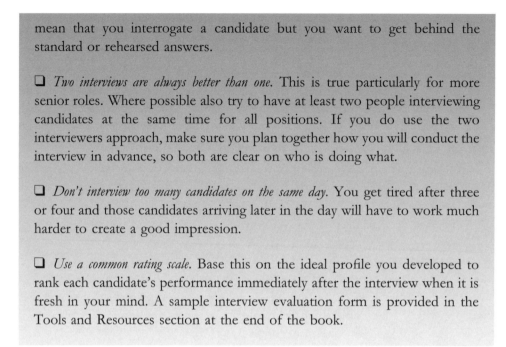

mean that you interrogate a candidate but you want to get behind the standard or rehearsed answers.

❑ *Two interviews are always better than one.* This is true particularly for more senior roles. Where possible also try to have at least two people interviewing candidates at the same time for all positions. If you do use the two interviewers approach, make sure you plan together how you will conduct the interview in advance, so both are clear on who is doing what.

❑ *Don't interview too many candidates on the same day.* You get tired after three or four and those candidates arriving later in the day will have to work much harder to create a good impression.

❑ *Use a common rating scale.* Base this on the ideal profile you developed to rank each candidate's performance immediately after the interview when it is fresh in your mind. A sample interview evaluation form is provided in the Tools and Resources section at the end of the book.

These simple tips will help you to improve the quality of the people you select to work in your hotel.

Some progressive hotels are further enhancing their recruitment process to help ensure they find the right people; often holding interviews in the evenings, or at weekends to test candidates' motivations. In some cases, potential candidates are even asked to work a shift or two, paid of course, before the final decision is made and members of the team they will be joining are given input into making the final decision to recruit or not.

Finally in this area, it goes without saying that diversity within your hotel should be embraced but also managed effectively to ensure that potential language barriers or cultural blockages which can arise are proactively dealt with through effective awareness and diversity programmes. If this is a major concern in your hotel, you should certainly develop a diversity policy and plan steps to address the issue as part of your overall strategy for employee engagement.

How can you provide clarity for your employees?

To engage employees to any level, you need to provide clarity for them about the hotel, their role and your expectations from them. So how will you provide this clarity?

For existing employees, you should communicate your vision and mission to them and provide regular updates on how the business is doing. There is no pretence that your employees will be running around the car park waving their arms in the air with excitement because you explain the big picture to them, but it is an important foundation for getting them to engage. The majority of people want their job to have some meaning for them, so helping them to understand what you are trying to achieve and how they can contribute to that is a useful early step.

When new employees join, you provide clarity for them by offering a comprehensive *induction*. It is surprising how frequently new team members are still thrown in at the deep end with very little support or guidance. This is a critical mistake, as everyone remembers their first day and how a new employee is treated in the beginning will strongly influence how they feel about working in your hotel.

Most employees start with high potential for engagement but this can quickly evaporate if their introduction to your hotel is poor. One employee summed up his experience of his first day well when he said 'it wasn't different than any other day really; in fact I should have seen the warning signs. It started off badly and got worse from there!'

It is important that an employee's early days at your hotel are memorable for the right reasons. When we refer to customers, we always say that you never get a second chance to make a good first impression and the same principle applies to new employees. You build their engagement from the outset when you induct them professionally; get it wrong and you do the opposite.

How you practically manage the induction process will of course depend on the specifics of your hotel. You may not personally deliver the induction yourself, but as the senior person you should always play an active role in it.

At a basic level, there are obviously legal requirements which must be complied with when a new employee starts, such as issuing contracts and informing them about relevant legislation governing their work. But our focus here is about providing them with clarity about the hotel and their role in it. To do this, all new employees should receive an induction which includes the following.

❏ *An introduction to your hotel, your vision and mission and the broader picture of what you are about.* Remember, simply putting a new employee in the care of an experienced member of staff does not guarantee that they are getting the right messages which you want to get across; you should certainly communicate your vision and expectations to all new employees at an early stage.

❏ *An explanation of what your expectations are of them in terms of their attitudes, behaviours and commitment to the hotel.* It is also essential that somebody explains to each new employee what is expected from them regarding their attitude and behaviour during their time at the hotel.

❏ *An introduction to their department.* Part of this means ensuring that their job description is properly explained and the relevant hygiene and safety points are covered. This element of their induction should result in the preparation of an individual training plan for their first few weeks, which ensures they are fully familiar with their department and can complete their duties to the standard you require.

You may use an induction handbook to support the process, but there is no substitute for face-to-face contact with a new employee.

Ongoing clarity for all your employees is sustained through the regular updates on how the hotel is doing mentioned earlier and when you provide structured individual feedback through a performance management system, which we will discuss later.

How can you build the competence of your employees?

Building employee competence contributes to engagement because it ensures that all employees are capable of doing their work to an equally high standard. This prevents disharmony in the ranks. Enhancing their capabilities also helps employees to grow and develop in their jobs and as such this makes them feel that they are progressing as individuals.

We will make a distinction here between training and development because although linked they are not necessarily the same thing. Training tends to have a narrower scope and concentrates on helping employees at all levels to develop skills which directly relate to their job. As such, it has a more immediate focus and can be either offered on or off the job.

Development, on the other hand, has a longer-term view than training because it is concerned with helping individuals to grow beyond the current requirements of their job. Everybody must be trained, but not all employees want or indeed are suitable for development and that's why we make the distinction.

MAKE TRAINING WORK FOR YOU AT THE HOTEL

You can only improve the competence of your employees if you offer regular, structured and effective training at the hotel which is at all times based on identified needs. Training begins for an employee during their induction, but it shouldn't stop there. Continuous training, both on and off the job is a feature of all excellent companies. Apart from the positive impact which training can have on engagement levels, having an effective approach in this area also leads to improved on-the-job performance and contributes to higher quality service delivery, which is good for the business.

On-the-job training

On-the-job training tends to be skills based and is aimed at helping an employee to do their job to the standard required. This is frequently an area of weakness in our industry. Nobody disagrees with the need to train on the job, but it doesn't always happen because there is never 'enough time'. Lack of time is a poor excuse and if your employees aren't competent, time is lost through lower productivity and poor service quality. In particular, when competence is low, someone ends up spending a lot of time correcting mistakes or dealing with the customer complaints and other problems which arise from employees' poor performance. So, you must find ways to ensure that logistical problems with on-the-job training are overcome.

The only way to address the on-the-job training issue effectively is to make it a mandatory requirement for all leaders that they fulfil their obligations regarding whatever training system you adopt at the hotel. As an example, the leadership competence model shown earlier contained a requirement to '*adopt a structured approach to training and developing their team*'. You should therefore ensure that whatever competence model you develop for your business defines leadership obligations regarding training. In particular, where you have performance-related-pay schemes for leaders, training should also be one of the areas upon which that performance is assessed.

Off-the-job training

Employees should also be provided with off-the-job training opportunities focusing on issues such as hygiene, health and safety, fire, first-aid and, of course, customer care. This again should not be an ad hoc activity but must be planned and budgeted for in advance each year as part of your overall strategy for engaging employees. This type of training also makes a hidden contribution to teambuilding when you bring employees from different departments together for training programmes.

At a management level, opportunities should be continuously provided for managers to develop their skills, particularly those related to whatever leadership competence model you agree.

Maximising training effectiveness

The key to maximising training effectiveness is to ensure that it continuously responds to defined needs. These might be identified through customer feedback, performance appraisals and indeed by direct requests from the employees themselves.

A related point here is that any training given, whether that's on or off the job, can only have a positive impact when it is delivered professionally. Anyone who is involved in training your employees should therefore have the talent and skills to do it well. Nothing will disengage employees more than having to sit through badly delivered training courses, or when they receive on-the-job training from someone who doesn't really know how to get their message across.

DEVELOP ENGAGED EMPLOYEES

Development is particularly geared towards employees who are fully engaged with your business. It is designed to help them to grow beyond their existing role and should again be based on specific, individual needs. There are many approaches you can take to developing your employees, none of which need to be overly formal; in fact the best development often happens without any formal structures in place.

Structured development activities might include coaching, mentoring, delegation and even job rotation and you should use all of them widely and encourage other leaders at the hotel to do the same. Sometimes, leaders can be short sighted with regard to developing certain employees. They often avoid it because although they can see an individual's potential, they are afraid that one day this person might outshine them. This is a mistake. Preventing engaged employees from developing will lead to resentment and, in any case, the better ones will move on in search of the opportunities they seek.

What can you do to increase cooperation between employees?

There are many simple, proactive steps which you can take to enhance cooperation and build team spirit between your employees, beginning with how you allocate the workload every day.

When rosters are prepared or as work is allocated each day, some leaders don't give enough consideration to who they assign to work with whom. As a result the same people often end up working together, so much so, that they can begin to believe that it is their right to be placed on the same shifts. This is natural human behaviour – people like to work with those they are closer to – but it can lead to cliques forming, which are essentially teams within teams. This can affect wider employee engagement, so do give some thought as to how you can plan and organise work to encourage greater intermingling of employees.

To break down the barriers which often build up between departments in hotels, it can also be helpful to allow people from one department to work in another for a short period, even just for part of a day. This takes some organising but is worth pursuing because it helps employees to understand what others go through in their jobs; it can change perceptions and lead to a reduction in the blockages between different teams.

Another area where you can maximise the potential for cooperation and build engagement in the process is to use *team-based approaches* to problem solving. There is tremendous scope for using teams, with individuals drawn from different areas, more widely in your hotel.

Here is a very simple example of how it can be done: one hotel manager wanted to see how the restaurant experience at his hotel compared to that of the nearest competitor. He put together a small team of staff, selected from different departments and agreed with them three key areas against which they would assess the offering in their competitor's restaurant: *product*, *service* and *price*. The manager then paid for this team to dine at the other hotel and experience what they had to offer.

After the experience, the team had to make a little presentation, nothing fancy, to the rest of the employees explaining how the competitor performed and offering ideas on what lessons could be learned from the experience and applied in the hotel restaurant. This approach is now a regular feature and is but one example of where team-based activities can be applied.

Finally in this area, don't forget the importance of the social aspect of work life and the contribution this can make to enhanced cooperation. You should encourage a structured approach to organising events away from work and in fact this can often best be arranged by employees themselves, with your guidance and supervision. The main point to note here is that events should involve more than a trip to the pub. There is nothing wrong with that, but activity-based outings have a greater potential for teambuilding.

How can you address the control issue?

To support the engagement effort, you and every leader at the hotel should be seen to maintain control on an ongoing basis; persistent underperformance should never be tolerated. This applies both in relation to how the job is done and to attitudes and behaviours demonstrated. If you have problems with disengaged individuals, begin by trying to coach and support them through it. However, at the end of the day, you can't save people from themselves and you will be better off without them if they fail to come onside. After all, that is why you have a disciplinary procedure.

THE IMPORTANCE OF FEEDBACK

As part of controlling performance, individual feedback is naturally vital and this should have both informal and formal components. Informal feedback should happen every day and forms a normal part of any leader's role. However, there should also be a systematic approach to appraising the performance of all employees at defined intervals. This might take the form of semi-formal job-chats on a quarterly basis with a more intense annual appraisal.

Individual appraisals are hugely important and highly effective in terms of building engagement, but only if they are well delivered. Sadly, appraisals are often seen as a hassle and as a result are poorly managed, so they often do more harm than good. Delivering an effective appraisal is a skill in its own right and those conducting them should be trained on how to do it well.

Appraisals also need to be planned in advance, with the employee provided with an opportunity to rate their own performance. The format for the appraisal itself should be one of a discussion and not an interview and be a participative event, not a dictatorial one. A suggested format for conducting an appraisal is provided under the Tools and Resources section at the end of the book.

The principles for making appraisals effective discussed earlier in relation to leadership naturally apply when appraising employees. To make the process worthwhile, specific criteria which summarise the expectations you have from your employees must be developed and used to measure performance. These criteria might relate to key elements of their job descriptions and employee profiles. A sample employee appraisal form based on the *what*, *how* and *who* is provided under the Tools and Resources section at the end of the book.

For an engaged employee, an appraisal offers an opportunity to receive recognition for their performance and can also allow you to identify ways in which you can further build that engagement. For those who are not engaged, they help you to determine why this is so, or at the very least to identify areas where they must improve. So, although appraisals do take time, it is time well spent in terms of employee engagement and ultimately business performance.

THE NEED FOR EMPOWERMENT

As well as maintaining control, you need to consider how you can release it as you seek to enhance engagement levels; employees need to feel empowered in their jobs. Sometimes in hotels we adopt a very narrow view of employee empowerment and it is often seen solely in the light of handling complaints where employees are provided with guidelines as to what they can and cannot do to resolve the problem. Whilst this is of course important, you should view the issue of empowerment in a wider context.

Empowerment in a true sense is really about involving employees in decision making, particularly where those decisions directly affect them. It is also about providing employees with a degree of autonomy to use their own initiative. At a simple level, as we have said, this can be in how they can handle a complaint but at a more challenging level, it could be to allow a team to prepare their own roster – with your guidance.

When employees are not empowered they feel, rightly or wrongly, that you don't trust them and the natural human reaction to that is to disengage.

What can you do to improve communication at the hotel?

Apart from the informal communication that happens every day in the business, you need to pay a lot of attention to the structural component of communication – the channels you have in place to communicate formally with your employees as a unit. Clearly, the channels you use will depend upon the size of your hotel but the suggestions here can be tailored to your needs.

In a small hotel you might do these things directly yourself, in a larger operation some of them will be the responsibility of the various leaders in the hotel. How you set about addressing the communication issue will also be dependent upon factors such as the extent of the language and cultural barriers you face in the hotel.

BRIEFINGS

Briefings are a great tool for daily communication and every shift in every department should begin with one. However, this rarely happens in hotels and outside of briefings given before functions or special events they aren't widely used. One supervisor explained a common reason why this is the case: 'There's no need for us to do them every day because what we do most days is pretty much the same, so we only hold them when something special is on'. This is actually how most people view briefings, but it is wrong and not holding them represents a major lost opportunity.

Briefings are designed to provide clarity as to what will happen on a given shift and for that reason alone they are beneficial because they focus on the job at hand. But they are more valuable for other reasons. By bringing everyone together for a few minutes each day, briefings allow *team morale and dynamic* to be gauged by the leader, simply by reading the collective mood. This is vital information which you don't get if you aren't seeing employees as a unit.

Briefings also reinforce the idea that all those attending are a team, even though that is never actually said. Finally, whilst on its own a ten-minute briefing achieves little, held every day over a year, well that's a lot of communicating, motivating, learning, listening and reinforcing.

MEETINGS

On a monthly basis, time should be set aside to meet with staff to talk through more in-depth aspects of work; this might be done at departmental level by the leader of each department. Time is always precious in a hotel but there is no justification in the world why an hour or so a month can't be devoted to this. If you don't, you are essentially sending out a subliminal message to your employees that they are unimportant.

As such, this should be another non-negotiable for your leaders – they must meet with their teams on a monthly basis, provide feedback to you on issues that arise and develop an action plan to address those issues. These meetings should have a set agenda so that a similar format applies for all departments and cover points such as:

❑ a review of department performance during the month

❑ feedback from customers over the month

❑ self-assessment of service quality and ideas/suggestions for service improvement

❑ department-related matters.

These meetings provide an opportunity for more in-depth, two-way communication with employees. As an aside, never put AOB (Any Other Business) on a work agenda – it only allows people to raise matters that you have had no time to think through, or in less technical terms to fire Scud missiles at you! It is a much more effective approach to allow employees to contribute to the agenda in advance, if there is something they want to raise. At least then you can come prepared.

Holding these meetings is one thing, but if they are to have any real impact, they need to be well managed. Unfortunately the majority of meetings in a work context are ineffective to some degree. Some tips for making meetings more effective are provided in the Tools and Resources section at the end of the book.

NON-VERBAL COMMUNICATION CHANNELS

As well as verbal communication, there are a number of non-verbal mechanisms to consider. It is always useful to have a central noticeboard where you can display information which is relevant to everyone such as the vision and mission for the hotel, positive feedback from customers, upcoming training courses and so on. But make sure any such boards are maintained and regularly updated; you can tell a lot about a hotel by looking at its staff noticeboard. Frequently, you find a general state of untidiness, with out-of-date or disfigured notices slowly fraying at the edges. This is often symbolic as to what's happening at the hotel generally in relation to employee engagement.

In a larger hotel you may also have a newsletter and these can be of value particularly when employees participate directly in producing it. There are also times when memos are necessary, but you should generally keep them to a minimum. Overuse of memos as a form of communication is essentially a waste of time; very few employees actually give them the attention they might warrant.

Internal emails have also become a feature of businesses today and naturally this facilitates transfer of information but there is no substitute for effective face-to-face communication.

How can you make work more challenging?

You should continuously explore ways in which your employees can be more challenged and this particularly applies to those who are already motivated and engaged. There are a number of actions you can consider to make work more challenging, some of which apply generally whilst others will depend on the motivations of the individual employee.

Not everyone wants to advance and progress in their careers and for those who don't, the key is to ensure that they engage to the extent that they work consistently to a high standard. But the majority of people like a challenge if it is presented in the right context.

For some this can mean having important tasks delegated to them, for others it might involve training them to work in other areas of the hotel. For everyone it should mean that they take a more proactive role in overall improvement efforts at the hotel through their participation in departmental meetings or by active involvement in cross-functional teams. Other points to consider include the following activities.

INVOLVING EMPLOYEES IN IMPROVEMENT INITIATIVES

Finding better ways of doing things at work should be an inclusive process and creates an ideal opportunity to challenge your employees. One simple approach to this can be to develop a *suggestions scheme*, whereby employees can propose ideas or solutions at work.

If you decide to go down that route, avoid using the 'suggestions box' approach, whereby a box is placed somewhere in the hotel and employees are expected to deposit slips of paper with their ideas in it. This rarely works very well. A far more effective system is to use the monthly departmental meetings as the vehicle for generating ideas and suggestions within certain boundaries. A set template to channel employee ideas is provided in the Tools and Resources section at the end of the book.

Encouraging employees to make suggestions and then, when they come up with something of value, recognising their contribution and allowing them to be involved in implementing their idea can give a real sense of challenge to work for the majority of employees.

CONSIDER MULTI-SKILLING/JOB ROTATION

For some employees, the opportunity to develop their skills or to work in other areas of the hotel can help add challenge to their working life, whilst at the same time enhancing their skills sets. Having multi-skilled employees is also of course beneficial for you, as it gives you more flexibility when it comes to rostering.

DEVELOP COMMUNITY LINKS

Developing links with your local community and working closely with charities, schools and associations can be a way of creating a sense of challenge for employees. Consider asking your employees for their opinions as to what they would be willing to do to support the local community and you might be surprised about the positive response you get.

These are just samples of what can be done to address the challenge issue, none of which are complicated or indeed difficult to implement, but they might require you to look at things from a new perspective.

How can you ensure that conflict doesn't affect engagement?

Destructive conflict can have far reaching consequences on overall engagement levels if it is not dealt with effectively, so you must pay particular attention to it. Most of us dislike dealing with destructive conflict and depending upon our own personalities, we have a tendency to either avoid it, or to try to battle down those involved. Neither of those approaches works. Avoiding it just means it gets worse but forcing people to stop, without addressing the root causes, only buries it and they simply hide it from you.

When you see destructive conflict happening between employees, you must make it clear to those involved that you are aware of what is going on and are not prepared to accept it. This is an important first step because you draw a line in the sand, so to speak. You then have to find out what is causing it, often by talking individually to those concerned. Unfortunately, in most cases, one will say it is black and the other will say it is white, so it can be hard to get to the root cause. But you have to try. If you can find out what the problem is, then you try to get them to sort it out with your help.

If you can't figure out what's causing it, or if your attempts at resolving the issue fail, then you move to imposing a solution; you can't get them to like each other, but you can define the behaviours that you will accept. If they persist with the conflict or don't abide by the solution you impose, then you have done all you can and continuing the conflict can only lead to one conclusion. You then move to the last resort and you follow whatever disciplinary procedures are relevant at the hotel.

Nobody likes to go down this route, but to allow the individuals concerned to continue the conflict not only affects the engagement levels of those involved, but can have a significant impact on that of other employees too.

In general, with regard to conflict, you need to:

❑ constantly monitor the climate amongst your employees

❑ make sure you do not inhibit constructive conflict, but do control it

❑ address destructive conflict as soon as you identify it and do not allow such situations to fester

❑ play a mediation-type role first, failing that you must impose the solution you expect and monitor compliance with it.

How can you address the compensation issue to raise engagement levels?

There is no easy answer to the pay aspect of employees feeling compensated; on the one hand, people want to be paid what they believe to be a fair return for their efforts (which for some individuals is often unrealistic), on the other hand, you have to keep your labour costs within affordable limits. You should also recognise that if you want to achieve excellence, then you need to recruit and retain the best employees and there is a cost attached to that.

The key issue here is productivity. The precise amount that you are paying people is less important than what you are getting in return. This is why some of the points we have already covered are so crucial: recruiting the best people available, addressing underperformance when it occurs and appraising performance. By dealing with these issues, you at least ensure that you are getting maximum value for the money you spend on labour.

Performance-related pay has grown in importance in our industry and you should explore how you might apply it in your hotel, or extend your current approach if it's already a feature. The first thing to consider here is the logic behind any such schemes. Any performance-related scheme must be based on an individual or team achieving a result which is above what is deemed the norm and shouldn't reward people for what they are expected to achieve in the first place.

A second concern is how such schemes are structured. For example, paying only the head chef for achieving the food cost target probably isn't a fair reflection of reality because others are involved in achieving that goal – even though that's usually how it works in the kichen. As an alternative approach, consider how you can more widely apply team-based incentives, as they have the benefit of recognising global rather than solely individual performance.

Whatever approach you adopt here, you should seek expert guidance on the design and implementation of such schemes, as getting it wrong can be very detrimental and ultimately costly to your business.

Another area linked to the compensation issue is the general conditions you offer for employees at work. One of the most common sources of the 'moan factor' for employees is often the quality of food provided in the canteen or even the general state of changing rooms. There is no excuse for this in any industry but in the hotel business, it beggars belief. Getting such working conditions right won't necessarily increase engagement, but it does remove a major source of disgruntlement.

RECOGNISE AND REWARD HIGH PERFORMANCE

Beyond the pay and conditions issues, you should also examine how people are recognised and rewarded when they do perform to a high standard. This can often be as simple as thanking them when they, individually or collectively, deliver good results for you.

Moving a step further, you can consider more formal recognition systems and many hotels today have an employee of the month scheme or similar. These are valid approaches, if they are well managed and based on defined criteria. In a small hotel, the pool of employees is naturally limited, so after a short period of time you can run out of people to award, so an employee of the quarter scheme might be more appropriate in that context.

Whatever approach you take, make sure that you:

❑ define specific criteria upon which the award is to be based. Often employees are nominated solely based on the opinion of their immediate leader. It needs to be more transparent than that. How can an employee strive to win the award, if they don't know what it is actually based upon?

❑ agree how the decision will be made, who will be involved in selecting the winner against the criteria

❑ identify how the winner will be recognised and whether there be an overall winner each year from those who won the monthly or quarterly award

❑ Make the award attractive – is it something that people would actually strive to achieve?

The added benefit of a well managed recognition scheme is that it enables you to promote 'excellence' attitudes and behaviours through the criteria that you define for achievement of the award.

In addition to the above options for recognising and rewarding employees, don't forget to promote any potential benefits to employees where it is within your capability to offer them. This could be insurance schemes, use of hotel facilities or special offers in other hotels you have associations with. It is not hard to establish links with other hoteliers where they can offer reduced rates for your employees and vice-versa. This can also apply with other local shops and businesses in your area.

How can you manage change to increase engagement?

It goes without saying that you should always be on the look out for better ways of doing things and even though the level of some changes may be minor, if they lead to improved team performance and better results, then they are worthwhile.

Change, when handled effectively will increase engagement; the opposite naturally applies. Here are some general points to consider in relation to handling change to maximise engagement.

❑ Define a structured framework for handling change in the business and apply it to all major change initiatives at the hotel.

❑ Change must be seen to lead to tangible benefits. If it doesn't, you will find that employee resistance to the change is greater. Avoid change just for the sake of it.

❑ Reactions to change vary, but most people fear it to some degree and the bigger the change the more people can worry about it. Handling change requires you to offer lots of support and guidance and in many cases you need to really sell the benefits of the change to get buy in.

❑ In general terms, the more involvement your employees feel they have in determining the nature and direction of changes affecting them, the easier it will be to get them to support the changes but also the more engaged they are likely to be.

❑ When you do make significant changes, you should set a timeframe for implementation and stick to it, as open-ended change can be disheartening.

❑ In any change process, show benefits as early as possible so that your employees see the value of it.

❑ When the change materialises, recognise the efforts of employees in making it happen.

You should also realise that any change process provides disengaged team members with a perfect opportunity to 'stir things up', so, if you have such characters, pay particular attention to the influence they are exerting at such times.

SUMMARY

The twelve factors covered here are the essentials for creating an environment where employees are more likely to engage. There is no pretence that you can address all these issues in a short period of time and in any case there is no magic formula on how to go about it. It is mostly common sense and involves applying a bit of creativity where possible.

The amount of effort required within the twelve factors will naturally depend upon what you do already. Whatever decisions you make about the way forward, doing nothing is not advisable because when we look again at the human equation identified earlier, you can quickly see that it is worth your while to engage your employees to the greatest extent possible.

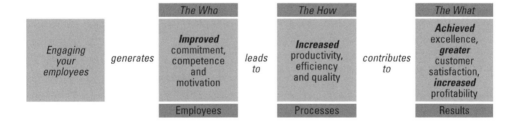

In the following chapter we will discuss how you can measure employee engagement levels over time.

9

How can you measure employee engagement levels over time?

HOW CAN YOU MEASURE EMPLOYEE ENGAGEMENT LEVELS OVER TIME?

As with everything you do under the four themes, you will want to know whether your efforts at engaging your employees are making a difference to the business. To determine this, you will need to measure it in some way. Earlier, the distinction was made between employee satisfaction and engagement and it will be explored further in this chapter.

Measuring employee engagement levels

Many companies today have some form of employee satisfaction survey. Whilst these are very beneficial, high satisfaction ratings do not necessarily convert to

Based on the results from your measures, learn the lessons so that you can make things even better.

Analyse the results and make improvements

Define the results you want to achieve

In this case, what do you actually want in terms of employee engagement?

Employee Engagement

Measure progress at defined intervals

Use your measures at defined intervals to identify what progress is being made.

Consider how you will measure progress

Take action to achieve the results you want

In this case, address the twelve factors which drive engagement.

In this case, how will you know that employee engagement is improving at the hotel? What measures will you use? Are the right systems in place to give you the information you need?

higher engagement as it is possible for an employee to be satisfied but not necessarily engaged. Therefore, we will focus on how to measure both satisfaction and engagement and our framework for managing continuous improvement can again be a useful guide here in terms of how to do so.

To effectively measure employee engagement, you need to consider the following issues.

Define the results you want to achieve

You already know from the previous chapter that there are twelve drivers of engagement. However, it is clear that you can't measure terms such as 'culture' or 'challenge', so the first hurdle you face in this area is to define more clearly what results you actually want under each of the twelve factors.

An example of how you might do this is shown below.

Factor	What outcomes do you want?
Leadership	❑ Employees have a positive impression of leadership at the hotel. ❑ Employees feel valued and respected by their leaders.
Culture	❑ Employees feel that the hotel shows general care and concern for their welfare. ❑ Employees feel proud about working at the hotel.
Composition	❑ Employees 'fit' with the culture of the hotel and work well with their colleagues. ❑ Employees respect diversity amongst those they work with and feel respected by others.
Clarity	❑ Employees understand what the hotel is trying to achieve and how they can contribute to that. ❑ Employees fully understand their job description and what is expected of them in terms of their performance.
Competence	❑ Employees receive regular training and coaching which helps them to do the job more effectively. ❑ Employees feel that they are growing and developing in their jobs.
Cooperation	❑ Employees feel that they get to work with different people in their department. ❑ Employees feel that teamwork is strong between departments at the hotel.
Control	❑ Employees feel that everyone in their team works to a high standard and that the workload is shared. ❑ Employees feel empowered at work and that they can use their own initiative.
Communication	❑ Employees feel that there is open, two-way communication at the hotel. ❑ Employees receive regular constructive feedback on their performance.
Challenge	❑ Employees feel a sense of challenge in their jobs. ❑ Employees feel that they can make suggestions about improving things at the hotel.
Conflict	❑ Employees feel that they can voice their opinions in a constructive manner on issues which concern them. ❑ Employees feel that the atmosphere at work is positive and that conflict is managed effectively.

Compensation	❑ Employees feel valued for the work they do at the hotel. ❑ Employees receive regular feedback and praise when they achieve something special at work.
Change	❑ Employees feel that they are kept informed about changes at the hotel. ❑ Employees feel that they can contribute to decisions that directly affect their work.

By defining these key outcomes, you now have something more solid to work with when it comes to measuring employee engagement. These are just suggestions of course and you might have different outcomes in mind. Whatever you decide, you should limit the number you seek to measure; otherwise it becomes an overly cumbersome process.

Take action to achieve the results you want

It is clear that if you don't actually take action within the twelve factors to enhance employee engagement then seeking to measure improvements will not be necessary, as you won't see any. Therefore it is important that you have an overall engagement strategy and from that you identify priority actions each year across the twelve factors and include them in your annual plan.

Consider how you will measure progress

Measuring employee engagement can occur at a number of levels moving from informal to more formal approaches. The degree of complexity you will adopt will depend upon the resources available to you but monitoring employee engagement does not have to be a costly exercise. Some general approaches to consider are defined here.

APPLY INFORMAL MEASUREMENTS

Informally, you can get a sense of how engaged your employees are through your regular interactions and discussions with them. You might even see evidence of it when you bring them together in groups at briefings or meetings. More formally, individual engagement levels can be determined during employee appraisals and they are an important tool in this regard.

DEVELOP AN EMPLOYEE ENGAGEMENT SURVEY

Developing and implementing an employee engagement survey requires a fair degree of planning to get it right. Before we look at how you might go about it, consider the following scenario for a moment.

In one hotel that I was involved with a number of years ago, the management team decided that it would be beneficial to introduce an employee satisfaction survey to gauge the mood of employees and to identify areas where improvements were required. Having conducted the survey it became clear that all was not well; not only was the response rate very low but quite a number of areas were negatively rated by those who did complete the survey. The management team reviewed the results and made lots of commitments to employees as to how things would improve from that point forward. A bit of good practice in action you might think. Unfortunately, it turned out not to be.

Despite all their promises, the management team didn't actually follow through and very few changes were seen. When the survey was conducted again the following year, not only was the response rate even lower but the negative ratings had worsened. The amazing thing was that the managers were actually surprised that this had happened!

The main point here is that you need to be very clear before you head down this road that if you do survey employee opinions and then don't act upon the results, you will end up in a far worse position than when you started. It hardly seems necessary to mention this, but many hotels do fall into this trap, so be warned.

The key to any good survey is getting the questions right; right in this case means that you are measuring both satisfaction and engagement. Your engagement survey must incorporate questions which are designed to test the outcomes you have defined for each of the twelve factors but also, and this is critical, to determine whether those outcomes are leading to greater engagement by your employees.

In terms of survey design, you could take the outcomes defined above for the twelve factors and translate them into a series of statements to be rated by employees which would give an indicator as to whether they were satisfied at work. Then by adding an additional statement for each factor you can determine whether this was translating into higher levels of engagement. Taking the leadership factor as an example, you would end up with the following statements to be answered by the employee.

Factor	Questions	Outcomes
Leadership	I believe that leadership at the hotel is effective. I feel valued and respected by my leaders at work.	*Satisfaction*
	The way I am led at work increases my willingness to give my all in my job	*Engagement*

A suggested engagement survey, incorporating these principles for all twelve factors is provided in the Tools and Resources section at the end of this book.

One question which often arises in relation to surveys of this nature is whether employees should complete it anonymously or not. The argument for anonymity is that by doing so employees are more likely to provide honest answers. The argument against is that you cannot follow up with an individual on any specific concerns they may have where negative ratings are given. Perhaps the best route to go on this is to give the employee the choice so that they can provide their name if they wish, but there is no problem if they don't.

USE HARD MEASURES

In addition to the overall rating you get from the engagement survey, you can again use your employee turnover ratio as an indicator of how satisfied and engaged your employees are. If turnover at your hotel, or within an individual department, is higher than the norm then this would indicate that there are problems that warrant investigation.

DO YOU HAVE THE NECESSARY SYSTEMS IN PLACE?

Once you have decided how you will measure employee engagement levels, you then need to make sure that you have the systems in place to produce the information you need. In this case, it will involve designing the survey and making the necessary arrangements to support its implementation. You can easily manage this survey in-house using a simple paper-based approach or an alternative relatively low cost, but effective, option to consider is to use an online survey platform, such as that provided by *surveymonkey.com*.

Such websites allow you to create your own survey and forward a link by email to your employees which they can complete online. You can then get tabulated results to support analysis. You could also consider contracting it out to an external company at a fairly reasonable cost.

Measure progress at defined intervals

Informal measurement of employee engagement levels should naturally be ongoing, but you must also decide upon the frequency for producing the more formal measures. At a minimum, you should conduct the engagement survey at least once a year, but ideally twice. Twelve months is a long time in business life and if the survey is only conducted annually, problems can go undetected which damages engagement. Normally the hard measure of employee turnover is produced on a monthly, quarterly or annual basis, depending upon the size of operation.

Analyse the results and make improvements

Based on the overall result from the employee engagement survey, you will know in general terms whether employee engagement is improving or not and over time you should see an upward trend in the overall scores you get. You should also consider how you might benchmark your result against comparable hotels, but again, to do so, such hotels would have to measure employee engagement using a similar methodology to you for the comparisons to be of any value.

The overall rating received for each individual factor will also help you to pinpoint particular areas where there might be problems affecting engagement levels. Although the survey tells you what employee perceptions are, it doesn't give you the causes of the results, so some further investigation will be necessary. You could include a comments section for each question you ask on the survey but this makes both the completion and analysis of the survey more cumbersome.

The survey is only intended as a snapshot and will give you a useful general overview. But you need more in-depth information to improve problem areas or just to get ideas on how you can make the positive results even better. One useful approach to getting the additional information you need is to establish a focus group representing a broad mix of employees across the hotel and meet with them to discuss the results of the survey. Through this feedback you can then pinpoint specific areas of improvement which you can work on in the following period.

Whatever you identify as needing attention, the critical point as we said is to take action to resolve the shortcomings. Employees tend to take a wait-and-see approach to surveys and if they notice improvements arising from them, then you will find that response rates will rise on subsequent surveys. In addition, the fact that you both listen to and act upon their feedback will in itself demonstrate that you value their input, which in turn enhances engagement.

SUMMARY

The suggestions here will give you some ideas as to how you might measure employee engagement in your hotel, or to improve on the approaches you already have in place. Simple, practical systems when applied consistently, can provide you with the information you need, so measuring employee engagement doesn't have to cost the earth.

Employee engagement is a major issue and one to which many owners and managers don't pay enough attention. In our industry, employees are the face of the organisation and without them the delivery of memorable service experiences is just not possible. Increasing engagement does take time, but armed with the information from these three chapters, you now have plenty of ideas to work with and you should start to take action in these areas as soon as you can, if you are truly serious about running a great hotel.

Finally, take a key message with you from Theme 3: great hotels need great people and you cannot realise your goals or achieve excellence at your hotel without having truly engaged employees.

THEME 4 – CAPTIVATE YOUR CUSTOMERS

Strive for total customer focus

CAPTIVATE YOUR
CUSTOMERS

Are you truly customer focused?

> *Quality in a service or product is not what you put into it. It is what the client or customer gets out of it.*
>
> Peter Drucker

The quality of service offered at your hotel is such a fundamental success factor that you could be forgiven for thinking that it needs no further emphasis here. After all, there isn't a hotel owner or manager in the world who doesn't proclaim their undying commitment to the customer, so much so, that the notion of customer as king has now perhaps attained cliché status.

Yet, despite all the promises, you frequently find shortcomings in the level of service provided in some hotels. That won't come as any surprise to you; in your own life outside of work, you are a customer and you will have encountered at first hand the effects of lack of customer focus. Sadly, commitments don't always translate into action when it comes to service.

No doubt you already devote a lot of attention to this area and you will know just how difficult it is to achieve service excellence, given the variety of inputs required to make that happen. You need the right culture at the hotel to facilitate it, there must be collective determination to realise it, strong leadership to drive it with engaged employees to deliver it every day. This is why we dealt with the preceding three themes first – get those right and quality service becomes an infinitely more achievable goal.

Our concern in the coming chapters will be to explore how to enhance service quality in your hotel to a level which gives you an edge; we will not discuss the consequences of poor service, for they are obvious. Great hotels, large and small, achieve excellence by getting the basics of service right first. Not only right, but consistently right. Then they take service delivery to another level – one which we will call *ServicePlusOne*.

In a nutshell, *ServicePlusOne* means striving to really captivate your customers. It is concerned with developing the capabilities within your hotel to offer a great service experience, which is focused on and meets customer expectations on a continuous basis. No easy task in itself. Having laid that solid foundation, *ServicePlusOne* involves augmenting the experience by incorporating a range of *Plus Ones* into service delivery which show true customer focus and demonstrate that the customer is, in fact, king.

These *Plus Ones* are often minor in nature, such as being proactive instead of reactive or remembering customer names or preferences, but when integrated into an already positive experience, they are major in how they impact on customer perceptions. As you begin to think about this important area, now is the time to ask yourself, *are you truly customer focused?*

Theme 4 examines how you can enhance quality across the totality of the customer experience by helping you to answer important questions such as:

❑ What is *ServicePlusOne* and why is it important?

❑ How can you attain *ServicePlusOne* at your hotel?

❑ How can you measure the impact of *ServicePlusOne* over time?

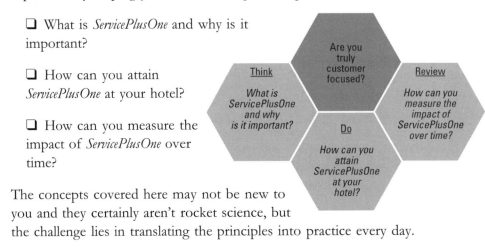

The concepts covered here may not be new to you and they certainly aren't rocket science, but the challenge lies in translating the principles into practice every day.

10
What is *ServicePlusOne* and why is it important?

THINK	WHAT IS *SERVICEPLUSONE* AND WHY IS IT IMPORTANT?

Have you ever wondered why similar hotels can be so radically different in terms of the experience they offer? Why is it that some are memorable, yet others are best forgotten? What makes one feel like a home from home, whereas another can make you want to get home as quickly as possible? These and related questions will preoccupy us now as we turn to the core of hospitality – the quality of service that you offer to your customers.

It should be obvious that if you provide poor service today you will be punished, regardless of how cheaply you price your offering. However, simply delivering good service is no longer a source of competitive advantage. To stand out you must reach for a higher goal and provide a customer experience that is above the norm; by doing so you increase your competitiveness within the markets you operate in. Of course, issues such as how you market your hotel impact heavily on success too. Many hotels end up diluting their marketing spend because when they do attract customers, they don't look after them to the level required to generate loyalty and increase retention.

Going back to basics

Although we will look beyond the basics here, in seeking to first define and later apply the concept of *ServicePlusOne*, it is helpful to step back for a moment and then build from there. To do this, you need to put yourself in the customers' shoes to remind yourself of the thought process that every customer works through every time they have a service encounter of any kind. As a customer, when you experience a service you undertake a mental journey of sorts, consisting of three stages:

Expectations ➡ **Experience** ➡ **Evaluation**

Before you have a service encounter you build up *expectations* about what's coming. These can be low level, for example, when you pop down to your local pub for a drink, or at a higher level if you, say, organise an important family event at a hotel or when you book your annual holiday. Regardless of the nature of the encounter there are always expectations.

Armed with those expectations, you then have the *experience*, which in a hotel context is a combination of a number of dimensions – the four Ps. The *physical* environment, the *products* offered and the *procedures* followed are the relatively tangible components and more easily managed, whereas the *people* aspect, involving as it does attitudes and behaviours, is less so.

Physical
The quality of the physical facilities.

Procedures
How efficiently the service is actually delivered.

The Experience

People
The employees you encounter and their attitudes and behaviours.

Products
The standard of the products such as food and beverages.

Once you have the experience, you then make a judgement or *evaluation* about what you encountered; what actually happened versus your expectations. This evaluation might again be low level and fleeting, or more intense depending upon the nature of the experience. But there is always a judgement made.

Of course, there is a fifth P to consider: Price. In short, did the experience represent value for money? Naturally value for money has different connotations for every customer, but we all want to feel that what we spent was worth it. Pricing structures are individual to each hotel so we won't directly address them here, other than to say that price is less important when the value the customer derives from the experience is high.

Here is an example of this thought process in action.

In the Customer's Shoes . . .

This week had been a nightmare for Mary and John. The kids had come down with the flu and had been kept home from school all week. So rather than her usual few quiet hours each day, Mary found herself stuck in the house. John had one of those weeks at work which made him wonder why he bothered. By Thursday night they were both at their wits' end and needed a night out, so they decided they would go for a meal on Friday evening.

On Friday morning Mary telephoned a local hotel. The receptionist who answered was very friendly. She wasn't sure of the opening times of the restaurant, as she was only new, but she offered to connect Mary to the Sunflower restaurant, so she could make the booking. A woman answered the phone in the restaurant. 'Is this the Sunflower?' asked Mary. 'Yes it is, what can I do for you?' replied the girl on the phone. 'I'd like to make a dinner reservation for two people for tonight if possible' . . . 'hang on I'll check,' came the reply and the woman went off to find out.

In the background Mary could hear the employee calling out to someone else whether they knew where the diary was. Mary waited and eventually the woman returned. 'Now, how many people was that for?' she asked. 'It's for two people at 9.00pm,' said Mary. 'And the name is?' asked the woman. 'You can reserve the table in the name of John Roche,' replied Mary. 'OK that's done, thanks, bye,' said the woman as she hung up. 'Er, could we have a table by the window?' . . . Mary was just in the middle of asking this when the phone went dead. 'Oh', said Mary to herself, 'she's in a bit of a hurry . . . but I'm sure we can sort it out tonight.'

All day Mary was looking forward to her night out. John arrived home at about 6pm and they started to get ready. Mary could tell he'd had a bad day as his thoughts were miles away. When the babysitter arrived they left and as they drove up the drive towards the hotel, John had started to relax a little. Mary mentioned the news about her sister getting married and he made some smart comment about love being blind which made them both laugh.

As they turned into the car park, they could tell that the hotel was quite busy. A security guard was on duty directing traffic. John couldn't find a space for some time and eventually squeezed in at the end of a row of cars. They were just getting out of the car when the guard came over. 'Hey, you can't park there,' he said. 'But this is the only place I could find,' replied John. 'Look, you'll have to move it anyway, you're blocking an exit,' said the guard. Normally John would have argued the point but he could tell by looking at Mary that it was the last thing she needed. 'You go ahead Mary and I'll find a space,' said John.

As Mary walked in she noticed how clean the front entrance looked. They obviously keep it nice, she thought to herself. As she waited in the lobby she noticed that they held weddings at the hotel. 'I must tell sis' about this place – it would be a nice venue for her wedding,' she thought. She also noticed there was a brochure stand and made a mental note to collect one on the way out.

When John arrived she could tell he was on a short fuse. 'We're a bit early, let's go for a drink first,' said Mary calming him down and they went to the bar. Once there, they were glad to see that there were some tables free, none of them were clean, but at least they had somewhere to sit.

They waited for a while for lounge service but finally John went to the bar. On his way back with the drinks he asked one of the lounge staff if he would come over and wipe the table. 'As soon as I get this order, sir,' was the reply. The waiter did eventually come over and Mary smiled to herself as she saw him coming, as he had his shirt sticking out at the back.

'Good evening,' he said and he nodded towards their drinks. John lifted both drinks and he wiped the table. 'You're busy tonight,' said Mary. 'No not really, we're just short-staffed that's all, so we're run off our feet. Can I get you anything while I'm here?' 'No thanks,' they replied and off he went.

When they had finished their drinks, they went to the restaurant. Upon entering, a girl at a little desk inside the door looked up briefly and asked them if they had a reservation. Mary said they had in the name of Roche for two people at 9pm. The girl looked through the diary but didn't seem to be able to find the booking. Noticing this, Mary said 'I telephoned today and made the booking with one of the girls.' 'Did you get her name?' asked the receptionist. 'No I didn't actually,' replied Mary. 'Well there's no booking here so you'll have to take a seat, we are very busy at the moment.'

Mary was really annoyed but she tried to stay calm, as she knew it wouldn't take much to set John off. 'Oh well these things happen,' she said as they sat down. After a few minutes a gentleman approached them. He introduced himself as the head waiter and apologised for the mix up. He explained that they were sorting out a table and that they could look through the menus while they were waiting. Mary asked if they could have a window table and he said that would be fine. He presented the menus, offered them an aperitif and then left, returning promptly with the drinks and promising that the table would be ready in a few moments.

After a short time, the head waiter reappeared and escorted them to their table. As they had already made their choices, he took the order and disappeared into the kitchen. A young girl brought them some bread and iced water. 'Good evening,' she said, 'my name is Sarah and I'll be looking after you tonight.' John and Mary now started to unwind. The food was very good for the most part and Sarah was very pleasant and attentive.

When the meal was over they went back to the bar for a quick drink before they set off home. John saw the barman checking his watch as they entered. 'Yes?' he said as they reached the bar. They ordered their drinks and sat down. 'That was a lovely meal, wasn't it?' asked Mary. 'Yes it was, although my dessert was a bit tasteless,' John replied. They chatted together for a while, but got the impression that the employees were looking to finish up. 'They've only just served last orders,' John said slightly irritated. 'I know,' said Mary, 'but let's go anyway, I'm tired.'

On the way home in the car Mary remembered that she had forgotten to take one of the wedding brochures for her sister. She thought about it for a while and decided that maybe she might be better off trying somewhere else . . .

This is not an unusual service experience by any means and there are both good and bad aspects to it. Overall, how would you describe it? You might conclude that it was inconsistent and didn't fully live up to expectations, but at the same time it was not a complete write-off either. Our stressed-out couple may well use the hotel again for a night out because for them it represents a fairly low-level encounter. However, they will think twice about using, or indeed recommending, the hotel for higher-level events, which would represent more risk.

Understanding the risk factor

An important message to take from our quick step back to basics relates to the risk factor and the rationale this provides for the need to strive to make *ServicePlusOne* a reality in your hotel.

For low-risk transactions, if the experience doesn't live up to expectations, there will of course be disappointment, but when a higher risk encounter goes astray that dissatisfaction is naturally magnified. For example, if you had a bad meal in your local pub, you wouldn't be happy about it, but if the food or service was poor at an important family event, you would be pretty annoyed.

Therefore the greater the risk factor associated with a service encounter (risk in the sense of the damage caused if something goes wrong), the more consideration the customer gives to venue selection and the higher their expectations. They need to have confidence and trust that the hotel will deliver. This goes some way to explaining why word of mouth and personal recommendations are so important for the reassurance they provide.

Hotels which continually underperform might survive, but they can never truly prosper because they lose out on the high-risk events as customers aren't convinced that they will come up trumps. But it is in these higher-level events where the real monetary value lies and you are more likely to secure this type of business when you consistently meet and, even better, exceed customer expectations.

What is *ServicePlusOne* (S + 1)

ServicePlusOne, or S + 1 as we will refer to it from here on, is about striving for excellence across the customer experience so that what you offer is demonstrably better than that of your competitors.

Naturally, the standard of service at your hotel will fluctuate to some degree on occasion; perfection is a worthy goal but you won't get it right every time because you are, after all, only human. However, it is the overall pattern of quality that matters and a good way of describing fluctuations in service delivery is to view it as being a quality continuum, based on your ability to respond to customer expectations.

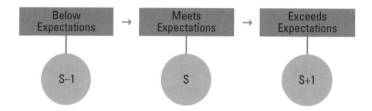

We can broadly describe three types of service quality across the continuum. When service falls *below expectations,* we can call it S−1. We are not talking about poor service here because that is unacceptable in a great hotel at any time, but on occasion, service can be inconsistent. An S−1 customer experience may not be all bad but, as in our earlier case study (which is a good example of S−1 by the way), it is all a bit hit and miss. When service *meets expectations* we can call it Standard, or S, and when the customer experience *exceeds expectations* it can be said to be S+1.

In any hotel, swings in the quality of service delivery between S−1 and S+1 do occur, but your goal must be to strive to continuously sustain it at the level of S+1, if you want to run a great hotel.

S+1 begins as a philosophy and hoping to attain it means having a real desire to excel by offering your customers a service experience which is second to none. In one sense, it involves repositioning your hotel culturally as well as operationally because S+1 is achieved as much through attitudes as it is through actions. In essence, a move towards S+1 involves shifting along the continuum as illustrated in the figure opposite.

The differences in a customer experience at the level of S+1 from that of S or even S−1 might be subtle, but they are powerful in terms of the impression they make. Here is a simple scenario of a repeat customer checking into a hotel to show the distinctions between a common service encounter at the three levels.

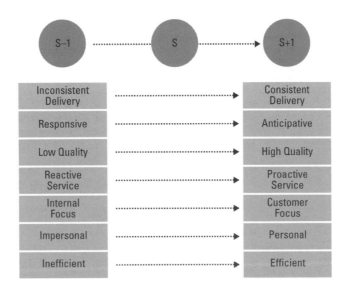

Service Experience at S−1

Receptionist:	Good evening sir, are you checking-in?
Guest:	Yes, I have a reservation in the name of David Brown.
Receptionist:	I see, yes here it is. Welcome to the hotel. It's for one night, is it?
Guest:	Yes, just tonight.
Receptionist:	Could I ask you to fill in your registration form, please.
Guest:	Certainly. May I borrow your pen?
Receptionist:	Sure . . . here you are . . . OK, thank you, sir. You will be paying by Visa is that correct?
Guest:	Yes.
Receptionist:	May I have your card for authorisation purposes please?
Guest:	Yes of course. Here it is.
Receptionist:	Thank you . . . here is your card sir. Now I'll just get your key.
Guest:	Actually, could I have a non-smoking room at the back of the hotel and, oh yes, a soft pillow?
Receptionist:	Ehm, let me check sir . . . yes, I do have a non-smoking room at the back, but I will have to contact housekeeping about the pillow. I will have them call you in your room . . . now, I have given you room 156 which is on the first floor and faces the back. Is there anything else?
Guest:	No, that's fine.
Receptionist:	OK, so. The lifts are just to your left. Have a nice evening sir and please let us know if you need anything during your stay
Guest:	Thank you.

Service Experience at S

Receptionist:	Good evening sir, may I help you?
Guest:	Yes, I have a reservation in the name of David Brown.
Receptionist:	Oh yes, here it is. You will be staying with us just for one night, Mr Brown, is that right?
Guest:	Yes, just tonight.
Receptionist:	Have you stayed with us before, Mr Brown?
Guest:	Yes, a few times.
Receptionist:	Oh, you are very welcome back to the hotel, it's nice to see you again, Mr Brown. Could I ask you to fill in your registration form, please? Here is a pen.
Guest:	Certainly.
Receptionist:	Thank you, Mr Brown . . . you will be paying by Visa, is that correct?
Guest:	Yes.
Receptionist:	May I have your card for authorisation purposes, Mr Brown?
Guest:	Yes of course . . . here it is.
Receptionist:	Thank you, Mr Brown. Would you like a wake up call in the morning and a newspaper perhaps?
Guest:	Yes at 6.30am and could I have *The Times* please.
Receptionist:	Would you like me to make a reservation for you for dinner this evening, Mr Brown?
Guest:	Yes, at 8.00pm please.
Receptionist:	Certainly, I will do that for you. Is there anything else you would like, Mr Brown?
Guest:	Actually, could I have a non-smoking room at the back of the hotel and, oh yes, a soft pillow?
Receptionist:	Yes of course . . . now let me see . . . I have given you room 156 which is at the back on the first floor. I will also have the pillow sent up to you. Are you familiar with our facilities?
Guest:	Yes, I am thanks.
Receptionist:	Would you like help with your luggage, Mr Brown?
Guest:	No that's fine, I can manage thanks.
Receptionist:	That's great, Mr Brown. The lifts are just to your left. Have a nice evening and please let us know if you need anything during your stay. Just dial 7 on your phone and we will be happy to help.
Guest:	Thank you.

Service Experience at S + 1

Receptionist:	Good evening sir, may I help you?
Guest:	Yes, I have a reservation in the name of David Brown.
Receptionist:	Oh yes, here it is. Welcome back Mr Brown, it is great to see you again. Here is your registration form, Mr Brown. Could you check if the details are the same as the last time and please just sign it at the bottom? Here is a pen.
Guest:	Certainly.
Receptionist:	Thank you, Mr Brown . . . you will be paying by Visa is that correct?
Guest:	Yes.
Receptionist:	May I have your card for authorisation purposes?
Guest:	Yes of course. Here it is.
Receptionist:	Thank you, Mr Brown. Would you like *The Times* in the morning as usual?
Guest:	Yes, thank you.
Receptionist:	What time would you like a wake up call for in the morning, Mr Brown?
Guest:	At 6.30am, please.
Receptionist:	That's fine . . . would you like me to make a reservation for you for dinner this evening, Mr Brown?
Guest:	Yes, at 8.00pm, please.
Receptionist:	Have you any preference for a table, Mr Brown?
Guest:	Actually, one to the side if you don't mind, not in the centre.
Receptionist:	I will organise that for you now . . . just to let you know that our restaurant manager, Paul, tells me that he will give you a quiet table towards the back of the restaurant because there is a large group in the front section, so it might be quieter for you there. Will that be alright for you, Mr Brown?
Guest:	Yes, that sounds perfect.
Receptionist:	Now, Mr Brown, I have given you a non-smoking room at the back of the hotel, which is on the same side that you requested the last time. It's 156 on the first floor. Is that suitable?
Guest:	Yes, thank you. I was just about to ask.
Receptionist:	And I will arrange for a soft pillow to be taken up to the room in the next few minutes.
Guest:	Oh, really, you remembered, that's great, thank you.

Receptionist:	Do you remember our facilities Mr Brown, or would you like me to run through everything again for you?
Guest:	No, I remember thanks.
Receptionist:	That's great, Mr Brown. Oh, we have recently redecorated the bar so you might like to have a drink there this evening before dinner. It's really nice what they have done, I'm sure you'll like it. We would be delighted to offer you a complimentary drink as a little thank you for your custom . . . Well, the lifts are just to your left, Mr Brown. Please, leave your luggage there and we will have it brought straight up for you.
Guest:	No that's fine, I can manage.
Receptionist:	Are you sure? Well, have a nice evening Mr Brown and please let me know if you need anything during your stay. Just dial 7 on your phone. My name is Sharon, or any of my colleagues will be happy to help at any time.
Guest:	Thank you.

Now, these three snapshots of a guest check-in may not seem dramatically different, but from the customers' perspective, they are. The experience at S−1 isn't that bad, or indeed unusual but it's very functional, reactive and somewhat impersonal, although the receptionist isn't unfriendly or rude in any way. The experience at level S is pretty good and would meet the expectations of most customers.

However, the S+1 encounter has that little bit extra – the *Plus Ones* – and although not earth shattering, they do show a greater focus on the customer and a genuine interest in their custom. These *Plus Ones* might seem insignificant and indeed taken in isolation they are, however, when found within the context of a good service experience they have the effect of turning it into a great one.

WHAT ARE *PLUS ONES* (+1s)?

In essence, *Plus Ones*, or +1s are anything which brings your level of service beyond basic expectations; there are an infinite number of potential +1s within the overall customer experience at your hotel. These +1s can be major or minor in nature and may be relevant to any of the four Ps that make up the customer experience:

❑ *Physical* They can be major issues when you design certain facilities specifically with guest needs in mind, such as a special secure floor for female executives in a corporate hotel.

146

❑ *Products*   They can be product related when you tailor products to meet specific customers' likes and dislikes.

❑ *People*   They can be all the minor things which employees can do to show positive attitudes and to signify to a customer that they are special. These can be as simple as name recognition or anticipating requirements rather than waiting to be asked. In fact the majority of +1s fall into this category and any time an employee does that little bit extra for a customer, it can be considered a +1. That is why employee attitude and engagement levels are so critical to delivering *ServicePlusOne*.

❑ *Procedural*   They can be procedural when you adjust how you do things to enhance the customer experience such as when you extend breakfast service times at weekends rather than expecting guests to make it down by 10am.

The +1s are therefore the icing on the cake but they won't have any impact without the cake. If you are not consistently meeting your customers' basic needs at level S, then seeking to add the +1s will not have the same impact.

Towards S + 1

As you seek to move up the quality continuum towards S+1 you face two intertwined challenges.

Levels S and S+1 go hand in hand and you cannot reach S+1 without achieving level S; you must consistently meet guest expectations before you can ever hope to exceed them. It is not a step-by-step process, but rather a matter of combining the two levels at the same time.

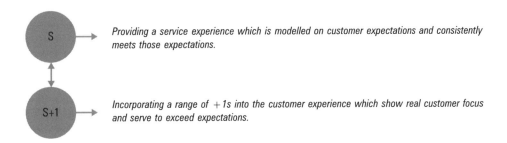

S — Providing a service experience which is modelled on customer expectations and consistently meets those expectations.

S+1 — Incorporating a range of +1s into the customer experience which show real customer focus and serve to exceed expectations.

Unfortunately, a lot of hotels don't get this balancing act right. Take the scenario of the check-in experience we saw earlier. Many hotels now have information systems in place which allow them to capture and use little details gleaned about customers from previous visits, such as their preferences for certain types of room or special requests about pillows; simple little touches which are positive in terms of the impression they give.

Despite the existence of these +1s, some hotels do not get the full benefit from using them because basic elements within the customer experience are lacking. This can range from minor flaws in bedrooms such as hairs in the bath, badly scuffed walls around the luggage rack, dirty ironing board covers or stained carpets to more major concerns such as unhelpful staff or erratic quality of food in the restaurant.

In one sense, hotels which let this happen are attempting to run before they can walk. They might have plenty of +1s, but the benefits are lost because they slip up on the fundamentals. So you need to see the addition of +1s as being the final piece of the puzzle, but you have to get the basics consistently right first.

Working towards S + 1 involves using the *Expectations–Experience–Evaluation* model as the basis for all your efforts in relation to enhancing the customer experience at your hotel. You will need to look at how well you understand your customers' expectations, how effectively you deliver on them and what they actually think about what you do. The *Expectations–Experience–Evaluation* framework is a very simple but effective tool to help you manage the customer experience and we will use it as the basis for the content of the following chapter.

SUMMARY

Understanding the concept of *ServicePlusOne* is easy; raising capabilities and performance at your hotel to the level required to achieve it is not. You need consistency, quality and efficiency and on top of that you must identify and integrate a range of +1s which are applicable at your hotel. How to achieve this in practice will be the focus of the following chapter.

Facilities, products and ideas can be fairly easily copied over time but truly excellent service can not be. So this is an area where there is potential for you to steal a march on your competitors. Your ability to make S + 1 a reality in your operation is not dependent upon the size, style or grade of your hotel although how you apply the principles covered here will of course depend upon your customer base, what you do already and the nature of the products and services you offer.

The only prerequisites to the attainment of S + 1 are your desire to be the best in terms of the customer experience you offer and that you have laid the groundwork by addressing the principles covered in the previous themes.

11

How can you attain *ServicePlusOne* at your hotel?

DO	**HOW CAN YOU ATTAIN *SERVICEPLUSONE* AT YOUR HOTEL?**

The scale of the task you face in attaining $S + 1$ at your hotel will naturally depend upon where you are starting from. You may have a lot to do or you may already be there and if you are, then well done; that's a big achievement. But don't stop there because you can always make things even better and there are no limitations as to how you can enhance the service experience.

For most hotels, there is probably a fair bit of work to be done to reach the level of $S + 1$. That's not because you don't already do things well but with so many inputs influencing its achievement, there's just so much to keep your eye on. In this chapter, we will explore how you might achieve it.

Laying the foundations for $S + 1$

Your efforts at attaining $S + 1$ actually begin when you develop your vision and mission where you broadly sketch out what you are trying to achieve in terms of your customers. It is here that you set the tone and context for service at your hotel. These general commitments provide the foundation for all other actions you will take in this area, so as a first step on the road to attaining $S + 1$, think hard about what it is you are trying to achieve in relation to service delivery.

In our hotel example from Theme 1, their vision and mission were:

Vision

To become the leading independent four star hotel in London *providing excellent products and services at reasonable prices to every customer, every time.*

> **Mission**
> *Our customers are our priority and we will provide them with a quality experience which is second to none.* We recognise the importance of our employees in achieving this and we will create a positive working environment which encourages their loyalty, commitment and hard work. We strive to be excellent leaders and will undertake all our business activities in an honest and ethical manner to provide a fair return on our investment.

Even a glance at these statements gives a sense that this hotel is pretty focused on its customers: phrases like *every customer, every time, customers are our priority* and *a quality experience which is second to none* are not vague terms, instead they send out a strong message about what this hotel is all about when it comes to their customers. And these weren't just flowery promises because they were translated into concrete goals which were:

Mission		Sample Goals
'Our customers are our priority and we will provide them with a quality experience that is second to none.'	→	❑ To increase the number of repeat customers to 40% within three years. ❑ To increase customer satisfaction levels to 90% within two years. ❑ To continuously increase our scores on internal and external quality audits.

The only way for this hotel to achieve these goals would be to develop a strategy centred on the application of the principles and practices of S + 1; otherwise they could not reach their customer retention and satisfaction targets, nor would they be living up to their vision and mission.

You must adopt a similar approach. First you will have to integrate your customer-related commitments into your vision and mission, then translate them into goals with a strategy designed to raise your game to the level required to attain S + 1. In essence, you should see the implementation of the principles and practices described here as being part of that strategy.

To help make S + 1 a reality, you can use the *Expectations–Experience–Evaluation* model as a tool to guide your efforts. As described, this model depicts what we all think about as customers when experiencing a service and the challenge for you will be to offer a customer experience which continually surpasses expectations. As you begin to reflect on how to do so, it is worth re-emphasising the extent of that challenge.

The challenge of the experience web

As well as their mental journey, your customers naturally undertake a physical one too when they visit your hotel. Everything that you do and everything you offer at your hotel impacts to some degree on that journey depending upon the type of customer involved. Certain components of what you offer, such as your website, or the way in which reservations are handled, actually help to build customer expectations, whereas other elements, such as the quality of food served in the restaurant, play a direct role in determining customer satisfaction regarding their experience.

This physical journey taken by the customer at your hotel may involve interaction with the following components, depending upon what you offer at your hotel.

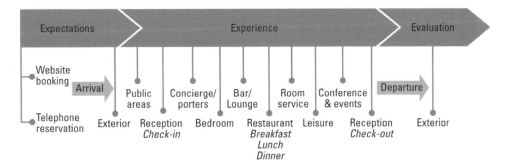

Some of your customers will naturally encounter all of these components during their stay whereas others will not, depending upon the type of customer they are or on the nature of their visit; and not necessarily in the precise sequence shown of course but you get the idea. For instance, corporate customers may not make the booking themselves, or someone popping into your bar for a drink may only encounter a limited number of these components.

Each of these components of the customer experience can be further divided into sub-components which relate to any, or all, of the 4Ps (Physical, Products, People and Procedures). For example, when you take the *exterior* component, you have to consider the car parking facilities, any grounds that you have, the exterior of the building and even security. In relation to the *restaurant* this can be further broken down into breakfast, lunch and dinner and within each of these areas, you have to consider the quality of the food and beverages served, efficiency of service and the personality and attentiveness of employees.

When you dissect the customer experience into its constituent parts, you find layers upon layers of intertwined components, all of which contribute in some way to the overall quality of the customer experience. It is in essence an *experience web*, with each sub-component having a greater or lesser impact on how the customer views their time spent at your hotel. This is what makes achieving S + 1 so challenging – how can you ensure that all of these components are consistently of a high standard and that the 4 Ps within the experience web are harmonised?

The route to achieving S + 1

You can only do this if you start to ask yourself some pretty tough questions about what you currently do, how well you do it and then by taking action to address any shortcomings identified. The type of questions you should consider includes the following.

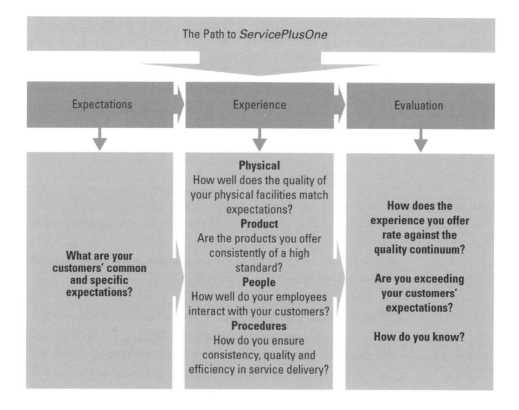

The Path to *ServicePlusOne*

Expectations

What are your customers' common and specific expectations?

Experience

Physical
How well does the quality of your physical facilities match expectations?
Product
Are the products you offer consistently of a high standard?
People
How well do your employees interact with your customers?
Procedures
How do you ensure consistency, quality and efficiency in service delivery?

Evaluation

How does the experience you offer rate against the quality continuum?

Are you exceeding your customers' expectations?

How do you know?

It is in the answers to these questions where you will find a route map to achieving S + 1. Let's explore these questions in greater detail.

What are your customers' common and specific expectations?

All of your practical efforts in progressing towards S+1 must begin with a thorough understanding of your customers' expectations; you need to consider

whether you and everyone at the hotel really understands what the common and specific needs of your customers are.

This may sound like kindergarten stuff and when you raise it with experienced hoteliers you are often met with only mildly concealed disdain, but it's amazing how quickly expectations can be forgotten when the pressures of running the hotel take over.

The Route to *ServicePlusOne*

Expectations	Experience	Evaluation
What are your customers' common and specific expectations?	**Physical** How well does the quality of your physical facilities match expectations? **Product** Are the products you offer consistently of a high standard? **People** How well do your employees interact with your customers? **Procedures** How do you ensure consistency, quality and efficiency in service delivery?	**How does the experience you offer rate against the quality continuum?** **Are you exceeding your customers' expectations?** **How do you know?**

Take this simple example: an obvious customer expectation when making a telephone reservation is that they can do so quickly and efficiently with the minimum of fuss. But it is not an unusual occurrence to phone hotels to make a reservation, particularly out of office hours, and be faced with a harried receptionist who is trying to deal with guests at the front desk, answer queries and take reservation calls all at the same time. This kind of thing regularly occurs in hotels, especially in smaller operations, and whilst from an operator's perspective the reasons for this are understandable, from a customer's point of view they are not. So understanding your customers' expectations is one thing but operating your hotel with those needs as a priority is another.

Therefore, as you aim for S+1, it is very beneficial to revisit this issue to determine how well you really know your customers' expectations. After all, how can you ever hope to exceed them, if you don't clearly define what they are in the first place? As you do this, it is a great learning exercise to involve your employees and this can be done for the hotel overall or broken down by department.

Of course, all customers have slightly different expectations and we will address this issue shortly, but our common needs are broadly the same. When you think about it, there are probably ten key things that customers expect for each component of the experience web. A sample for the check-in component is provided below.

Reception – Check-in

General Expectation	As part of this, your customers expect that:
Your customers expect that their check-in will be handled efficiently, that they will feel welcomed to the hotel and valued as a customer. →	1. The reception desk and lobby area will be clean, tidy and well presented. 2. The appearance and hygiene of employees will be good and that they will be wearing name badges. 3. They will be promptly acknowledged upon arrival and a warm welcome will be given with appropriate eye contact and a smile. 4. Their booking will be in the system and the details will be correct as per the reservation made. 5. The check-in procedure will be handled efficiently and smoothly. 6. A morning call and newspaper will be offered to them. 7. The hotel facilities will be explained to them. 8. Help will be offered with their luggage, or, if not provided as a service, then at least clear directions will be given to their room. 9. The employee will be smiling and courteous throughout the check-in process and will interact well with them making them feel valued as a customer. 10. The check-in will be ended in a friendly manner and that they will be wished a pleasant stay.

There is nothing in the above which you could argue against as these points are fairly typical of what customers expect, even if they don't analyse it to the extent that we have done. Examples of common customer expectations for all elements of the experience web can be found in the Tools and Resources section at the end of the book.

Now that you have clarified common expectations, you need to consider how you can first meet and exceed them. But before you do so, give some thought as to how you can define the specific expectations that your customers have.

SPECIFIC GUEST EXPECTATIONS

A more challenging task, but crucial in terms of attaining $S+1$, is to identify specific customer expectations; the better you become at doing this, the more you will be in a position to demonstrate real customer focus at your hotel.

To define specific needs, you must focus on your customer segments, i.e. corporate, leisure, groups, conference, wedding, or whatever they may be. For example, speed and efficiency are more likely to be of greater concern to corporate clients than for leisure guests, or a suitable location for photographs will of course be high on the list for wedding clients.

For each of your segments, you should try to determine what their specific expectations within the experience web may be. From that, you need to consider whether you are meeting them on a consistent basis. There are a number of mechanisms you can use to source this information and they relate to what we said earlier at the outset of this book about stakeholder focus – if you truly believe that customers are part of your business, then you will take time to pinpoint their needs. Some approaches to help you to get a feel for specific customer expectations include the following.

❑ *Feedback* The range and scope of your feedback mechanisms are vital and we will address this area in the following chapter. The one downside of feedback from a needs identification perspective is that it is received after the experience has taken place. However, over time, by listening to what your customers tell you, it is possible to adjust what you do to better meet their specific needs in future.

❑ *Focus groups* Bringing together small groups of key clients from within your market segments provides you with an ideal opportunity to identify specific customer needs. It also shows that they matter to you and is a great way to build relationships with them. The more you adopt this approach, the more you demonstrate true customer focus.

❑ *Reservation processes* In terms of defining specific guest expectations, your reservations processes, including online and telephone, for all relevant elements within the experience web (accommodation, conference, restaurant etc.), are critical. The enquiry or reservation process, when handled professionally, can both raise customer expectations and provide you with the perfect opportunity to gather information on their specific needs.

Apart from the essential information you need to secure a booking, you should also consider what additional details you can glean from your customers, which would help you to enhance the customer experience. Unfortunately, many hotels miss this opportunity through poor handling of enquiries and reservations. At one end of the scale, we highlighted earlier the harried receptionist who through no fault of her own is too busy to do anything but get the bare minimum of information required to take the booking. At the other end of the scale, some hotels have over-structured their approach to reservations to the extent that callers are required to supply so much information, most of which is of more benefit to the marketing department than it is to enhancing service delivery, that it actually turns customers off. So, it is a matter of getting the balance right.

Recently, when booking a small meeting room at a hotel, I was asked a question as part of the reservation process which stood out. Having gathered the usual information such as numbers, timings, equipment and so on, the conference organiser asked me what the purpose of the meeting was and how they could help to make it a success. This stood out as a simple example of seeking to find out that little bit extra which showed genuine concern for meeting my expectations. It certainly did make a positive impression which was lived up to during the event. Even after an excellent experience on the day, the organiser still took time to sit with me at the end of the meeting to review how it went and to find out if there was anything else they could do to make it even better next time.

It is only by getting closer to your customers that you will generate the information you need to build a great customer experience. Naturally this requires systems and procedures in place to capture and then utilise what you find out, but there is no alternative if you are serious about attaining $S + 1$.

Building a better customer experience

Having defined what your customers' expectations are, you then need to ask yourself how well you currently meet them on a consistent basis. Enhancing the customer experience means answering key questions in relation to the four Ps within the experience web.

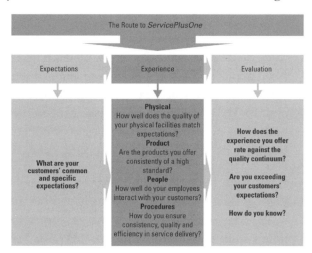

1. **Physical** How well does the quality of your physical facilities match expectations?

2. **Product** Are the products you offer consistently of a high standard?

3. **People** How well do your employees interact with your customers?

4. **Procedures** How do you ensure consistency, quality and efficiency in service delivery?

By answering these questions, you will be in a position to identify where the current shortcomings are in relation to meeting your customers' expectations; in effect, you are trying to pinpoint your $S - 1$ performance areas.

HOW WELL DOES THE QUALITY OF YOUR PHYSICAL FACILITIES MATCH EXPECTATIONS?

The design and maintenance of your facilities are, of course, critical in creating a positive customer experience. We will focus less on design issues here, not that they are unimportant but because you are likely to be restricted in this area, for now at least, as a result of financial constraints.

However, at any stage in the future when you do undertake capital projects at the hotel, make sure that customer needs are paramount in how facilities are designed. You would think this doesn't need to be mentioned but travel around and you will constantly find, even in new builds, aspects of design which are far from customer-centric. This can be as minor as noisy air conditioning units in bedrooms or more considerable general design flaws such as poor elevator positioning, which require customers to undertake long walks to and from their designated bedroom.

Whereas you may have to live with design flaws, at least in the medium term, the area of maintenance is entirely within your sphere of control. There is no excuse for the poor maintenance and upkeep of facilities or indeed equipment. Attention to detail in these areas must be a priority at the hotel and there should be robust procedures in place to deal with ongoing routine maintenance problems to minimise the inconvenience caused to guests. In addition, you should also have a wider maintenance programme to keep your property looking fresh; it is amazing how often even recently built hotels look tired and worn out after short periods.

Maintenance is of course a cost centre and often one of the first areas to be cut back in a downturn. But the simple fact remains that you cannot offer a great experience if visually your hotel, or elements within it, are in poor shape. Effective maintenance can also extend operational life, so in that sense it should also be seen as an investment and not solely a cost.

ARE THE PRODUCTS YOU OFFER CONSISTENTLY OF A HIGH STANDARD?

The products you offer at the hotel must be of a high standard if you want to enhance the customer experience. This clearly applies to the food and beverages you offer, but you may also provide additional leisure, health and beauty products at the hotel and the same principles apply to those.

In particular, getting food quality right is always a challenge but inconsistency in product quality damages your reputation with customers. Often when you stay in a hotel for any length of time, you see the same dish presented differently, or worse still tasting great on one occasion but less so the next. This is unacceptable from a customer's perspective, because they don't get a discount when quality doesn't live up to expectations, so in a sense they feel cheated.

HOW WELL DO YOUR EMPLOYEES INTERACT WITH YOUR CUSTOMERS?

We have already emphasised the importance of engaged employees in running a great hotel and, as part of that, highlighted issues such as effective recruitment, training and teamwork. Although we will touch on the training issue later in this chapter, there is not much more to be said in this area; you should recognise that all your efforts toward attaining $S+1$ will be wasted, if your employees are not behind you in seeking to be the best.

After all, you can have beautiful physical facilities, quality products and efficient procedures but if your people don't interact well with your customers, then you can never achieve $S+1$. Success is ultimately dependent upon employee attitudes and their desire to create a customer experience which stands out.

For each of these first three questions in relation to the quality of experience you offer, it is critical that you compare what you do with your competitors to ensure that you are a leader in these areas amongst your competitive set.

HOW DO YOU ENSURE CONSISTENCY, QUALITY AND EFFICIENCY IN SERVICE DELIVERY?

We now come to the most challenging issue you face in managing the customer experience – how to define procedures which meet guest expectations and how to get your employees to work to them all the time. It is the holy grail of hotel operations and you will already have struggled with this issue at some point; you will likely have spent significant time pulling your hair out trying to get consistency in service delivery from all your employees.

Undoubtedly you will have come across terms such as standard operating procedures, standards of performance, SOPs, or similar to define how things should be done at the hotel. Often, hotels end up with reams of paper and manuals full of standards with accompanying procedures only to find them gathering dust on shelves somewhere but adding little value to daily operations in terms of enhancing the customer experience.

Whatever route you take to addressing this issue it has to work; simple, practical approaches are better than having cumbersome paper-bound systems which only serve to frustrate and de-motivate employees. The approach you take here must also lead to a situation where again you outshine your competitors. Service delivery at your hotel must be second to none.

Despite all the challenges associated with this area, and those challenges are indeed significant, you cannot ignore it because unless there is a 'right' way of doing things, how can you ever hope to meet guest expectations never mind exceed them? In the absence of defined standards with clear procedures on how to meet them, you end up with slight variations of service delivery which leads to an erratic customer experience and you end up operating at the level of $S-1$.

There are admittedly no easy solutions here but many of the problems associated with this important area arise from a lack of understanding and poor application of the concept of standards and procedures. This is further compounded by the terminology used, which is, at best, mind numbing and certainly not conducive to generating passion and enthusiasm. As we work through this important area, we will examine how you might overcome some of these problems.

Changing mindsets

You already know that to achieve the level of $S+1$ you must first reach level S, whereby service delivery is based on, and meets, common guest expectations in terms of consistency, quality and efficiency. For this you cannot avoid having some form of standards and related procedures which describe how to achieve that standard.

Part of the problem here is that many employees and indeed managers do not fully understand what standards and procedures are all about and in fact see them in a negative rather than a positive light. Here is a not uncommon extract from the many workshops which I have delivered on the subject over the years.

As you all know, the purpose of our workshop today is to focus on standards of performance here at the hotel.' Blank stares all round ranging from disinterest to despair. *'Let's start with an easy question. What's the difference between a standard and a procedure?'* Silence. Growing despair amongst some. *'OK, what is a standard then?'* Furtive glances between participants. *'The way we're supposed to do things.'* Great, an answer. Not a very good one but it's a start. *'No that's a procedure,' shouts another.* Confusion abounds, well, at least amongst those still conscious.

'OK, let's try another tack. When a guest phones down to room service and orders a pot of tea, what do they mean?' All are attentive now, only because they are wondering why they are being asked such a stupid question. *'A pot of coffee?'* replies the previously most disinterested participant, sensing an opportunity to relieve the boredom by having a go at the tutor. *'No, it's definitely a pot of tea, but from a customer's perspective what would matter about the tea?'* Again silence, but some sniggers. *'That it was hot.'* Great. *'And in a clean pot.'* We're on a roll now. *'What else would be important?' 'That there was milk and sugar.'*

And on it goes ... this is not an exaggeration of the kind of thing that happens when you address the issue of standards and procedures with employees and before you say it, it's not down to tutor incompetence! Unfortunately, most employees don't really get the full picture regarding standards and procedures, so let's clarify that once and for all.

Taking the pot of tea example, a customer wants their tea to be hot, served in a clean pot, on a clean tray that is well presented and has all the necessary accompaniments, and so on. These are natural basic expectations. Standards and procedures are supposed to be about helping us to meet those expectations consistently.

❑ A *standard* is simply what we are trying to achieve; to meet the customer expectation.

❑ A *procedure* is what we must actually do in order to achieve that standard.

It's amazing how often this is not understood. Don't get me wrong, it's not because people are stupid, it's more a case that the concept is rarely explained in meaningful terms. Employees often believe that standards and procedures are something they are being forced to do, or what the boss wants, when in reality they are completely geared towards the customer.

So, in seeking to address this issue, you first need to consider how you can achieve greater clarity and understanding about standards and procedures in the hotel. A related problem here is the terminology used. Words like standards and procedures scream conformity and rigidity and they certainly don't instil any sense of excitement or interest. In fact, they are likely to have the opposite effect. As you review your approach to this area, why not consider doing away with this sort of terminology as a starting point to reinvigorating your approach? Of course, it requires more than a cosmetic change of wording and we will address the substance shortly.

Perhaps replacing the term *standard* with *service goals* might be helpful because everyone can grasp the concept of a goal and it has more positive connotations. Maybe you could also do away with the term *procedures* and simply call them *service steps*, in the sense that they are the steps to achieving the goals. We will use these terms from now on but they are obviously only suggestions and you get the point – call them what you want but don't underestimate the importance of phraseology in setting the right tone about this important area. You also need to recognise that there must be meat on the bones too, which will be our next concern.

160

In seeking to create service goals and steps you should realise that if you were to define goals and steps for every single thing you do in relation to service delivery across all aspects of the experience web, you will end up with literally hundreds of them. This will add no value to the business and you will end up with a paperwork mountain which only serves to drive you and your employees around the twist. A more effective approach is to identify key service goals and focus on those; when you achieve them consistently you can build from there.

Defining service goals

The first task is to define your service goals and these should be based on the customer expectations which you identify. This is easily done for common guest needs and simply means translating the expectations we highlighted earlier for all elements of the experience web into short, snappy goals which might read something like this:

Component of the Experience Web	Customer expectations	Our service goals
Website/online bookings	Your customers expect that your website will look professional, be easy to use and will provide them with the relevant information they need about your hotel.	*Our website will at all times offer an informative and user-friendly resource to customers, which creates a positive impression for the hotel.*
Telephone reservation	Your customers expect that when they call your hotel they will be dealt with in a friendly and positive manner and that their booking will be taken professionally and efficiently.	*We will handle all telephone enquiries and reservations in a professional, friendly and personal manner.*
Exterior	Your customers expect that your hotel will be easy to find and when they get there that the exterior of the hotel will create a positive first impression.	*The exterior and surroundings of our hotel will be well maintained to create a positive first impression and will be safe and secure for our customers at all times.*
Public areas	Your customers expect that the public areas of your hotel will offer a safe, comfortable and relaxing environment during their visit.	*The public areas of our hotel will be well maintained and presented at all times to offer a pleasant, comfortable and secure environment for our guests.*
Check-in	Your customers expect that their check-in will be handled efficiently, that they will feel welcomed to the hotel and valued as a customer.	*All our customers will receive a professional, efficient and friendly check-in which makes them feel welcome and valued by us.*
Concierge/porters	Your customers expect that porters will be polite, friendly and attentive to their needs.	*Our porters will interact professionally with our customers at all times and perform their duties to a high standard.*
Bedroom	Your customers expect that they will get a clean, warm and comfortable bedroom which will have all the amenities they need for a pleasant stay.	*Our bedrooms will always offer a pleasant and comfortable environment for all our customers during their stay.*

Bar/lounge	Your customers expect that the surroundings in the bar/lounge will be pleasant, the products offered will be good and that service will be personal and attentive.	*Our bar/lounge will offer a welcoming and pleasant environment for our customers and service will be attentive, friendly and efficient at all times.*
Restaurant	Your customers expect that the surroundings in the restaurant will be pleasant, the products offered will be good and that service will be personal and attentive.	*Our restaurant will offer a welcoming and pleasant environment for our customers and service will be attentive, friendly and efficient at all times.*
Room service	Your customers expect that when they order room service the order will arrive promptly and the quality and presentation of the food/beverages will be high.	*All room service calls will be handled professionally and efficiently and items served will be consistently of a high standard and delivered on time.*
Breakfast	Your customers expect that the surroundings in the breakfast room/restaurant will be pleasant, the products offered will be good and that service will be personal and attentive.	*Our breakfast room/restaurant will offer a welcoming and pleasant environment for customers and service will be attentive, friendly and efficient at all times with buffet presentation continuously of a high standard throughout service.*
Conference and events	Your customers expect that the facilities, products and service provided will contribute to the success of their conference or event	*Service and product quality in our conference and events area will always be of high quality to facilitate successful outcomes for our customers' events.*
Leisure	Your customers expect that your leisure facilities will offer a safe, hygienic and relaxing environment for them to enjoy their chosen leisure pursuit.	*Our leisure facilities will be maintained to a high standard at all times and the quality of service will ensure that all our customers enjoy their time spent in this area.*
Check-out	Your customers expect that their check-out will be handled efficiently and that they will feel valued as a customer.	*All our customers will receive a professional, efficient and friendly check-out, which demonstrates that we value their custom and ends their visit on a high note.*

Essentially what we have done here for each component of the experience web is to translate the overall guest expectation into a service goal. These service goals must then set the boundaries for what you are trying to achieve in terms of service delivery. They are:

❑ challenging because the aim is to achieve them *all the time*

❑ relevant because they are based *specifically* on what your customers generally expect

❑ easy to communicate to your employees because they *simplify* what it is you are trying to achieve for your customers.

Naturally, you may end up with different service goals and you may decide to have more or less of them, but the principles remain the same; they are of value because they make you truly customer focused.

Defining service steps

Like any goals, you will actually have to do something to achieve them and this is the hard part. For each goal you identify, you then need to consider how you will give guidance to your employees on how to consistently achieve that goal. Do you need a written and documented service step for every goal, or will you allow your employees to work on their own initiative?

In developing the service steps to guide employees on how to achieve the service goals, only use written formats when it is really essential. A good quality photo depicting the end result you want, supported by effective on-the-job training can be more beneficial than written materials. For example, a photo showing the correct tray set-up for room service orders when linked to high quality training would be more helpful than a written service step explaining how to do it. However, for some tasks, such as taking a reservation, you will probably need to write service steps as the visual approach won't work.

In developing service steps, use a simple template and keep them short and to the point. Here is a sample of how this might look for check-in (see page 164), showing the link from the *customer expectations* to the *service goal* to the *service steps*.

The left-hand column shows the customer expectations of check-in which we defined earlier. The right-hand column shows both the service goal and the steps required to achieve it; this column is all you need to provide to employees. You will note that the service steps are simply the ten things that customers expect translated into guidance steps for your employees. If all your employees were to consistently adhere to these ten steps then you would be meeting guest expectations on a consistent basis.

To support this check-in example, you might need to define what the correct 'check-in procedure' is but do you need to have another written set of instructions for this? Probably not, because by the time you are finished you will just end up with that mountain of paper you are trying to avoid. What you will need to do is to ensure that there is a defined procedure for check-in, communicate that through training and monitor performance through supervision and coaching.

Naturally, you need to develop service steps following these general principles for all the service goals you define, but this example will serve as an indicator as to how you might go about that task. The full list of customer expectations across the experience web provided in the Tools and Resources section will also be of help to you here.

Check-in

Expectation *Your customers expect that their check-in will be handled efficiently, that they will feel welcomed to the hotel and valued as a customer.*		Service goal *All our customers will receive a professional, efficient and friendly check-in which makes them feel welcome and valued by us.*
As part of this, customers expect that:		**Service steps**
1. the reception desk and lobby area will be clean, tidy and well presented.	→	1. Ensure that the reception desk and lobby area are kept clean and tidy at all times.
2. the appearance and hygiene of employees will be good and that they will be wearing name badges.	→	2. Ensure that your hygiene and appearance is excellent at all times and adheres to the hotel dress code. Always wear your name badge.
3. they will be promptly acknowledged upon arrival and a warm welcome will be given with appropriate eye contact and a smile.	→	3. Acknowledge our customers promptly upon arrival and always offer them a warm welcome and make good eye contact with them. Smile!
4. their booking will be in the system and the details will be correct as per the reservation made.	→	4. Ask the customer how you can assist them and check that their reservation details are in the system. Confirm the details of their stay back to the customer to ensure accuracy.
5. the check-in procedure will be handled efficiently and smoothly.	→	5. Complete check-in efficiently and smoothly at all times according to our agreed procedure.
6. a morning call and newspaper will be offered to them.	→	6. Check with the customer if they would like a morning call and a newspaper and ensure that their request is immediately entered onto the system.
7. the hotel facilities will be explained to them.	→	7. Explain the hotel facilities to the customer when offering the key card to them.
8. help will be offered with their luggage, or, if not provided as a service, then at least clear directions will be given to their room.	→	8. Offer the customer help with their luggage and contact the porters to assist them. Provide clear directions to the guest as to how to get to their room.
9. the employee will be smiling and courteous throughout the check-in process and will interact well with them and make them feel valued as a customer.	→	9. Ensure that you are positive and friendly towards the customer at all times throughout check-in and chat with the guest so that they feel that you really care about them.
10. the check-in will be ended in a friendly manner and that they will be wished a pleasant stay.	→	10. End every check-in by providing your name to the customer as a contact point during their stay and wish them a pleasant stay.

Application of service goals and steps

Whatever approach you adopt in relation to service goals and steps, it is how they are used on a daily basis in your hotel which ultimately matters; if they do not become the norm for employees then you have wasted your efforts. To achieve this requires the following.

❑ *Effective on-the-job training*   Unless all employees are trained on how to follow the service steps, you can never consistently meet customer expectations, or in other words, attain level S. For this, you need structured, ongoing and effective on-the-job training delivered by individuals who actually have the required skills to train to a high standard.

As part of this, make sure that the relevant service goals and steps are clearly visible for employees in every department. In addition, each week there should be an emphasis on a 'goal of the week', whereby particular attention is devoted to that one particular goal on a rolling basis. This helps to keep the goals fresh in everyone's minds. For new employees, specific training on the service goals and steps should naturally form part of their induction training plan.

❑ *Supervise delivery of service steps and goals*   There is no replacement for continuous supervision as a means of ensuring that service steps are followed for all areas of the experience web, so that the service goals are achieved. The old adage of 'management by walking around' applies nicely here. If underperformance in this regard is overlooked, then over time the service steps are seen as optional and eventually become irrelevant.

❑ *Measure how well you are doing*   An important feature in determining the effectiveness of service goals and steps will be to measure their delivery in a structured way. This will involve employees assessing their own performance but will also require external measurement. We will return to this in detail in the following chapter.

By applying this approach to the design and application of service goals and steps or whatever you decide to call them, you will find that the consistency, quality and efficiency of service delivery will improve over time and you will raise service performance from $S-1$ to S. This alone is a major achievement and from that you can focus on bringing your service to the level of $S+1$.

Raising your game to reach $S+1$

Once you attain consistency and quality in service delivery through the application of service goals and steps, you can then focus on adding little touches which will differentiate your service experience from that provided by other hotels. This is the essence of $S+1$; get the basics consistently right and then add value through the $+1$s.

As mentioned, these $+1$s may be relevant to physical, product, people or procedural elements within the customer experience. They can be designed to meet specific customer expectations identified from your interactions with your key customer groups. Most of the time though, the +1s are common sense and can be very simply applied, such as through the little things that your employees say or do to make your customers feel special.

On some occasions +1s might require a cost input. For example, in one hotel which I have stayed in frequently, retiring for the night meant getting out of bed to switch off various lamps, all with separate controls. Following consistent feedback from guests all the rooms were rewired over time so that all lights could be switched off from a single main switch beside the bed. Not a major +1, but it was commented on positively by customers.

Many hotels decide to formalise their +1s and actually build them into their service steps, so that they become standard practice. You might do this too for the +1s that you feel are non-negotiable, but a better approach is to encourage your employees to use their initiative in this area.

One way of achieving this is to provide general training to your employees on the concept of S+1 and then allow them in teams to identify potential +1s in their department. You will find they come up with lots of good examples, particularly if you have engaged employees. Once they have devised potential +1s, you can then decide if you are happy with them and make appropriate arrangements to facilitate their implementation.

When a 'menu' of potential +1s is agreed for each department, allow your employees to use them as and when they feel appropriate depending upon the customer involved. In esssence, this approach empowers your employees, gives them a greater sense of ownership for service delivery and indeed creates a challenge around the issue. This is a far more effective approach than trying to standardise everything.

Remember, you achieve standardisation (S) by ensuring that your employees aim for the service goals by following the service steps, but you allow employees to pick and choose from the menu of agreed +1s as and when they feel it will make the greatest difference to the customer. Your customers will feel and appreciate the spontaneity and you will exceed their expectations (S+1).

SUMMARY

In this chapter, we have identified practical steps you can take to achieve $S+1$ at your hotel. There is no pretence that the guidance here will solve all your problems related to service delivery and it is always easier to talk about it than to make it happen in practice.

However, the advantage of the approach outlined here is that it builds a simple and easy to apply framework around the only thing which really matters in hotels – customer expectations. It works because customers like consistency and they also feel more valued and special because of the application of the $+1$s into the overall service experience.

The focus in the following chapter will be, as it has been for every theme, to explore ways in which you can measure the effectiveness of your efforts to implement the principles and practices of $S+1$.

12

How can you measure the impact of *ServicePlusOne* over time?

A couple of months ago, whilst checking into a budget hotel in London, I was asked by the receptionist if I would be rushing away the following morning or whether I would have time to meet with the General Manager for breakfast. Having the time to spare I accepted the offer and at the appointed time the following morning was shown into a small conference room where the General Manager was entertaining a number of customers to breakfast.

During the thirty-minute encounter, the manager chatted informally with those present asking a series of questions relating to our perceptions of the service experience at the hotel, whilst a microphone placed in the centre of the table recorded our responses. Although an informal setting, it was clear that he was exploring particular aspects of service delivery and his questions spanned the 4 Ps. This was a fairly simple but effective way in which to get some invaluable qualitative feedback from customers and was apparently a weekly occurence at the hotel.

The Route to *ServicePlusOne*

Expectations → Experience → Evaluation

What are your customers' common and specific expectations?

Physical
How well does the quality of your physical facilities match expectations?
Product
Are the products you offer consistently of a high standard?
People
How well do your employees interact with your customers?
Procedures
How do you ensure consistency, quality and efficiency in service delivery?

How does the experience you offer rate against the quality continuum?

Are you exceeding your customers' expectations?

How do you know?

Measuring the impact of S + 1

To continuously enhance the service experience you offer at your hotel you will need to really listen to your customers; and not just listen, but to act on what you learn. As part of your efforts to apply the principles of S+1, you need a clear picture of what you do well at your hotel and more importantly from an improvement perspective, what you don't do so well.

Developing a comprehensive customer feedback system takes time and depending upon what you have in place already, you should start with a basic, user-friendly approach and build from there. Our continuous improvement model can again be helpful here as you seek to determine the effectiveness of your efforts in achieving S+1.

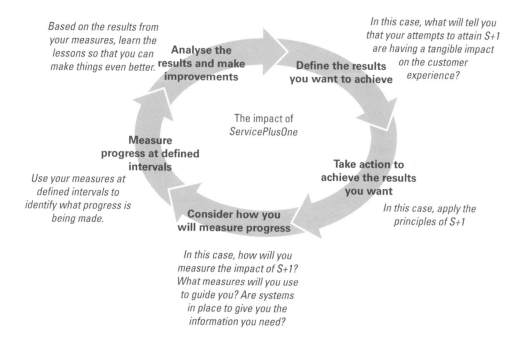

Measuring the impact of S+1 will require you to consider the issues in the following sections.

Define the results you want to achieve

The obvious result here is that you want your customers to be satisfied with the experience you offer. However, customer satisfaction is a very broad term so in seeking to measure this you will need to define it somewhat more specifically. You will want to know how the experience you offer rates against the quality continuum, and whether you are actually exceeding your customers' expectations? As you set out to achieve S+1, you are therefore seeking to address the two key issues we saw earlier.

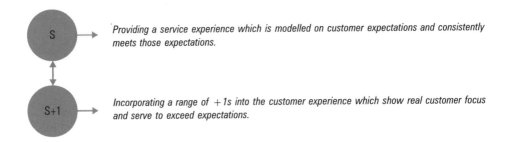

Consequently, you need to measure results in two areas.

1. *Are you consistently meeting customer expectations? In other words, have you achieved level S?*

   One result you want is to know whether you are meeting your customer expectations consistently. Are you achieving your service goals and are the service steps being followed by employees? Have you achieved level S in terms of the quality of the service experience?

   Attaining your service goals, based as they are on customer expectations, is a key driver of customer satisfaction and you will want evidence as to whether you actually achieve them consistently. Whatever your service goals are, your target will be to realise them 100 per cent of the time.

2. *Are you exceeding your customers' expectations? In other words, have you achieved level S + 1?*

   The second result you want here is to determine whether the overall service experience is exceeding customer expectations. In other words, have you achieved S + 1?

Using these two perspectives, you will have a clear indication that you are achieving your service goals (S) and whether you are exceeding customer expectations (S + 1). How you will answer these questions will have important implications for the types of measurements you will use, as we shall see in a moment.

Take action to achieve the results you want

It is clear that unless you apply the principles of S + 1 as highlighted, you will not see any resulting improvement in customer satisfaction levels. As you well know, changing customer perceptions takes time, so the sooner you begin to address the concepts covered the better.

Consider how you will measure progress

Given that you want to evaluate two areas, this will require two different but mutually supportive approaches to measurement.

1. HAVE YOU ACHIEVED LEVEL S?

To measure whether the experience you offer at the hotel does actually deliver on your service goals and adheres to the service steps, you need to assess the quality of service delivery across all elements of the experience web. This can be achieved in a number of ways.

Self-assessment

It is a very good idea to allow employees to assess their own performance in relation to the quality of service they offer. On a monthly basis, employees in each department should, as a team, assess their own performance in achieving their service goals and to determine whether or not they follow the service steps consistently. This could be done as part of the monthly meeting discussed previously. The benefit of this approach is that it involves employees in defining their own strengths and areas for improvement and increases their levels of ownership for what they do, or don't do.

It is not complicated to organise a basic self-assessment framework for each department and employees could rate their own performance using a simple template, an example of which is shown for check-in below.

Check-in

Rating	1	2	3	4	5
	We are very weak in this area	We are weak in this area	We are average at this area	We are strong in this area	We are very strong in this area
Service Goal – are we achieving it?					
All our customers receive a professional, efficient and friendly check-in which makes them feel welcome and valued by us					
Service Steps – do we follow them?					
1. We always ensure that the reception desk and lobby area are kept clean and tidy at all times.					
2. We always ensure that our hygiene and appearance is excellent at all times and adheres to the hotel dress code. We always wear our name badges.					
3. We always acknowledge our customers promptly upon arrival, offer them a warm welcome and make good eye contact with them. We always smile.					
4. We always ask the customer how we can assist them and check that their reservation details are in the system. We always confirm the details of their stay back to the customer to ensure accuracy.					
5. We always complete check-in efficiently and smoothly at all times according to our agreed procedure.					
6. We always check with the customer if they would like a morning call and a newspaper and we always ensure that their request is immediately entered onto the system.					
7. We always explain the hotel facilities to the customer when offering the key card to them.					
8. We always offer the customer help with their luggage and we always provide clear directions as to how to get to their room.					
9. We ensure that we are positive and friendly towards our customers at all times throughout check-in and we chat with them so that they feel we really care about them.					
10. We always end check-in by providing our name to the customer as a contact point during their stay and we always wish them a pleasant stay.					

You can see that this template simply coverts the *service goals* and *steps* for check-in into statements which can be self-assessed by the reception team. You can apply the same principles for all departments, so that you have a self-assessment checklist for each element of the experience web.

Using this approach, employees can define their own areas for improvement and given that they are involved in the process, they are more likely to make an effort to improve on any shortcomings they identify. This is a particularly effective approach where you have engaged employees and can also serve to build engagement as it involves employees in decision making related to their area. As such it should be encouraged at your hotel.

External assessment

Self-assessment is useful for the reasons described above, but the true test of whether you are achieving your service goals can only come from assessing quality from the customers' perspective. To achieve this, you should consider introducing some form of *mystery guest* mechanism to your hotel if you don't already have one in place.

Again, a simple checklist for use as part of the mystery guest process can be developed simply by rewording your service goals and steps into criteria which can be assessed by a mystery guest, as shown below for the check-in component of the experience web.

Check-in

Service Goal	Excellent 2 points	Average 1 point	Poor 0 Points	Comments
A professional, efficient and friendly check-in was provided which made me feel welcome and valued.				

Service Steps	Excellent 2 points	Average 1 point	Poor 0 Points	Comments
1. Reception desk and lobby area were clean, tidy and well presented.				
2. Appearance and hygiene of employees was good and they were wearing name badges.				
3. Prompt acknowledgement upon arrival was given and a warm welcome with appropriate eye contact and a smile was evident.				
4. Booking was in the system and the details were correct as per the reservation made.				
5. Check-in was handled efficiently and smoothly.				
6. Morning call and newspaper were offered.				
7. Hotel facilities were explained.				
8. Help was offered with luggage and clear directions provided on how to get to the room.				
9. Employee was smiling and courteous throughout the check-in process and did interact well making me feel valued.				
10. Check-in was ended in a friendly manner and I was wished a pleasant stay.				

A full mystery guest checklist for all elements of the experience web is provided in the Tools and Resources section at the end of this book.

Using the mystery guest approach can be very effective and when applied properly will help you to determine whether your service goals are being achieved and if the service steps you have agreed with your employees are actually being followed consistently. Using the above checklist, or similar, you can quite easily generate an overall result for the hotel as a whole based on the simple rating scale and break it down by each component of the experience web.

2. HAVE YOU ACHIEVED LEVEL S + 1?

The second area you must consider from a measurement perspective is how you will determine if you are exceeding your customers' expectations. To establish this, you will need to hear directly from your customers and the important consideration here will be the scope and breadth of your feedback mechanisms.

Many hotels over-rely on comment cards as their main source of customer feedback, but comment cards are limited for a number of reasons. First, customers tend to only complete them if they are either very happy or unhappy, so they often only give a picture of the extremes. Second, only a very small percentage of customers actually fill them out, and whilst you can increase the completion rate by prompting guests in subtle ways, they remain a useful but limited tool.

If you really want a comprehensive customer feedback system, then you need to align your approach against your customer base or segments. For example, if corporate clients form the largest proportion of your customer mix, you will naturally want to hear more from them. But you still need to hear back from all the segments as well. This will involve introducing a range of feedback mechanisms covering all customer types, which at the same time have commonality in design and content, so that you can amalgamate the results into an overall customer satisfaction percentage.

Therefore you will need to consider a range of tools to get feedback from your customers:

❏ Comment cards

❏ Customer surveys – online

❏ Focus groups

❏ Face-to-face or telephone interviews

For example, you might use the comment card approach for accommodation users, or in ground floor areas such as the bar and restaurant. You could use a follow-up online survey again for accommodation guests, or conference and event clients. Focus groups and interviews could be beneficial for key customers from whom you get a lot of business. Whatever mix of feedback tools you use, the critical point is that they give you the information you need and that you are targeting as high a percentage of customers in each segment as possible to enable you to define patterns in responses.

The design and structuring of questions is critical because you want to get as much information as you can, but at the same time keep it short enough to encourage response rates. You will also want to ensure that similar questions are asked in all the feedback mechanisms you use, so that you can actually compare and analyse the results.

One way of ensuring this consistency of approach is to ask questions in all survey methods based on criteria relating to the four Ps – Physical, Products, People and Procedures – as shown in the sample for check-in below:

Check-in

Component of experience web	Below expectations	Met expectations	Exceeded expectations	Comments
Quality of maintenance and appearance of reception.				
Appearance and attitude of employees.				
Efficiency and attentiveness of service during check-in.				
Overall sense of welcome to hotel.				

These criteria provide an example of the type of feedback you might seek from customers in relation to the check-in component of the experience web. A full set of suggested criteria for all areas is provided in the Tools and Resources section at the end of the book.

Using these criteria as a guide, you can devise comment cards, online surveys, telephone call-backs and even key customer questionnaires. As well as these feedback mechanisms, you can also use these questions during focus group sessions to give you more detailed qualitative information about how your customers view what you offer. Because you ask similar things in all surveys, you can compile an overall satisfaction rating for the hotel.

DO YOU HAVE THE NECESSARY SYSTEMS IN PLACE?

Whatever approaches you adopt for measuring customer feedback, you will naturally need to ensure that you have the necessary systems in place to support the implementation of your ideas and bridge any existing gaps.

Measure progress at defined intervals

The two forms of measurement, mystery guest visits and customer satisfaction surveys, have different objectives so the frequency of their use will naturally differ.

MYSTERY GUEST VISITS

You should seek to hold mystery guest visits as often as possible because a one-off or infrequent snapshot of the experience web is of little value. It is the overall pattern of consistency which emerges over time that is of interest to you and ideally you should look at conducting these visits monthly, or at a minimum quarterly.

In terms of organising the mystery guest visits there are many external companies which offer such a service and if you choose this route you need to ensure they actually measure what you want; you need to align their assessment template with your service goals and steps. Obviously, using external firms has a cost attached, but, like everything else, it is the value you get in return which is the issue here.

If in your situation, the cost of using an external agency is prohibitive, don't discount the idea completely – there may be alternative low-cost solutions. In some small hotels, the owner/manager often gets colleagues and friends to perform the mystery visit, but unless they have some experience and use an agreed measurement template this can have little value as the feedback is scattered and often overly subjective.

One hotel owner struggling with this issue approached a local university which ran a masters course in hotel management and agreed with the Dean that students on the programme would conduct mystery guest visits to the hotel. In return the hotel offered the University the use of a small meeting room for faculty meetings on a weekly basis. A little creativity goes a long way.

CUSTOMER SATISFACTION SURVEYS

Customer satisfaction surveys should be ongoing so that you have a continuous flow of feedback to work with. Customers should be encouraged to complete comments cards, so you will need employee support here. If you develop an online survey for accommodation users, this should be sent to each customer immediately after their visit, having attained their permission to do so first. Every conference or event should receive a follow-up call, or online survey shortly after their event.

You should set specific targets for the overall response rates you want for each survey tool you use and summary data should be compiled on a monthly basis, so that you can monitor trends over time.

Analyse the results and make improvements

The various quality assessment and feedback mechanisms are only of value if you do something with the information you receive, so you must take action to make improvements based on what you learn.

When a mystery guest report is provided to the hotel, it is critical that you analyse the shortcomings and define a plan of action to address the areas for improvement. The compiled monthly results from your various customer feedback tools should also be reviewed and problem areas highlighted with action taken to implement corrective measures where service delivery is shown to be below standard.

Where possible, it is also helpful to benchmark your results against other comparable hotels because this gives you a stronger indication as to how you are performing against your peers.

At all times you should involve employees as much as you can in determining how things can be improved based upon what your customers are telling you. The team-based approaches to problem solving or the suggestions scheme discussed under Theme 3 are ideal for facilitating this.

SUMMARY

The concept of being close to your customers is at the heart of the $S + 1$ philosophy; truly customer focused hotels excel at listening to and learning from their guests. If you genuinely believe that your customers are stakeholders in your hotel, then you will take a proactive approach in this area.

Measurement systems do not have to be complicated, nor should it be a drain on resources to implement the ideas discussed. What is required is a real commitment to put your customer at the centre of everything you do, followed by consistency in approach, application and follow up.

The quality of service provided in your hotel is the key to your success and the focus in these three chapters has been to give you some ideas as to how you can build on the positive things you do already in this area. You now have plenty of tools and resources to help you analyse what you currently do and implement improvements, so that you can truly say the service you offer is second to none.

Finally, take a key message with you from Theme 4: customers demand excellence in service today and simply being good is no longer good enough. You need to excel in service delivery to really captivate your customers.

MAKE IT HAPPEN

First steps towards excellence

MAKE IT
HAPPEN

Where to now?

Introduction

We have intentionally covered a lot of ground throughout this book and a holistic view has been taken of achieving excellence. We have explored important themes such as how to define the overall direction for your hotel, enhance leadership effectiveness, engage your employees and captivate your customers. Not all of the content will have been new to you, but hopefully you will have gained fresh insights into these critical issues.

The real work starts now, in the sense that, if you want to derive any benefits from the book, then you will need to take concerted action to apply the concepts at your hotel in future. Naturally, what you need or indeed decide to do will depend on where you are currently as a business, but you should be proactive in making changes based on your new insights. Obviously, you cannot expect to see results overnight, but unless you lay the groundwork now, you won't ever see any.

This final section is intended to support you as you define and implement measures in relation to the four themes. Each of the four themes is briefly summarised and then an action checklist is provided to guide you as to actions you might take in your hotel. A simple diagnostic is also included for each theme which will help you, at some point in the future, to gauge how well you are progressing.

MAKE IT HAPPEN

THEME 1 – DEFINE DIRECTION

Theme 1 emphasised that the achievement of excellence doesn't just magically happen and if you really want to run a great hotel, then you need a planned route to take you there. In other words, you need a strategic map. The purpose of the map is to help you to strengthen your stakeholder focus and develop a longer-term view with regard to the development of your hotel. It focused on the definition of goals across key business dimensions to guide all your efforts at achieving excellence in future.

Key messages from Theme 1

❑ Lack of direction for your hotel will lead to problems sooner or later because focusing only on the short term is essentially self-defeating.

❑ A strategic map provides the focus needed to not only excel but also to achieve lasting business success because it creates a framework for business development.

❑ Creating a strategic map for your hotel begins with a mindset. It involves having a stakeholder focus and placing your primary stakeholders at the forefront of decision making for your hotel.

❑ The key elements of your strategic map include:

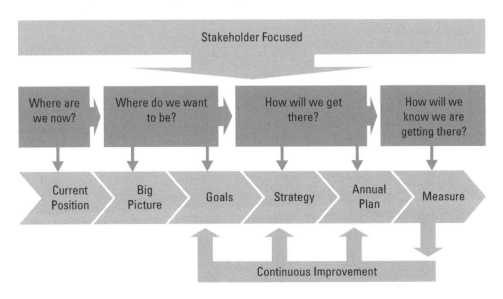

181

❑ Answering the question *where are we now?* means clearly understanding what strengths, weaknesses, opportunities and threats are currently facing your business.

❑ Defining *where do we want to be?* involves considering the big picture by preparing a vision and mission for your business and from that defining specific and measurable goals which are stakeholder focused.

❑ You answer the question *how will we get there?* by identifying overall strategies to realise your goals and from that preparing an annual plan to take you there.

❑ Finding answers to *how will we know we are getting there?* involves measuring progress against your goals, learning the lessons from the results you get and taking action to continuously improve.

Success in business life comes from being outcome-focused and in such a volatile environment as the hotel industry, the need for direction is even greater. Achieving excellence is not a game of chance.

Moving forward with Theme 1 – Action Checklist

To help you apply the concepts covered in Theme 1, the following checklist will be useful in focusing your thoughts.

THEME 1 – ACTION CHECKLIST	✓
Reflect on how a strategic map might be useful in the context of your hotel.	☐
Think about what elements of the strategic map you might already have in place and where the gaps lie.	☐
Identify the primary and secondary stakeholders for your hotel.	☐
Define the specific needs of your Primary Stakeholders. *Consult with them as part of that process.*	☐
Reflect on how well you currently meet those needs and what you don't do so well.	☐
Answer the question *where are we now?* in relation to your hotel and ensure that you have the appropriate data to answer the related sub-questions. Prepare a SWOT analysis for your hotel based on facts, not opinions.	☐
Define *where do we want to be?* by preparing or revising your vision and mission statements to reflect what achieving excellence will mean in your hotel.	☐
Finalise your vision and mission and communicate them widely and frequently to your key stakeholders.	☐
Consider how you will keep your vision and mission alive and meaningful within the hotel.	☐
Convert your vision and mission into specific *goals* and ensure that they are SMART and stakeholder focused.	☐
Consider *how will we get there?* and define the strategies you will need to follow to achieve these goals.	☐
Review the current approach to annual planning at your hotel. Ensure that it enables you to identify actions related to implementing your strategies.	☐

Prepare an annual plan which defines the actions to be implemented in the coming year to progress towards your goals.	☐
Consider *how will we know we are getting there*? Review how you currently measure performance at your hotel. Identify the gaps in your current approach.	☐
Define the measures you require to track progress towards your goals and ensure that your measures relate to all your stakeholders.	☐
Consider whether your existing information systems are sufficient to give you the information you need to produce these measures.	☐
Implement the necessary systems and procedures to provide you with the data you need.	☐
Reflect on how you currently manage continuous improvement and think about how you might enhance this in future.	☐
Define an effective process for managing continuous improvement which meets your specific needs.	☐

Defining direction for your hotel should be your primary concern as everything else must stem from that. Start the process soon!

Reviewing progress under Theme 1 – Diagnostic

To help you to gauge how effective you have been in applying the principles and practices of Theme 1 in the future, the following diagnostic might be helpful.

THEME 1 – DIAGNOSTIC

Objective					
There is a clear direction for your hotel with measurable goals and related strategies and action plans.					

What you should be doing in your hotel to achieve this:
1. Become stakeholder focused.
2. Create a strategic map for your hotel.
3. Define measures to monitor progress.
4. Review actual results against your goals.
5. Make continuous improvement a feature within your hotel.

Rating	*We are very weak in this area*	*We are weak in this area*	*We are average at this area*	*We are strong in this area*	*We are very strong in this area*
1. Become stakeholder focused					
The Primary stakeholders in our hotel have been defined and their needs identified					
Structured channel(s) are in place which facilitate stakeholder involvement in the running of our hotel					
Information gained from these channels is used to guide the development of our strategic map					
2. Create a strategic map for your hotel					
The vision for our hotel has been developed and communicated					
Our mission is clearly defined and communicated and relates to all our primary stakeholders					
Our vision and mission have been translated into SMART goals which guide decision making					
Broad strategies have been agreed to help us achieve our goals					
An annual plan is prepared according to an agreed timeline which defines specific actions to implement our strategies					
3. Define measures to monitor progress					
The measures we need to help us track progress against each of our goals have been defined					
The necessary systems are in place to generate the information we need for these measures					

4. Review actual results against your goals					
Actual performance against our goals is reviewed at defined intervals					
Our performance is also benchmarked against industry norms					
5. Make continuous improvement a feature within your hotel					
The results of our analysis of actual performance against our goals is used to define improvement areas with input from stakeholders					
Defined improvements are agreed and implemented on a regular basis					

Completing this diagnostic in say six months will help you to identify what progress you have made in applying the principles covered in Theme 1.

MAKE IT HAPPEN | **THEME 2 – LEAD TO SUCCEED**

Theme 2 concentrated on leadership and specifically how you can make it more effective at your hotel. It focused on defining a leadership competence model which describes what you expect from your leaders and explored how you, and all leaders at the hotel, can enhance your leadership capabilities.

Key messages from Theme 2

❑ You cannot manage people towards excellence, you can only ever hope to lead them there.

❑ You shouldn't ignore the human equation in our industry. It is only through the *commitment*, *competence* and *motivation* of your employees that you achieve greater *productivity*, *efficiency* and *quality* – all of which contribute to the achievement of *excellence*, *customer satisfaction* and in turn to the overall *profitability* of your hotel.

❑ Leading and managing is not the same thing. A leader thinks and therefore acts differently from a manager, although they carry out the same functions and want the same results.

❑ Whereas management, particularly old-style approaches, seeks to push employees towards goals, leadership is about trying to attract them there by first attracting them to you in the way you think and act as a leader.

❑ Leadership means genuinely seeing your employees as stakeholders in your hotel and acting in a way that reflects your belief.

❑ Effective leaders recognise that they need certain personal qualities to succeed. A first practical step in seeking to improve your ability to lead is to increase your self-awareness in relation to the leadership profile.

❑ Leaders need certain attributes to succeed: *driving*, *directing* and *drawing* qualities. Effective leaders need strengths across a range of them.

❑ Leading in practice every day is essentially about managing relationships and every skill you have helps in some way. The ability to communicate and to apply different leadership styles are core competences.

❑ Developing your ability to communicate is such an important area in business, and in life generally, that not improving isn't an option. You certainly cannot be a good leader without mastering the art of communication.

❑ Leadership styles are a balance between the amount of direction and control you exercise over employees versus the involvement and autonomy you allow them.

❑ Measuring leadership effectiveness requires you to define a competence model to describe what you expect from leaders. It then involves using tools such as self-assessment, appraisals and employee feedback to help you determine if leadership effectiveness is improving over time. From that you should learn the lessons from the results you get and take action to continuously improve.

Moving forward with Theme 2 – Action Checklist

To help you to apply the concepts covered in Theme 2, the following checklist will be useful in focusing your thoughts.

THEME 2 – ACTION CHECKLIST	✓
Ensure that your vision and mission broadly describe what you are trying to achieve as leaders.	☐
Ensure that you have specific business goals to aim for in relation to leadership.	☐
Reflect on what leadership means to you and consider whether you buy into the idea of the *need to lead*.	☐
Consider the three dimensions of work and which of these you focus on most on every day.	☐
Think about the differences between leading and managing and where you think you fit currently.	☐
Talk to the other leaders in the hotel whom you depend upon to ensure that they too understand the need to lead.	☐
Define a leadership competence model to reflect your expectations of leaders at the hotel. Use this model to guide all your efforts in enhancing leadership effectiveness.	☐
Consider your own personal qualities and whether you have what it takes to make an effective leader. Identify your areas for improvement.	☐
Consider your current skills as a communicator and identify how you can improve in this area.	☐
Reflect on the leadership styles you adopt and consider whether you are flexible in your approach. Think what you can do to improve.	☐
Think about the other leaders in your hotel and consider their capabilities in relation to their personal qualities, communication skills and leadership styles.	☐
Devise a plan to improve the quality of leadership at the hotel. Include both personal actions and proposals related to improving the performance of other leaders at the hotel.	☐

Review how you currently measure leadership effectiveness at the hotel. Identify the gaps in your current approach.	☐
Think about whether your existing systems are sufficient to give you the information you need to measure leadership effectiveness to the level required. Develop the necessary systems to provide the data you need.	☐

Leadership effectiveness is such an important area that you should give it plenty of attention. Having direction is one thing but unless you can lead people there, it will have no value. Changing your own approach to leadership and that of others is not going to be easy, but with desire and determination it can be done. You should also think heavily about how you recruit leaders in future so that you are bringing people into the hotel that have the right mindset and competences.

Reviewing progress under Theme 2 – Diagnostic

To help you to gauge how effective you have been in applying the principles and practices of Theme 2 in the future, the following diagnostic might be helpful.

THEME 2 – DIAGNOSTIC

Objective					
A commitment to leadership effectiveness is evident at the hotel.					

What you should be doing in your hotel to achieve this:
1. Develop a leadership competence model.
2. Consider the leadership profile.
3. Develop leadership competences.
4. Apply effective leadership styles.
5. Measure leadership effectiveness.

Rating	*We are very weak in this area*	*We are weak in this area*	*We are average at this area*	*We are strong in this area*	*We are very strong in this area*
1. Develop a leadership competence model					
Leadership is a concept we believe in and this influences how we interact with our employees					
A leadership competence model has been developed at the hotel					
2. Consider the leadership profile					
All leaders at the hotel have identified their areas for improvement against the leadership profile					
Practical steps have been defined to help us, individually and collectively, to improve in this area					
3. Develop leadership competences					
All leaders at the hotel have identified their strengths and areas for improvement against the competence model					
Specific training has been given to all leaders on how they can improve their skills					
Additional practical steps such as coaching and mentoring have been defined to help us improve in this area					
4. Apply effective leadership styles					
The acceptable styles of leadership at the hotel have been agreed between all leaders					
Specific training has been given to all leaders on how they can apply leadership skills more effectively					
Additional practical steps have been defined to help us improve in this area					
5. Measure leadership effectiveness					
Criteria and systems have been agreed to measure leadership effectiveness based on our competence model					
Feedback gained from the feedback mechanisms is discussed and potential areas for improvement identified					
Additional practical steps have been defined to help us improve in this area					

Completing this diagnostic in say six months will help you to identify what progress you have made in applying the principles covered in Theme 2.

MAKE IT HAPPEN

THEME 3 – ENGAGE YOUR EMPLOYEES

Theme 3 addressed the issue of employee engagement and was based on the premise that you cannot achieve your goals or deliver excellence without having truly engaged employees. Employee engagement is primarily concerned with raising performance to maximise the *contribution* that employees make to your hotel.

Key messages from Theme 3

❑ *Twelve factors* have been proven to drive employee engagement.

❑ *Effective leadership* is central to increasing employee engagement and there is a direct correlation between leadership effectiveness and engagement levels.

❑ You cannot improve employee engagement without the right *culture* and certain cultures enhance engagement, whereas other destroy it.

❑ The *composition* of any team impacts heavily on individual engagement and you can have a direct impact in this area through your recruitment processes.

❑ Lack of *clarity* and direction causes frustration and will lead to disengagement and, in particular, your approach to induction is vital here.

❑ *Competence* matters because when some employees are not fully competent, others have to compensate for those weaknesses which will affect engagement. Most employees want to learn and grow in their jobs.

❑ The levels of *cooperation* in your business are both a driver of employee engagement and a reflection of it.

❑ *Control* is important when it comes to employee engagement. You must control behaviour and performance to ensure that all employees work to the required standard but you also need to release control and empower employees where possible.

❑ *Communication* is a key driver of employee engagement. You must consider the styles, channels, frequency and effectiveness of communication at your hotel.

❑ An important factor in determining levels of engagement is how *challenging* employees believe their work to be. The more challenged they are the more likely they are to engage.

❑ *Conflict* is a feature of all organisations and when it is mismanaged, it will have a detrimental impact on employee engagement.

❑ *Compensation* relates to broad issues such as how your employees are rewarded for performance beyond the norm.

❑ Too much *change* can be frustrating for many people, particularly if it isn't leading to improvements, but too little can lead to stagnation. Change and innovation processes, when well managed, can contribute to improved engagement.

Moving forward with Theme 3 – Action Checklist

To help you apply the concepts covered in Theme 3, the following checklist will be useful in focusing your thoughts.

THEME 3 – ACTION CHECKLIST	✓
Ensure that your vision and mission broadly describe what you are trying to achieve for your employees.	☐
Ensure that you have specific business goals to aim for in relation to your employees.	☐
Consider how engaged your employees currently are. Use the twelve factors to assess the current situation in your hotel.	☐
Ensure that you address the *leadership* issue as it will help to improve engagement levels.	☐
Think about the current *culture* at your hotel and identify areas for improvement.	☐
Review the *composition* of your employees. Does the mix work? Define steps to improve your recruitment and selection process.	☐
Consider whether there is *clarity* amongst your employees regarding what you are trying to achieve but also what you expect from them. In particular, improve your induction of new employees.	☐
Think about whether your employees are *competent* to the level you need them to be. Are some people carrying others? Is there real potential for people to develop? Enhance your approach to training and development to bridge the gaps you identify.	☐
Take proactive steps to improve *cooperation* levels amongst your employees. In particular, use team-based approaches to problem solving.	☐
Ensure that the *control* of employee behaviour and performance is effective at the hotel. Consider how you might increase empowerment for your employees.	☐

Review the current effectiveness of *communication* at the hotel. Think about individual styles, the channels you use and the frequency of communication with employees. Take proactive steps to address any problems you identify.	☐
Identify ways in which you can increase the *challenge* of work for your employees.	☐
Explore how *conflict* is managed at all levels in the hotel. Are there simmering conflicts which are creating a bad atmosphere? Think about how you might deal with such issues.	☐
Consider the *compensation* issue. Define ways in which you can better compensate people for above the norm performance.	☐
Think about how *change* is currently managed at the hotel. Is it an inclusive process or forced from the top down? Identify ways in which you can manage change more effectively in future.	☐
Consider how you will measure employee engagement and put systems in place to facilitate that.	☐

Employee engagement is a significant challenge. Tackling the issue requires you to adopt a holistic approach to the 12 factors and to proactively implement measures which will lead to improvements in the overall environment at work.

Reviewing progress under Theme 3 – Diagnostic

To help you to gauge how effective you have been in applying the principles and practices of Theme 3 in the future, the following diagnostic might be helpful.

THEME 3 – DIAGNOSTIC

Objective					
Employee engagement is strong at the hotel.					

What you should be doing in your hotel to achieve this:
1. Focus on employee engagement.
2. Review your current approach to employee engagement.
3. Provide training for leaders related to employee engagement.
4. Develop and implement a strategy to enhance engagement.
5. Measure employee engagement.

Rating	We are very weak in this area	We are weak in this area	We are average at this area	We are strong in this area	We are very strong in this area
1. Focus on employee engagement					
Employees are genuinely viewed as stakeholders in our hotel					
Engaging our employees is a concept we believe in and this influences how we interact with them					
2. Review your current approach to employee engagement					
A review of our current approach to employee engagement against the 12 factors has been conducted					
Areas for improvement in relation to employee engagement have been defined					
3. Provide training for leaders related to employee engagement					
All leaders at the hotel have received training in relation to improving employee engagement					
The ability of each leader at the hotel to engage their employees is reviewed during their annual appraisal					
4. Develop and implement a strategy to enhance engagement					
An overall strategy for enhancing employee engagement has been developed and linked to our mission and related goals					
Key actions to address the areas for improvement in employee engagement have been agreed and a plan formulated					
Key actions for addressing these areas for improvement have been included as part of the annual plan for the hotel					

5. Measure employee engagement				
An approach to measuring employee engagement has been developed at the hotel				
Information gained from the feedback mechanisms is discussed and potential areas for improvement identified				
Practical steps have been defined based on this feedback				

Completing this diagnostic in say six months will help you to identify what progress you have made in applying the principles covered in Theme 3.

MAKE IT HAPPEN

THEME 4 – CAPTIVATE YOUR CUSTOMERS

Theme 4 focused on the heart of hospitality and explored issues surrounding the achievement of excellence in service delivery. It avoided overly complicated approaches to managing service quality in favour of practical, easy to implement solutions based on the concept of S+1, whereby you seek not only to meet customer expectations but to exceed them.

Key messages from Theme 4

❏ Achieving S+1 requires the right culture to facilitate it, collective determination to realise it, strong leadership to drive it and engaged employees to deliver it every day.

❏ S+1 means striving for excellence across the customer experience, using the *expectations–experience–evaluation* model to guide you.

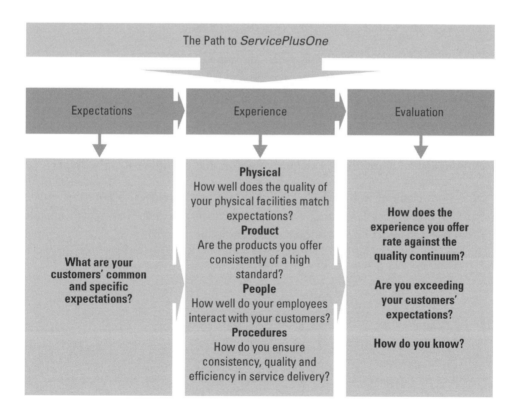

The Path to *ServicePlusOne*

Expectations	Experience	Evaluation
What are your customers' common and specific expectations?	**Physical** How well does the quality of your physical facilities match expectations? **Product** Are the products you offer consistently of a high standard? **People** How well do your employees interact with your customers? **Procedures** How do you ensure consistency, quality and efficiency in service delivery?	**How does the experience you offer rate against the quality continuum?** **Are you exceeding your customers' expectations?** **How do you know?**

❑ The experience, in a hotel context, is a combination of the four Ps: physical, products, your people and procedures.

❑ S+1 can be viewed as the pinnacle of a quality continuum, based on your ability to respond to customer expectations. Service can either fall below, meet or exceed expectations. Naturally, your goal should be to exceed them.

❑ S+1 is about getting the basics consistently right first and then enhancing the service experience by adding +1s, which show a greater focus on the customer and a genuine interest in their custom.

❑ Achieving S+1 starts when you develop your vision and mission and when you translate those sentiments into concrete goals relating to your customers. The implementation of the principles and practices of S+1 should be seen as your strategy for achieving your goals in relation to your customers.

❑ The practical steps in progressing towards S+1 should begin with a thorough understanding of your customers' common and specific expectations.

❑ Enhancing the customer experience means answering key questions in relation to the four Ps within the experience web.

❑ You must define *service goals* which are aimed at meeting guest expectations and develop *service steps* which provide guidelines to employees on how to achieve those goals. Training and buy-in from employees are key factors in making this approach work.

❑ The final piece of the puzzle are the +1s which you can agree with your employees and allow them a degree of autonomy on how to apply them.

❑ A core element in making S+1 a reality is getting closer to your customers by defining and implementing a range of feedback mechanisms, which include mystery guest visits and customer satisfaction surveys.

Moving forward with Theme 4 – Action Checklist

To help you to apply the concepts covered in Theme 4, the following checklist may be useful in focusing your thoughts:

THEME 4 – ACTION CHECKLIST	✓
Ensure that your vision and mission broadly describe what you are trying to achieve for your customers.	☐
Ensure that you have specific business goals to aim for in relation to your customers.	☐
Identify your current strengths and areas for improvement in relation to the quality of service delivery at your hotel. Talk to key customers to get a clearer picture. Where would you place your hotel on the quality continuum in relation to $S+1$?	☐
Reflect on how well you presently understand your customers' common and specific expectations for the key elements of the experience web.	☐
Review how well the quality of your physical facilities currently matches your customers' expectations.	☐
Consider whether the products you offer at present are consistently of a high standard and take steps to address problems identified.	☐
Think about how well your employees currently interact with your customers. Do they make a real difference to the customer experience?	☐
Reflect on how you currently ensure consistency, quality and efficiency in service delivery.	☐
Identify clear service goals which are based on your customers' expectations to guide your efforts at attaining $S+1$.	☐
Define service steps for each of these goals and communicate them to employees through training and coaching.	☐
Involve your staff in agreeing a 'menu' of potential $+1$s for each area of the experience web and provide them with general guidance as to how and when they might apply them.	☐

Review your current approach to obtaining customer feedback. Is it effective in the sense that it provides you with the information you need across all your customer segments?	☐
Define a mechanism to give you an insight into the quality of service delivery using a mystery guest approach.	☐
Identify the customer feedback mechanisms appropriate for your hotel and take the necessary action to implement them.	☐

Captivating customers is a priority for all hotels, so making your operation stand out from the crowd in terms of service delivery is an uphill struggle. There are no easy answers, however the principles of S+1 simplify what is required, yet are robust enought to make a real and lasting difference to the customer experience.

Reviewing progress under Theme 4 – Diagnostic

To help you to gauge how effective you have been in applying the principles and practices of Theme 4 in the future, the following diagnostic might be helpful.

THEME 4 – DIAGNOSTIC

Objective *Customers are at the heart of everything you do.*					
What you should be doing in your hotel to achieve this: 1. Focus on your customers. 2. Review your current approach to managing customer service. 3. Define your customers' expectations. 4. Develop and implement a strategy to achieve S + 1. 5. Measure customer satisfaction.					
Rating	*We are very weak in this area*	*We are weak in this area*	*We are average at this area*	*We are strong in nthis area*	*We are very strong in this area*
1. Focus on your customers					
Customers are genuinely viewed as stakeholders in our hotel					
Defined mechanisms are in place which enable us to listen to and learn from our customers					
2. Review your current approach to managing customer service					
A review of our current approach to managing customer service has been conducted					
Immediate areas for improvement in relation to customer service have defined					
3. Define your customers' expectations					
Generic and specific customer expectations for all elements within the experience web have been defined					
Defined *service goals and steps* have been agreed at the hotel which are geared to meeting these customer expectations					
4. Develop and implement a strategy to achieve S + 1					
An overall strategy for achieving S + 1 has been developed and linked to our mission and related goals					
Areas for improvement in relation to each of the 4Ps have been integrated into the strategy					
Key actions for addressing these areas for improvement have been included as part of the annual plan for the hotel					

5. Measure customer satisfaction					
Systems have been defined to measure customer satisfaction at the hotel					
Feedback gained from these measurements is discussed and corrective actions identified					
Practical steps have been defined based on this feedback to help us improve the service experience we offer					

Completing this diagnostic in say six months will help you to identify what progress you have made in applying the principles covered in Theme 4.

THE FUTURE

LOOKING AHEAD

By now it should be clear to you that strategic focus and clear direction are essential components in achieving excellence. So too are strong leadership, engaged employees and captivated customers. Without an integrated and consistent approach to implementing the necessary measures within our four themes, you cannot run a great hotel.

The support offered here is intended to smooth your journey to excellence. The information has been presented in a manner which strips away the jargon and unnecessary complexity often associated with the four themes, so that you can apply the concepts for the benefit of your operation. Naturally, you can't address all the issues raised in the short term, but you should chip away at them on a regular basis, using this book as an important reference point to guide your efforts. And you need to stick with it if you want to make a lasting impact on your own performance and that of your hotel.

Finally, if you take anything from this book it should be that there are few rewards for finishing second. Acclaim rightly goes to the winner and the runner up is quickly forgotten, even more so the also-rans. In any walk of life, achievement and excellence get all the attention and it's no different in the hotel industry. If you really want your hotel to stand out in a crowded marketplace today, just competing isn't enough; you need to win. To do that, you must excel.

TOOLS AND RESOURCES

TOOLS AND RESOURCES

Tools and resources

A number of tools and resources are provided here which will help you to apply some of the key concepts covered under the four themes. Electronic versions of these documents are available by contacting the author at info@htc-consult.com

Theme 1 – Planning Template

This template may be helpful when preparing your strategic map.

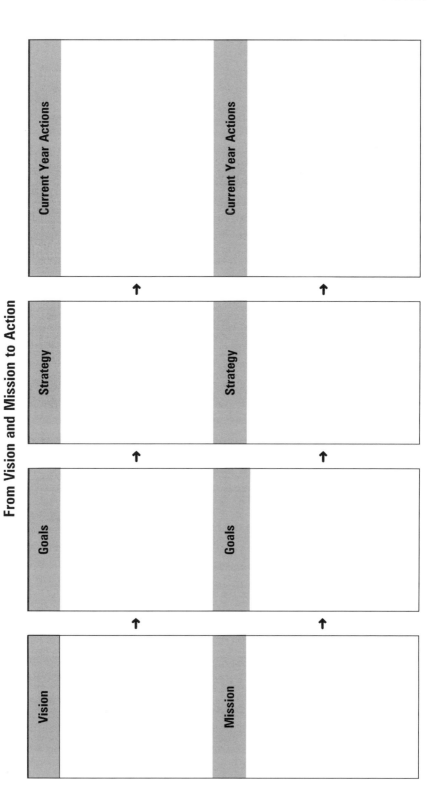

From Vision and Mission to Action

Theme 2 – Leadership Profile Self-Assessment

Statements	Exactly like me	Very like me	Somewhat like me	A little like me	Not like me at all
	5	**4**	**3**	**2**	**1**
1. I genuinely believe that our employees are stakeholders in the hotel					
2. I understand the hotel's vision and mission and regularly communicate this to my team					
3. I am strongly committed to the hotel and to my team					
4. I am highly self-motivated and can raise my performance, even when I don't necessarily feel like doing so					
5. I am passionate about achieving excellence at the hotel					
6. I have high levels of energy and enthusiasm					
7. I am genuinely concerned about the welfare of my team					
8. I take proactive measures to create a positive working environment for my team					
9. I make a conscious effort to be open and honest with my team					
10. I work hard at seeing things from other peoples' perspectives					
11. I always try to be objective when dealing with my team members					
12. I have excellent levels of self-control and can prevent individuals, or situations from making me act in a way which I later regret					
13. I am competent at what I do and I have a strong understanding of both the hotel industry in general and hotel operations in particular					
14. I am good at analysing problems and finding creative ways of improving how we do things at the hotel					
15. I am consistent in my behaviour and approach and I do not change what I think, or want from one day to the next					
16. I am approachable and willing to listen to my team members' concerns					
17. I don't let things at work get me down and I always try to see the bright side of things					
18. I can build trust between myself and other people					
19. I notice when members of my team are having problems and I make a point of helping them					
20. I work hard to meet my commitments to my team mates and colleagues					
Column score					
Overall total					

Scoring: 76–100: You seem to have the right qualities to support you as a leader. 51–75: There is a good foundation there. 26–50: You have a lot of work to do to develop your leadership qualities. 0–25: Did you score it correctly? On a separate sheet of paper, summarise your strengths and areas for improvement with regard to the leadership profile. Look particularly at your lower scoring answers and this will give you some indication as to the personal qualities and behaviours which you need to particularly focus on to improve.

Theme 2 – Communication Skills Self-Assessment

Statements	Exactly like me / 5	Very like me / 4	Somewhat like me / 3	A little like me / 2	Not like me at all / 1
Please tick the box under the score which you feel best describes you.					
1. I am open minded and am willing to change my viewpoint based on the valid opinion of others					
2. I prepare for all communications and think things through before I speak					
3. I always tailor my message to suit the person(s) I am talking to					
4. I find it easy to listen to what other people have to say without interrupting					
5. I am good at making eye contact with people when I am talking to them					
6. I am not intimidated by situations where I must communicate with difficult employees					
7. I am confident when I talk to people and speak clearly without mumbling					
8. I am good at getting my point across in a clear, concise manner without waffling					
9. I find it easy to concentrate on what others are saying and don't lose my focus					
10. I don't start planning my response whilst the other person is talking					
11. I don't think that my opinion is the most important in the room					
12. I only speak up if I have something valuable to contribute to the conversation and I avoid talking just for the sake of it					
13. I make a conscious effort to match my body language to the message I want to convey					
14. I am good at reading the body language of others					
15. I can keep my cool when talking to other people even if I feel angry about what they say					
16. When other people in the group are quiet, I encourage them to contribute					
17. I don't shout and point at people when we have a heated conversation					
18. When group discussions get heated, I am good at keeping everyone calm and on the point					
19. I feel comfortable holding meetings					
20. I am good at summarising the key points of conversations which I have with people					
Column score					
Overall total					

Scoring: 76–100 : You seem to have good communication skills. 51–75: There is a good foundation there. 26–50: You have a lot of work to do to develop your communication skills. 0–25: Did you score it correctly?

On a separate sheet of paper, summarise your strengths and areas for improvement with regard to your ability to communicate. Look particularly at your lower scoring answers and this will give you some indication as to what aspects of communication you need to focus on.

Theme 2 – Leadership Style Self-Assessment

Statements	Please tick the box under the score which you feel best describes you.				
	Exactly like me	Very like me	Somewhat like me	A little like me	Not like me at all
	5	**4**	**3**	**2**	**1**
1. I believe that my real authority as a leader comes not from my title or position, but from how I behave and interact with my team					
2. I regularly think about how I lead others and I am constantly trying to improve my performance					
3. I always lead by example					
4. I treat all my team members equally and fairly					
5. I am not aggressive in my leadership style					
6. My team members would not consider me to be a bully					
7. I have the ability to be flexible in how I apply my leadership style in practice					
8. I can actively apply different styles to match the requirements of each given situation					
9. When an individual is not performing to standard, I can deal with it in an effective manner					
10. I do not lose my temper with difficult team members					
11. I have consistently shown an ability to bring people back on track when they underperform					
12. I encourage my team members to be more involved in decision making					
13. I allow my team members a degree of autonomy when appropriate					
14. I regularly acknowledge the efforts of my team members					
15. I give my team members praise when it is justified					
16. I ensure that high performing team members have the ability to develop their skills even further					
17. I delegate to these high performing team members					
18. I believe that I am a positive role model for my team					
19. I make a conscious effort to build team spirit					
20. I do not let conflict fester in the team but proactively address it					
Column score					
Overall total					

Scoring: 76–100: You seem to have a good approach to leadership. 51–75: There is a good foundation there. 26–50: You have a lot of work to do to develop your leadership potential. 0–25: Did you score it correctly?

On a separate sheet of paper, summarise your strengths and areas for improvement with regard to leadership. Look particularly at your lower scoring answers and this will give you some indication as to the areas you need to focus on.

Theme 3 – Suggested Interview Plan

WELCOME

During this initial phase of the interview you should do the following.

❑ Establish rapport – break the ice. A relaxed candidate will perform better.

❑ Explain the purpose of the interview/outline the format for the interview with approximate timings.

❑ Inform the candidate that you will be taking notes.

ACQUIRE INFORMATION

This phase should form the bulk of the interview from a time perspective. During this stage you are seeking to get as many relevant details from the candidate as possible, so that you can make an informed decision about their suitability against the profile.

❑ Begin with the general questions moving to the more specific.

❑ Use effective question technique to explore background, attitudes, suitability etc., relevant to the employee profile. Focus most on the attributes.

❑ Probe the candidate to explore any information 'gaps', but not to the extent that you end up interrogating them.

❑ Let the candidate speak, use your listening skills! Apply the 80/20 rule; they talk for 80 per cent of the time, not you.

Remember, just as you assess the candidate they are also assessing and making some judgements about you and the hotel.

SUPPLY INFORMATION

Once you have obtained all the relevant information you need, then you should allow the candidate to ask you questions about the position. You should ensure that you do the following.

❑ Provide an overview of the hotel, what you are trying to achieve etc.

❑ Outline their job description in greater detail, giving details of their potential role in the company.

❏ Provide the candidate with details on the salary and conditions associated with the position.

❏ Answer any remaining interviewee questions.

PLAN AND PART

The final part of the plan is designed to ensure that both parties leave the interview fully aware of the next steps in the selection process. During this phase you should do the following.

❏ Ask to check references.

❏ Discuss salary if not mentioned already.

❏ Give a timetable for the decision and how they will be notified.

❏ Thank them.

In some cases you may wish to provide the candidate with a tour of your facilities. This can be done at this stage; if you are incorporating this into the interview, then you should inform them of this at the outset.

Remember, you can learn as much about a candidate as you walk them to and from an interview as you can during it because they are more relaxed and less rehearsed.

Theme 3 – Sample Interview Evaluation Form

	Area	Poor 1	2	Average 3	4	Excellent 5	Comments	Totals
The What	Education/qualifications/training							
	Work experience							
The How	Skills and knowledge							
	Communication skills							
The Who	Personality/disposition							
	Personal attributes							
							Total score	

Overall Summary/Comments

Decision Appoint/Call for 2nd Interview   Y/N

Theme 3 – Suggested Format for an Appraisal Discussion

INTRODUCTION

❑ Welcome

❑ Break the ice

❑ Explain purpose, format, time, their/your role

❑ Tell them that you will be taking notes

❑ Emphasise objective of appraisal.

REVIEW PERFORMANCE

❑ Encourage employee to review their overall performance since last appraisal

❑ Use question technique and listening skills to get them to open up

❑ Praise performance where appropriate

❑ Review specific performance under each appraisal heading

❑ Seek the employee's opinion first

❑ Discuss strengths/areas for improvement

❑ Give feedback on performance

❑ Agree rating.

Appraisals should not be a matter of simply agreeing a rating against each heading. The discussion around their performance in that area is the most important thing, with praise offered where the employee is strong and areas for improvement identified. The rating given should be an agreement following the evaluation of performance. It should *never* become a discussion such as this one.

Leader: What rating did you give for this area

Employee: I gave it a four

Leader: Actually I think you're only a three there because I wasn't happy with how you performed in that area. And what did you give for the next heading?

Appraisals of this nature are of no value because there is no acknowledgement of strengths or discussion and agreement as to the areas to improve. An employee will not, and indeed cannot improve their performance, if they don't know what needs improving and if they feel that what they do well has not been recognised.

SUMMARISE STRENGTHS AND EXPLORE AREAS FOR IMPROVEMENT

Having worked through the headings on the appraisal form, the appraiser should do the following.

❑ Summarise the strengths identified

❑ Discuss in detail the causes of the areas for improvement identified

❑ Seek the employee's opinion on how they can improve

❑ Identify training and development needs.

AGREE ACTION

❑ Discuss how to maintain their strengths

❑ Agree action to improve areas for improvement

❑ Agree personal objectives

❑ Gain their commitment

❑ Outline next steps

❑ Sign off agreed appraisal form.

Theme 3 – Sample Employee Appraisal Criteria and Evaluation Form

Name: **Date:**

Area	Poor 1	2	Average 3	Excellent 4	5	Comments	Total
The What							
Achieved specific targets assigned for them by their immediate supervisor							
Clearly understands their role and delivers on their responsibilities							
Demonstrates strong customer orientation and interacts well with customers							
Contributes positively to the smooth running of the department							
Adheres to all relevant hygiene, safety and other work-related regulations							
The How							
Maintains high levels of personal appearance at all times							
Consistently demonstrates good timekeeping and attendance							
Shows a willingness to develop their skills and knowledge							
Continuously carries out their work to a high standard							
Willingly participates in service improvement efforts							
The Who							
Demonstrates commitment to the hotel's vision and mission							
Continuously maintains a positive attitude at work							
Maintains high levels of energy, enthusiasm and professionalism							
Consistently interacts well with their colleagues and contributes positively to team spirit							
Shows initiative and an ability to solve problems relevant to their work							
						Total score	

Summarise strengths and areas for improvement

Personal development plan

The appraisal criteria shown here are intended as a guide and will give you some ideas to work with.

Theme 3 – Suggested Structure for an Effective Meeting

BEFORE THE MEETING

Consider the following.

- ❏ What is the purpose of the meeting/what do I want to achieve?

- ❏ Who actually needs to be there?

- ❏ What is the most appropriate time to hold the meeting?

- ❏ Where is the best place to hold the meeting?

- ❏ What will be discussed – the agenda?

- ❏ Ensure that everyone attending is clear on what will and won't be discussed.

DURING THE MEETING

- ❏ Start on time. Don't reward latecomers by waiting.

- ❏ Follow a clear structure: *introduction, main body, conclusion.*

Introduction

- ❏ Greeting and welcome

- ❏ State the purpose/time of the meeting

- ❏ Outline the agenda points

- ❏ Encourage participation – through you!

- ❏ Emphasise time constraints

- ❏ Allocate responsibilities, i.e. note-taker/timekeeper.

Main body

Introduce each agenda point, making initial points for discussion. As discussion takes place it is essential to do the following.

❏ Maintain control/participation

❏ Keep the discussion on track

❏ Allow involvement from all participants

❏ Prevent conflict from getting out of hand

❏ Keep to allocated time

❏ Summarise agreement/action on each agenda point before moving to next.

Close

❏ Finish on time

❏ Summarise all the points agreed

❏ Ensure that each participant is clear about the action they must take following the meeting and the completion date for the action

❏ Thank everyone for attending and for participating

❏ Remind any latecomers of the necessity for arriving on time in future.

AFTER THE MEETING

❏ Minutes are not required, just action points. What, by when, by whom etc.

❏ Follow up to make sure that allocated responsibilities/tasks are actually completed.

❏ It is also useful to discuss with the participants how they felt the meeting went. Feedback is always useful to help make the next one better.

Theme 3 – Sample Ideas Generation Form

Help us on our journey to excellence! *We welcome your ideas or suggestions in any or all of the following areas. Please tick the box which best describes your idea and provide details below.*	
Improving the service experience for our customers	☐
Making us more productive or efficient at what we do	☐
Helping us to improve communication at the hotel	☐
Creating a better atmosphere at work or improving teamwork	☐
Helping us to reduce our costs or wastage of resources	☐
Helping us to be more environmentally friendly	☐
Creating a safer environment for us and/or our customers	☐
Any other ideas/suggestions	☐

Briefly tell us about your idea/suggestion:

Thank you for your idea. We will respond to you shortly.

Theme 3 – Sample Employee Engagement Survey

Factor	Questions	Rating				
		1	2	3	4	5
Leadership	I believe that leadership at the hotel is effective					
	I feel valued and respected by my leaders at work					
	The way I am led at work increases my willingness to give my all in my job					
Culture	I believe that the hotel genuinely cares about my welfare and there is a good atmosphere at work					
	I am very proud that I work at this hotel					
	The culture at this hotel encourages me to put more effort into my job					
Composition	I respect the people that I work with and feel respected by them					
	I regularly get opportunities to work with different people at the hotel					
	The mix of people in my team works well and brings the best out in me					
Clarity	I understand what the hotel is trying to achieve and how I can contribute to that					
	I am clear about my job description and what is expected of me in terms of my performance					
	My understanding of my role and the hotel's goals makes me more committed to this hotel					
Competence	I receive regular training and coaching which helps me to do my job more effectively					
	I feel that there is potential for me to grow and develop as an individual in my job					
	The training and development I receive at the hotel helps me to be better at what I do					
Cooperation	I feel that everyone works well together in our department and we are supportive of one another					
	I feel that teamwork between departments is strong at the hotel					
	The positive levels of cooperation and teamwork at the hotel makes me work hard so as not to let my teammates down					
Control	I believe that everyone in my team works to a high standard and the workload is shared					
	I am empowered in my job and can act upon my own initiative					
	The guidance I am given and the autonomy I am allowed makes me more productive at what I do					
Communication	I feel there is open, two-way communication at the hotel					
	I receive regular, constructive feedback on my performance					
	The quality of communication at the hotel keeps me informed and I do a better job as a result of that					

Challenge	I feel challenged at work						
	I have opportunities to make suggestions as to how we can improve						
	There is a sense of challenge in my job and this makes my job more interesting						
Conflict	I can voice my opinions in a constructive manner about issues that concern me						
	I believe that the working atmosphere in our department is positive and that conflict is managed effectively						
	There is an absence of conflict at work and this helps me to do a better job						
Compensation	I feel valued for the work that I do at the hotel						
	I regularly receive praise when I do my job well or achieve something special at work						
	The recognition I get for my efforts makes me want to contribute more in my job						
Change	I am kept informed about changes that take place at the hotel						
	I can contribute to decisions which affect me directly						
	Change is well handled at the hotel so I do my best to make the changes work						
General	I feel fulfilled by my job at the hotel						
	I would like to continue working here for the next year and beyond						
	I am happy to go the extra mile in this job						
	I want to help make this hotel a success						
	Totals						
	Maximum score	200					
	% Score						

Rating scale:
1 = Disagree strongly
2 = Disagree somewhat
3 = Neither agree nor disagree
4 = Agree somewhat
5 = Agree strongly

You can see that for each of the 12 factors, the first two statements explore satisfaction, whereas the third tries to determine if this is impacting on an employee's engagement level. The final general questions give a sense of overall engagement. You might feel that this survey is very long and you could reduce the number of statements if you wish but in its current format it shouldn't take more than 15 minutes to complete.

The advantage of this survey is that it will give you an overall indication of employee engagement levels and will also allow you to identify which of the 12 factors receive poor ratings. If you already have a survey in place, does it provide you with the information on employee engagement that you need, or do you need to adjust it?

Theme 4 – Common Customer Expectations Across the Experience Web

1. WEBSITE/ONLINE BOOKINGS

General expectation	As part of this, customers expect that:
Your customers expect that your website will look professional, be easy to use and will provide them with the relevant information they need about your hotel.	1. The website will be easy to access. 2. The website will project a professional image for the hotel. 3. The website will have appropriate information and contact details. 4. The website will offer a user-friendly and efficient approach to making a reservation. 5. Their request for information/reservation will be replied to promptly and accurately. 6. The cancellation policy will be outlined during The booking process. 7. They will receive confirmation when a booking is made which outlines appropriate details such as dates, rate etc. 8. Any special requests made as part of the reservation will be responded to appropriately. 9. Their details will be treated confidentially and will not be used for other purposes unless authorised by them. 10. The security of their personal information is assured when using the site.

2. TELEPHONE RESERVATION

General expectation	As part of this, customers expect that:
Your customers expect that when they call your hotel they will be dealt with in a friendly and positive manner and that their booking will be dealt with professionally and efficiently.	1. The call will be answered promptly and an appropriate greeting will be given by the employee. 2. Their requirements will be clearly established by the employee and options to meet those needs will be explained. 3. The employee will demonstrate good knowledge of what is on offer at the hotel and that the correct rate will be quoted, with what it includes explained to them. 4. The booking will be taken efficiently by the employee and the method of confirmation will be explained to them. 5. The cancellation policy and any restrictions on the booking will be clearly outlined by the employee. 6. The details of the reservation will be repeated back to ensure that no mistakes or confusion exist. 7. The main facilities at the hotel will be explained by the employee and that directions to the hotel will be offered. 8. The employee will demonstrate by their approach to the call that the hotel values the customer's business. 9. The employee will be friendly, helpful and efficient throughout the call and that the call will not feel rushed. 10. The call will be ended by the employee in a friendly way and that they will be thanked for their business.

3. EXTERIOR

General expectation		As part of this, customers expect that:
Your customers expect that your hotel will be easy to find and when they get there that the exterior of the hotel will create a positive first impression.	➡	1. There will be clear directional signage to the hotel which will be easy to see, particularly at night. 2. Any grounds around the hotel will be tidy and well maintained. 3. The car park will be easy to access, amply lit at night with parking spaces clearly marked. 4. Pathways and pavements will be clearly marked and easy to negotiate. 5. Special access arrangements are available for those with sensory or physical disabilities. 6. Security around the hotel will be good and provide a safe and secure environment. 7. Smoking areas, where provided, are clean and tidy. 8. The maintenance and presentation of the hotel exterior will make a positive first impression on them. 9. Front steps will be safe and easy to use. 10. Entrance doors will be in working order and well presented.

4. PUBLIC AREAS

General expectation		As part of this, your customers expect that:
Your customers expect that the public areas of your hotel will offer a safe, comfortable and relaxing environment during their visit.	➡	1. The public areas will be clean and tidy at all times. 2. Lighting, heating and music will create a pleasant ambience. 3. The overall standard of maintenance throughout the hotel will be good. 4. Safety concerns will be a priority and customer welfare will never be jeopardised. 5. Security at the hotel will be discreet, but effective. 6. Services such as payphones or wireless etc. will be in full working order. 7. There will be clear signage throughout all public areas which facilitate ease of movement. 8. Lifts will be clean and presentable and in full working order. 9. The toilets will clean and tidy throughout the visit and will be regularly serviced. 10. There will be constant evidence of management presence at the hotel.

5. RECEPTION – CHECK-IN

General expectation	As part of this, your customers expect that:
Your customers expect that their check-in will be handled efficiently, that they will feel welcomed to the hotel and valued as a customer.	1. The reception desk and lobby area will be clean, tidy and well presented. 2. The appearance and hygiene of employees will be good and that they will be wearing name badges. 3. They will be promptly acknowledged upon arrival and a warm welcome will be given with appropriate eye contact and a smile. 4. Their booking will be in the system and the details will be correct as per the reservation made. 5. The check-in procedure will be handled efficiently and smoothly. 6. A morning call and newspaper will be offered to them. 7. The hotel facilities will be explained to them. 8. Help will be offered with their luggage, or if not provided as a service then at least they will be given clear directions to their room. 9. The employee will be smiling and courteous throughout the check-in process and will interact well with them and make them feel valued as a customer. 10. The check-in will be ended in a friendly manner and that they will be wished a pleasant stay.

6. CONCIERGE/PORTERS

General expectation	As part of this, your customers expect that:
Your customers expect that porters will be polite, friendly and attentive to their needs.	1. The porters/concierge desk will be clean, tidy and well presented. 2. Hotel literature and local information will be clearly visible and available. 3. The appearance and hygiene of porters will be good and that they will be wearing name badges. 4. Porters will be helpful and friendly and attentive to their needs. 5. Porters will respond to information requests in an efficient and timely manner. 6. The porter will escort them to their room in a professional manner, pointing out the hotel facilities as appropriate. 7. The porter will handle their luggage with due care and attention. 8. The porter will place their luggage in an appropriate position in room. 9. The porter will explain the use of room facilities to them. 10. The porter will end the interaction in a friendly manner and they will be thanked.

7. BEDROOM

General expectation	As part of this, your customers expect that:
Your customers expect that they will get a clean, warm and comfortable bedroom which will have all the amenities they need for a pleasant stay.	1. The bedroom will create a positive first impression and will smell clean and fresh. 2. The overall cleanliness and hygiene of the bedroom will be good. 3. The overall standard of maintenance in bedroom will be good. 4. All facilities in room will be in full working order – TV, iron, trouser press, tea/coffee making facilities etc. 5. An adequate supply of quality clothes hangers will be available. 6. The overall cleanliness and maintenance of the bathroom will be good. 7. Clean, fresh towels will be available. 8. The standard of the bathroom accessories will be good. 9. The bath/shower will be in good working order and safe for use. 10. The bedroom will offer an overall environment which will be conducive to a pleasant stay.

8. BAR/LOUNGE

General expectation	As part of this, your customers expect that:
Your customers expect that the surroundings in the bar/lounge will be pleasant, the products offered will be good and that service will be personal and attentive.	1. They will be promptly acknowledged upon entering the bar/lounge and a warm welcome will be given with appropriate eye contact and a smile. 2. The appearance and hygiene of employees will be good and that they will be wearing name badges. 3. The atmosphere in the bar and the presentation and quality of facilities will be of the standard expected. 4. Their order will be taken in a pleasant and professional manner. 5. The drinks will be served in a timely and efficient manner. 6. Employees will interact well with them and make them feel valued. 7. The tables will be regularly cleared in a professional manner. 8. Employees will be observant and anticipate their needs during service. 9. Employees will interact well with them and make them feel valued. 10. The presentation of the bill and subsequent payment will be dealt with in a professional manner and that they will be thanked on departure.

9. RESTAURANT

General expectation		As part of this, your customers expect that:
Your customers expect that the surroundings in the restaurant will be pleasant, the products offered will be good and that service will be personal and attentive.	→	1. They will be promptly acknowledged upon entering the restaurant and a warm welcome will be given with appropriate eye contact and a smile. 2. The appearance and hygiene of employees will be good and that they will be wearing name badges. 3. The atmosphere in the restaurant and the presentation and quality of facilities will be of the standard expected. 4. They will be seated in a professional manner and that the menu/wine list will be presented professionally, any specials or off-dishes explained to them and a drink will be offered. 5. The tables will be correctly and hygienically presented with appropriate accompaniments relevant to the meal service. 6. The order will be taken professionally and accurately by the employee. 7. The food and beverages will be served at the appropriate pace and that the quality and presentation will be good. 8. Employees will be observant and will anticipate their needs during service. 9. Employees will interact well with them and make them feel valued. 10. The presentation of the bill and subsequent payment will be dealt with in a professional manner and that they will be thanked on departure.

10. ROOM SERVICE

General expectation		As part of this, your customers expect that:
Your customers expect that when they order room service that the order will arrive promptly and the quality and presentation of the food/beverages will be good.	→	1. The telephone will be answered promptly and professionally with an appropriate greeting given to them. 2. The room service order will be taken in a friendly, helpful manner and repeated to them to ensure accuracy. 3. The call will be ended in a friendly manner and they are thanked by the employee with an approximate time for delivery given. 4. The items ordered will be delivered within the stated time. 5. The tray/trolley will be well presented, with the correct food/beverage items and accompaniments supplied. 6. The employee will leave the tray/trolley in an appropriate position in the room. 7. The employee will check with the guest for satisfaction before leaving the room. 8. A room service docket will be presented for signing and arrangements for collecting the tray/trolley will be outlined. 9. They will be thanked by the employee on departure. 10. The food/beverage items delivered will be well presented, at the right temperature and that the quality of items will be good.

11. RESTAURANT – BREAKFAST

General expectation	As part of this, your customers expect that:
Your customers expect that the surroundings in the breakfast room/restaurant will be pleasant, the products offered will be good and that service will be personal and attentive.	1. They will be promptly acknowledged upon entering the restaurant and a warm welcome will be given with appropriate eye contact and a smile. 2. The appearance and hygiene of employees will be good and that they will be wearing name badges. 3. The atmosphere in the breakfast room/restaurant and the presentation and quality of facilities will be of the standard expected. 4. They will be seated in a professional manner and that breakfast service will be explained and a menu will be presented, if appropriate. 5. The tables will be correctly and hygienically presented with appropriate accompaniments relevant to breakfast service. 6. The order will be taken professionally and accurately by the employee and/or that the buffet presentation will be appealing. 7. The food/beverages will be served at the appropriate pace and that the quality and presentation of the food will be good. 8. Employees will be observant and will anticipate their needs during service. 9. Employees will interact well with them and make them feel valued. 10. The presentation of the bill and subsequent payment will be dealt with in a professional manner and that they will be thanked on departure.

12. CONFERENCE AND EVENTS

General expectation	As part of this, your customers expect that:
Your customers expect that the facilities, products and service provided will contribute to the success of their conference or event.	1. The conference and events area will be easily accessible and will make a positive first impression. 2. They will be greeted in a professional manner by an employee and a warm welcome will be given with appropriate eye contact and a smile. 3. They will be shown to their conference room and assistance offered with bringing any equipment/materials to the room. 4. An employee will check with them that the room is set up as agreed and that arrangements and logistics for the event will be reconfirmed. 5. The atmosphere, presentation and quality of facilities will be of a standard expected. 6. All equipment in the room is of good quality and in full working order. 7. Any coffee breaks, meals etc will be served at the correct time and that the quality and presentation will be good. 8. Employees will be observant and will anticipate their needs during the event. 9. Employees will interact well with them and make them feel valued throughout the event. 10. The presentation of the bill and subsequent payment will be dealt with in a professional manner and that they will be thanked on departure.

13. LEISURE

General expectation	As part of this, your customers expect that:
Your customers expect that your leisure facilities will offer a safe, hygienic and relaxing environment for them to enjoy their chosen leisure pursuit. →	1. The leisure facilities will smell clean and fresh and will create a positive first impression. 2. They will be promptly acknowledged upon arrival in the facility and that a warm welcome will be given with appropriate eye contact and a smile. 3. The appearance and hygiene of employees will be good and that they will be wearing name badges. 4. The facilities will be explained to them and special attention brought to any safety considerations. 5. The overall cleanliness and hygiene of the facilities will be good. 6. The overall standard of maintenance of the facilities will be good. 7. All relevant safety procedures will be in place to ensure their safe usage of the facility. 8. Employees will be observant and anticipate their needs throughout their time in the facility. 9. Employees will interact well with them and make them feel valued throughout their time in the facility. 10. The presentation of the bill for any charges incurred and subsequent payment will be dealt with in a professional manner and that they will be thanked on departure.

14. RECEPTION – CHECK-OUT

General expectation	As part of this, your customers expect that:
Your customers expect that their check-out will be handled efficiently and that they will feel valued as a customer. →	1. The reception desk and lobby area will be clean, tidy and well presented. 2. They will be promptly acknowledged and a warm greeting will be given with appropriate eye contact and a smile. 3. The appearance and hygiene of employees will be good and that they will be wearing name badges. 4. That they will be checked for satisfaction about their stay. 5. That any problems regarding their stay will be appropriately addressed. 6. The bill will be presented in a professional manner and charges clearly explained. 7. The payment process will be handled efficiently and a receipt offered. 8. Help will be offered with luggage and directions offered with their onward journey, if appropriate. 9. The employee will be smiling and courteous throughout the check-out process and will interact well with them during service. 10. They will be thanked for their business and will be encouraged to return.

Theme 4 – Sample Mystery Guest Survey Template

1. WEBSITE/ONLINE BOOKINGS

COMPONENT OF EXPERIENCE WEB	Excellent 2 points	Average 1 point	Poor 0 points	Comments
Service goal				
Website offers an informative and user-friendly resource to customers which creates a positive impression for the hotel				
Service steps				
1. Website was easy to access 2. Website projected a professional image for the hotel 3. Website provided appropriate information and contact details 4. Website offered a user-friendly and efficient approach to making the reservation 5. Requests for information/ reservation were replied to promptly and accurately 6. Cancellation policy was outlined during the booking process 7. Confirmation of booking was received which outlined the appropriate details 8. Special requests were responded to appropriately 9. Details provided were treated confidentially 10. Security of personal information was assured when using the site				

2. TELEPHONE RESERVATION

COMPONENT OF EXPERIENCE WEB	Excellent 2 points	Average 1 point	Poor 0 points	Comments
Service goal				
Telephone enquiry and reservation handled in a professional, friendly and personal manner				
Service steps				
1. Call was answered promptly and an appropriate greeting was given by the employee				
2. Requirements were clearly established by the employee and options to meet those needs were explained				
3. Employee demonstrated good knowledge of what is on offer at the hotel and the correct rate, with what it includes, was quoted and explained				
4. Booking was taken efficiently by the employee and the method of confirmation was explained				
5. Cancellation policy and any restrictions on the booking were clearly outlined by the employee				
6. Details of the reservation were repeated back				
7. Main facilities at the hotel were explained by the employee and directions to the hotel were offered				
8. Employee demonstrated by their approach to the call that the hotel valued the business				
9. Employee was friendly, helpful and efficient throughout the call and the call did not feel rushed				
10. Call was ended by the employee in a friendly way and the caller was thanked for their business				

3. EXTERIOR

COMPONENT OF EXPERIENCE WEB	Excellent 2 points	Average 1 point	Poor 0 points	Comments
Service goal				
Exterior and surroundings of the hotel were well maintained, created a positive first impression and were safe and secure				
Service steps				
1. Clear directional signage to the hotel was visible and easy to see at night 2. Grounds around the hotel were tidy and well maintained 3. Car park was easy to access, amply lit at night with parking spaces clearly marked 4. Pathways and pavements were clearly marked and easy to negotiate 5. Special access arrangements were available for those with sensory or physical disabilities 6. Security around the hotel was good and provided a safe and secure environment 7. Smoking areas were clean and tidy 8. Maintenance and presentation of the hotel exterior did make a positive first impression 9. Front steps were safe and easy to use 10. Entrance doors were in working order and well presented				

4. PUBLIC AREAS

COMPONENT OF EXPERIENCE WEB	Excellent 2 points	Average 1 point	Poor 0 points	Comments
Service goal				
Public areas were well maintained and presented at all times and offered a pleasant, comfortable and secure environment				
Service steps				
1. Public areas were clean and tidy at all times 2. Lighting, heating and music did create a pleasant ambience 3. The overall standard of maintenance throughout the hotel was good 4. Safety concerns were a priority and customer welfare was never jeopardised 5. Security at the hotel was discreet, but effective 6. Services such as payphones or Wi-Fi etc. were in full working order 7. Clear signage was available throughout all public areas which facilitated ease of movement 8. Lifts were clean and presentable and in full working order 9. Toilets were clean and tidy throughout the visit and were regularly serviced 10. Management presence was continuously evident at the hotel				

5. RECEPTION – CHECK-IN

COMPONENT OF EXPERIENCE WEB	Excellent 2 points	Average 1 point	Poor 0 points	Comments
Service goal				
A professional, efficient and friendly check-in was provided which made me feel welcome and valued				
Service steps				
1. Reception desk and lobby area were clean, tidy and well presented 2. Appearance and hygiene of employees was good and they were wearing name badges 3. Prompt acknowledgement upon arrival was given and a warm welcome with appropriate eye contact and a smile was evident 4. Booking was in the system and the details were correct as per the reservation made 5. Check-in was handled efficiently and smoothly 6. Morning call and newspaper were offered 7. Hotel facilities were explained 8. Help was offered with luggage 9. Employee was smiling and courteous throughout the check-in process and did interact well making the customer feel valued 10. Check-in was ended in a friendly manner and customer was wished a pleasant stay				

6. CONCIERGE/PORTERS

COMPONENT OF EXPERIENCE WEB	Excellent 2 points	Average 1 point	Poor 0 points	Comments
Service goal				
Porters interacted professionally at all times and performed their duties to a high standard				
Service steps				
1. Porters/concierge desk was clean, tidy and well presented 2. Hotel literature and local information was clearly visible and available 3. Appearance and hygiene of porters was good and they were wearing name badges 4. Porters were helpful, friendly and attentive 5. Porters did respond to information requests in an efficient and timely manner 6. Porter did escort customer to their room in a professional manner and pointed out the hotel facilities as appropriate 7. Porter did handle luggage with due care and attention 8. Porter did place luggage in an appropriate position in room 9. Porter did explain the use of room facilities 10. Porter did end the interaction in a friendly manner and thanked customer				

7. BEDROOM

COMPONENT OF EXPERIENCE WEB	Excellent 2 points	Average 1 point	Poor 0 points	Comments
Service goal				
Bedroom offered a pleasant and comfortable environment during the stay				
Service steps				
1. Bedroom did create a positive first impression and did smell clean and fresh				
2. Overall cleanliness and hygiene of the bedroom was good				
3. Overall standard of maintenance in bedroom was good				
4. All facilities in room were in full working order				
5. Adequate supply of quality clothes hangers was available				
6. Overall cleanliness and maintenance of the bathroom was good				
7. Clean, fresh towels were available				
8. Standard of bathroom accessories was good				
9. Bath/shower were in good working order and safe for use				
10. Bedroom did offer an overall environment which was conducive to a pleasant stay				

8. BAR/LOUNGE

COMPONENT OF EXPERIENCE WEB	Excellent 2 points	Average 1 point	Poor 0 points	Comments
Service goal				
Bar/Lounge offered a welcoming and pleasant environment and service was attentive, friendly and efficient				
Service steps				
1. Prompt acknowledgement was forthcoming upon entering and a warm welcome was given with appropriate eye contact and a smile				
2. Appearance and hygiene of employees was good and they were wearing name badges				
3. Atmosphere in the bar and the presentation and quality of facilities was of the standard expected				
4. Order was taken in a pleasant and professional manner				
5. Drinks were served in a timely and efficient manner				
6. Employees did interact well and made the customer feel valued				
7. Tables were regularly cleared in a professional manner				
8. Employees were observant and did anticipate needs during service				
9. Employees did interact well and make the customer feel valued				
10. Presentation of the bill and subsequent payment was dealt with in a professional manner and customer was thanked on departure				

9. RESTAURANT

COMPONENT OF EXPERIENCE WEB	Excellent 2 points	Average 1 point	Poor 0 points	Comments
Service goal				
The restaurant offered a welcoming and pleasant environment and service was attentive, friendly and efficient				
Service steps				
1. Prompt acknowledgement was forthcoming upon entering and a warm welcome was given with appropriate eye contact and a smile				
2. Appearance and hygiene of employees was good and they were wearing name badges				
3. Atmosphere in the restaurant and the presentation and quality of facilities was of the standard expected				
4. Customer was seated in a professional manner and the menu/wine list was presented professionally, any specials or off-dishes were explained and a drink was offered				
5. Tables were correctly and hygienically presented with appropriate accompaniments relevant to the meal service				
6. Order was taken professionally and accurately by the employee				
7. Food and beverages were served at the appropriate pace and the quality and presentation was good				
8. Employees were observant and did anticipate needs during service				
9. Employees did interact well and make the customer feel valued				
10. Presentation of the bill and subsequent payment was dealt with in a professional manner and customer was thanked on departure				

10. ROOM SERVICE

COMPONENT OF EXPERIENCE WEB	Excellent 2 points	Average 1 point	Poor 0 points	Comments
Service goal				
Room service call was handled professionally and efficiently and items served were of a high standard and delivered on time				
Service steps				
1. Telephone was answered promptly and professionally and an appropriate greeting was given 2. Room service order was taken in a friendly, helpful manner and repeated to ensure accuracy 3. Call was ended in a friendly manner and caller was thanked by the employee and an approximate time for delivery given 4. Items ordered were delivered within the stated time 5. Tray/trolley was well presented, with the correct food/beverage items and accompaniments supplied 6. Employee did leave the tray/trolley in the appropriate position in room 7. Employee did check with the guest for satisfaction before leaving the room 8. Room service docket was presented for signing and arrangements for collecting the tray/trolley were outlined 9. Customer was thanked by the employee on departure 10. Food/beverage items delivered were well presented, at the right temperature and the quality of items was good				

11. RESTAURANT – BREAKFAST

COMPONENT OF EXPERIENCE WEB	Excellent 2 points	Average 1 point	Poor 0 points	Comments
Service goal				
Breakfast room/restaurant offered a welcoming and pleasant environment and service was attentive, friendly and efficient with buffet presentation continuously of a high standard throughout service				
Service steps				
1. Prompt acknowledgement was forthcoming upon entering and a warm welcome was given with appropriate eye contact and a smile				
2. Appearance and hygiene of employees was good and they were wearing name badges				
3. Atmosphere in the breakfast room/restaurant and the presentation and quality of facilities was of the standard expected				
4. Customer was seated in a professional manner and breakfast service was explained and a menu presented				
5. Tables were correctly and hygienically presented with appropriate accompaniments relevant to breakfast service				
6. Order was taken professionally and accurately by the employee and buffet presentation was appealing				
7. Food/beverages were served at the appropriate pace and the quality and presentation of the food was good				
8. Employees were observant and did anticipate needs during service				
9. Employees did interact well and made the customer feel valued				
10. Presentation of the bill and subsequent payment was dealt with in a professional manner and customer was thanked on departure				

12. CONFERENCE AND EVENTS

COMPONENT OF EXPERIENCE WEB	Excellent 2 points	Average 1 point	Poor 0 points	Comments
Service goal				
Service and product quality in the conference and events area was of high quality and facilitated a successful outcome to the event				
Service steps				
1. Conference and events area was easily accessible and did make a positive first impression				
2. Customer was greeted in a professional manner by an employee and a warm welcome was given with appropriate eye contact and a smile				
3. Customer was shown to their conference room and assistance was offered with bringing any equipment/ materials to the room				
4. Employee did check with customer that the room was set up as agreed and arrangements and logistics for the event were reconfirmed				
5. Atmosphere, presentation and quality of facilities were of a standard expected				
6. Equipment in the room was of good quality and in full working order				
7. Coffee breaks, meals etc. were served at the correct time and the quality and presentation was good				
8. Employees were observant and did anticipate needs during the event				
9. Employees did interact well and made the customer feel valued throughout the event				
10. Presentation of the bill and subsequent payment was dealt with in a professional manner and customer was thanked on departure				

13. LEISURE

COMPONENT OF EXPERIENCE WEB	Excellent 2 points	Average 1 point	Poor 0 points	Comments
Service goal				
Leisure facilities were maintained to a high standard and the quality of service ensured that an enjoyable time was spent in this area				
Service steps				
1. Leisure facilities did smell clean and fresh and did create a positive first impression				
2. Prompt acknowledgement was forthcoming upon entering and a warm welcome was given with appropriate eye contact and a smile				
3. Appearance and hygiene of employees was good and they were wearing name badges				
4. Facilities were explained and special attention was brought to any safety considerations				
5. Overall cleanliness and hygiene of the facilities was good				
6. Overall standard of maintenance of the facilities was good				
7. Relevant safety procedures were in place to ensure safe usage of the facility				
8. Employees were observant and did anticipate needs throughout the time in the facility				
9. Employees did interact well and made the customer feel valued throughout their time in the facility				
10. Presentation of the bill for any charges incurred and subsequent payment was dealt with in a professional manner and customer was thanked on departure				

14. RECEPTION – CHECK-OUT

COMPONENT OF EXPERIENCE WEB	Excellent 2 points	Average 1 point	Poor 0 points	Comments
Service goal				
A professional, efficient and friendly check-out was received which demonstrated that the customer was valued and ended the visit on a high note				
Service steps				
1. Reception desk and lobby area were clean, tidy and well presented 2. Prompt acknowledgement was forthcoming upon entering and a warm welcome was given with appropriate eye contact and a smile 3. Appearance and hygiene of employees was good and they were wearing name badges 4. Satisfaction regarding the stay was checked 5. Any problems regarding the stay were appropriately addressed 6. Bill was presented in a professional manner and charges were clearly explained 7. Payment process was handled efficiently and a receipt was offered 8. Help was offered with luggage and directions were offered with the onward journey 9. Employee was smiling and courteous throughout the check-out process and did interact well during service 10. Customer was thanked for their business and encouraged to return				

Theme 4 – Sample Criteria for Integrating into Customer Feedback Surveys

1. WEBSITE/ONLINE BOOKINGS

COMPONENT OF EXPERIENCE WEB	Below expectations	Met expectations	Exceeded expectations	Comments
Ease of access and navigation				
Quality of information				
Efficiency of reservation process				
Speed of response and confirmation				

2. TELEPHONE RESERVATION

COMPONENT OF EXPERIENCE WEB	Below expectations	Met expectations	Exceeded expectations	Comments
Promptness of response to call				
Attitude and friendliness of employee				
Efficiency of reservation process				
Sense of value felt as a customer				

3. EXTERIOR

COMPONENT OF EXPERIENCE WEB	Below expectations	Met expectations	Exceeded expectations	Comments
Ease of access to hotel				
Quality of maintenance and appearance				
First impressions of hotel				
Sense of security				

4. PUBLIC AREAS

COMPONENT OF EXPERIENCE WEB	Below expectations	Met expectations	Exceeded expectations	Comments
Quality of maintenance and appearance				
Overall ambience in hotel				
Cleanliness of toilets				
Quality of services available				

5. RECEPTION – CHECK-IN

COMPONENT OF EXPERIENCE WEB	Below expectations	Met expectations	Exceeded expectations	Comments
Quality of maintenance and appearance of reception				
Appearance and attitude of employees				
Efficiency and attentiveness of service during check-in				
Overall sense of welcome to hotel				

6. CONCIERGE/PORTERS

COMPONENT OF EXPERIENCE WEB	Below expectations	Met expectations	Exceeded expectations	Comments
Quality of maintenance and appearance of concierge/porter's desk				
Appearance and attitude of employees				
Efficiency and attentiveness of service				
Quality of literature/ information available				

7. BEDROOM

COMPONENT OF EXPERIENCE WEB	Below expectations	Met expectations	Exceeded expectations	Comments
Cleanliness and maintenance of bedroom and bathroom				
Quality of products and equipment provided				
Attention to detail in preparation of room				
Overall quality of environment				

8. BAR/LOUNGE

COMPONENT OF EXPERIENCE WEB	Below expectations	Met expectations	Exceeded expectations	Comments
Quality of maintenance and appearance of bar/lounge				
Appearance and attitude of employees				
Efficiency and attentiveness of service				
Quality of food/beverages				

9. RESTAURANT

COMPONENT OF EXPERIENCE WEB	Below expectations	Met expectations	Exceeded expectations	Comments
Quality of maintenance and appearance of restaurant				
Appearance and attitude of employees				
Efficiency and attentiveness of service				
Quality of food/beverages				

10. ROOM SERVICE

COMPONENT OF EXPERIENCE WEB	Below expectations	Met expectations	Exceeded expectations	Comments
Promptness of response to call				
Efficiency and attentiveness of employee during call				
Appearance and attitude of employee during delivery				
Timeliness of delivery and quality of food/beverages				

11. RESTAURANT – BREAKFAST

COMPONENT OF EXPERIENCE WEB	Below expectations	Met expectations	Exceeded expectations	Comments
Quality of maintenance and appearance of restaurant				
Appearance and attitude of employees				
Efficiency and attentiveness of service				
Presentation of buffet and quality of food/beverages				

12. CONFERENCE AND EVENTS

COMPONENT OF EXPERIENCE WEB	Below expectations	Met expectations	Exceeded expectations	Comments
Quality of maintenance and appearance of event facilities				
Appearance and attitude of employees				
Efficiency and attentiveness of service during event				
Quality of food/beverages				

13. LEISURE

COMPONENT OF EXPERIENCE WEB	Below expectations	Met expectations	Exceeded expectations	Comments
Quality of maintenance and appearance of leisure facilities				
Appearance and attitude of employees				
Efficiency and attentiveness of service				
Overall impression				

14. RECEPTION – CHECK-OUT

COMPONENT OF EXPERIENCE WEB	Below expectations	Met expectations	Exceeded expectations	Comments
Quality of maintenance and appearance of reception				
Appearance and attitude of employee				
Efficiency and attentiveness of service during check-out				
Overall sense of being valued as a customer				

15. GENERAL

COMPONENT OF EXPERIENCE WEB	Below expectations	Met expectations	Exceeded expectations	Comments
Appearance and maintenance of hotel facilities				
Employee attitude and appearance				
Efficiency and attentiveness of service				
Quality of products				
Value for money				
	Yes		No	Comments
Would you return again?				
Would you recommend us to others?				

Index

MASTERING BOOK-KEEPING

Dr Peter Marshall

An accredited textbook of The Institute of Chartered Bookkeepers.

This updated 8th edition contains extracts from ICB, AAT, OCR and AQA sample examination papers.

'This book has been planned to cover the requirements of all the major examining boards' syllabuses and achieves all it sets out to do.' – *Focus on Business Education*

'Presented in a clear and logical manner – written in plain English.' – *Learning Resources News*

'This book has great potential value.' – *Educational Equipment Magazine*

ISBN 978-1-84528-324-7

THE SMALL BUSINESS START-UP WORKBOOK

Cheryl D. Rickman

'I would urge every business adviser in the land to read this book.' – Sylvia Tidy-Harris, Managing Director of www.womenspeakers.co.uk

'Inspirational and practical workbook that takes you from having a business idea to actually having a business. By the time you have worked through the exercises and checklists you will be focussed, confident and raring to go.' – www.allthatwomenwant.co.uk

'A real "must have" for anyone thinking of setting up their own venture.' – *Thames Valley News*

'. . . a very comprehensive book, a very readable book.' – *Sister Business E-Zine*

ISBN 978-1-84528-038-3

START AND RUN A SANDWICH AND COFFEE BAR

Jill Sutherland

In this step-by-step guide, the owner of a multi-award winning sandwich and coffee bar tells how you, too, can turn your passion for food into a successful business. Jill Sutherland's comprehensive guide will take you on a stage-by-stage guide to your first year, from idea to opening and then to becoming established. Packed with top tips, real-life examples, checklists and anecdotes, this book provides you with practical and realistic advice from someone who has been there and done it. In it you'll learn how to develop and research your sandwich bar 'idea'; write a professional business plan; find the right shop unit, and fit it out; find and manage suppliers; manage food hygiene, and health and safety; create your menu and source produce; budget, forecast and manage cash flow; launch and generate publicity and employ and manage staff.

ISBN 978-1-84528-333-9

HOW TO START AND RUN AN INTERNET BUSINESS

Carol Ann Strange

'An excellent definitive guide.' – *Jobs & Careers*

This book will guide you through the process of establishing a profitable online venture and steer you towards success. You'll learn how to generate online income; create a reliable and appealing virtual shop window; optimise your web venture for growth; generate more profit from affiliate schemes and other prospects and become a successful internet entrepreneur

ISBN 978-1-84528-356-8

WAKE UP AND SMELL THE PROFIT
52 guaranteed ways to make more money in your coffee business

John Richardson and Hugh Gilmartin

'A quite brilliant new book on cafe operation.' – *Coffee House Magazine*

'It should come with a health warning that it should not be read at bedtime, since you wont sleep after it, as your mind will be buzzing with great ideas.' – Robert Bligh – Just Bean Espresso Bar

'A really fun read, full of proven ideas and sensible advice to make money but also enjoy your business at the same time. A must for anyone wanting to start a coffee bar and many operators would benefit from a read as well.' – Steve Penk – UK National Co-Ordinator & Director of the Speciality Coffee Association of Europe

'A quite brilliant new book on cafe operation . . . sometimes all of us are lucky enough to learn from those who have turned their mistakes into practical experience, such as in this exceptional new book from Ireland's 'Coffee Boys', John Richardson and Hugh Gilmartin.' – Ian Boughton – *Coffee House Magazine*

'Asolutely nobody should open a coffee shop without first reading this book. We have already incorporated it into our training program and manuals.' – Se Gorman – Entrepreneur and National Barista Champion 2006 and 2007 Indiego Publications

ISBN 978-1-84528-334-6

PREPARE TO SELL YOUR COMPANY

L B Buckingham

Selling your company is a trying time, similar to selling your house. For those unfamiliar with this process, the challenging thoughts will be: 'How do I start?'; 'Who can help me?'; 'How much can I get for the business?'; 'Who is most likely to buy it, and where do I find them?'; 'When should I do it?' This book will answer all your questions. Easy to read, it covers all the practical aspects of preparing your business for sale. It will show you just how a potential acquirer will view a company that is up for sale. This will enable you to develop a business profile that will attract buyers – and maintain their interest until completion, and build into the business those aspects that will encourage a buyer to increase their bid. This book will take you through the sale process: preparation, marketing, acceptance of offer, the 'due diligence examination' (the vendor's nightmare), successful completion, and beyond.

ISBN 978-1-84528-328-5

How To Books are available through all good bookshops, or you can order direct from us through Grantham Book Services.

Tel: +44 (0)1476 541080
Fax: +44 (0)1476 541061
Email: orders@gbs.tbs-ltd.co.uk

Or via our website
www.howtobooks.co.uk

To order via any of these methods please quote the title(s) of the book(s) and your credit card number together with its expiry date.

For further information about our books and catalogue, please contact:

How To Books
Spring Hill House
Spring Hill Road
Begbroke
Oxford OX5 1RX

Visit our web site at
www.howtobooks.co.uk

Or you can contact us by email at info@howtobooks.co.uk